Going to My Father's House

Going to My Father's House

A History of My Times

Patrick Joyce

VERSO

London • New York

For the immigrants and those who come after them, and with deepest love for my grandchildren, Isaac and Jonathan Joyce, and Orlagh Joyce-Young.

First published by Verso 2021
© Patrick Joyce 2021

1 3 5 7 9 10 8 6 4 2

Verso
UK: 6 Meard Street, London W1F 0EG
US: 20 Jay Street, Suite 1010, Brooklyn, NY 11201
versobooks.com

Verso is the imprint of New Left Books

ISBN-13: 978-1-83976-324-3
ISBN-13: 978-1-83976-326-7 (US EBK)
ISBN-13: 978-1-83976-325-0 (UK EBK)

British Library Cataloguing in Publication Data
A catalogue record for this book is available from the British Library

Library of Congress Cataloging-in-Publication Data

Names: Joyce, Patrick, 1945– author.
Title: Going to my father's house : a history of my times / Patrick Joyce.
Description: London ; New York : Verso Books, 2021. | Includes
  bibliographical references and index. | Summary: "A historian's personal
  journey through immigration, home, and the questions of nationhood"—
  Provided by publisher.
Identifiers: LCCN 2021012068 (print) | LCCN 2021012069 (ebook) | ISBN
  9781839763243 (hardback) | ISBN 9781839763267 (ebk)
Subjects: LCSH: Joyce, Patrick, 1945– | Historians—England,
  Northern—Biography. | Joyce family. |
  Irish—England—London—Biography. |
Immigrants—England—London—Social
  conditions—20th century. | Connemara (Ireland)—Biography. | Wexford
  (Ireland : County)—Biography. | England—Biography.
Classification: LCC D15.J69 A3 2021 (print) | LCC D15.J69 (ebook) | DDC
  941.085092 [B]—dc23
LC record available at https://lccn.loc.gov/2021012068
LC ebook record available at https://lccn.loc.gov/2021012069

Typeset in Minion Pro by MJ&N Gavan, Truro, Cornwall
Printed and bound by CPI Group (UK) Ltd, Croydon CR0 4YY

Contents

Decades later that child's grandchild's
speech stumbles over lost
syllables of an old order.

John Montague, 'A Severed Head',
from *The Rough Field*

Introduction

I am always going to my father's house, I am always going home.

Novalis

This book began as a history of my parents, written for my children. It was in this regard personal but also universal, for in my act of writing I joined hands with how most of humanity apprehends the past, namely through the family that has gone and is to come. The time that is most presently and intimately the past, and the hoped for future, is the time of the family. It is as if the family is the door which is the one most open to us, the one from which the light of the past shines brightest.

As in many such acts of remembrance, my aim was to take the existence of my parents out of the historical obscurity from which they came, for they were poor and without a voice. They were immigrants from an Ireland that now seems centuries not decades ago. What I began to write was a bequest to the future, so that their lives were not forgotten and would be part of possible futures, if only those of my grandchildren. I thought that my posterity in this time of great change might even, in the relatively short period between my writing and their reading, be already too far hurled into the future to make sense of their own lives without knowing more of the worlds from which they came.

What I wrote I also considered to be something of a homage to my parents; I can find no better word. 'Homage' because of the debt I owe them, which was the life they made for my brother and me in London, and the Irishness they gave us.

That dual debt of gratitude, for that which was made in the new place and that which was carried from the old one, is one that immigrant children from everywhere always have. So, in discharging this debt I found that I was also telling a bigger story: one of the emigrant, the immigrant, and their children. Homage involves the show of public respect, and as I wrote I realized I wanted to mark their lives more widely than my family alone, and so the historical details started to accrue. I am by occupation and preoccupation a historian, so that the banking up of historical details is second nature to me.

As I wrote, then, what I set down became a book, and one in which its author figured more and more. A historian needs evidence, and short of a few letters – though many photographic 'snaps' – there was little to record the memory of my parents. Therefore I become, in some way, one of the few remaining 'documents' that mark their time on earth. Their memory depended on my memory, and I realized that I was part of their story too, of what they passed on into history.

And so these pages, 'A history of my times' (if I may be permitted so grand a term), tell something of my life. However, the book is neither a memoir nor a history, but is located somewhere between the two. Being, as I find myself, between the two – or in an Irish phrase, *idir eatarthu*, of and between two things at the same time – my hope is that I can see both better. I could not find many precedents for what I was doing, so I just did it, in a sense being led by the writing, by the pleasure of it, by where the words led me as they came out from some unknown place within. Unknown, but I have always tried to prime that place, make it ready, by knowing at least some of the history I guessed might be waiting there.

For me, then, being between history and memory means embedding my own memories in historical writing, as a way of making them speak with greater purpose and direction than they might otherwise have done. Alone they are limited to a single life, and in this case the mundane one of a scholar, for

2

whom much of life is sedentary and lived in the head. However, if I embed memory in history, being between the two also means doing the reverse, embedding history in memory, so that in my attempt to write a 'history of my times', it is memory itself that is forever prompting the history, taking it off in different directions, along jagged, uneven paths, into subjects and times that history writing does not usually attend to; into the silences of time that might be better listened to this way. 'Memory' – mine or that of any person – is, of course, more than an individual matter, so this collective memory is my subject too, in war and peace both.

'A history of my times' has a different sense, too. What time is and where 'our times' come from are central concerns in what follows: my times extend back over more than my life alone and that of my parents. We live in several times, not just one, and the past is constantly at work in our lives, forever becoming the present and so shaping the future. Nonetheless, I have lived a certain span of years, those between 1945 and now, when I write this; inevitably, I talk about my generation, before we all fade away. So I am not interested in writing a memoir, in which the 'I' is the composer busily arranging the score of her or his life. I do not want, I am not interested in, revealing an inner life, though it is true that one cannot altogether avoid the inner in recounting the outer, as the reader will find.

My way forward has much in common with that of Czeslaw Milosz in his *Native Realm*, first published in 1959, though our books are very different in many other respects, and he is a man of my father's generation, only a year separating them. The introduction to his book, which he subtitles a 'search for self-definition', concludes with words whose simple eloquence I borrow now:

The vision of the small patch on the globe to which I owe everything suggests where I should draw the line. A three-year-

3

old's love for his aunt or jealousy towards his father take up so much room in autobiographical writings because everything else, for instance a history of a country or a national group, is treated as something 'normal' and, therefore, of little interest to the narrator. But another method is possible. Instead of thrusting the individual into the foreground, one can focus attention on the background, looking upon oneself as a sociological phenomenon. Inner experience, as it is preserved in the memory, will then be evaluated in the perspective of the changes one's milieu has undergone. The passing over of certain periods important for oneself, but requiring too personal an explanation, will be a token of respect for those undergrounds that exist in all of us and are better left in peace. Yet one can avoid the dryness of a scholarly treatise because the outside world will be coloured by memory and subjective judgement.[1]

I have been a witness to three epochal historical transformations: the end of the old peasant order; the passage from world war to peace, and the decline of the old manual working class. Yet as the work developed, and as the historical circles widened, I needed to keep history and memory together, and so find things that resonate with both and make listening to the silences of time easier. I needed things both solid and symbolic, things that speak widely. I found these in three figures: the house, the road, and the grave. These are real – the house and not just the home; the road and not just travelling; real and not only figurative graves, that of my parents in Irish and Catholic west London, for instance.

At the same time, what could be symbolically more rich than these three figures? Indeed, they seem almost overloaded with significance, age-old as they are, their richness extending across many cultures. The house, the road, and the grave; stability, movement and separation, the ending that is death. Other things too, of course, are represented by these three – the house confining as well as nurturing, roads taken and not taken, the grave a beginning rather than only an ending. I write about another real thing: walls – those of houses, but also of cities; walls in the head, too.

I take my first bearings in my father's house in Joyce Country, in the Galway and Mayo of north Connemara. Joyce Country, mapped as such by the eighteenth century, is Dúiche Sheoighe in Irish. The critic Patrick Sheehan has used the road, the house, and the grave to triangulate 'Galway space'.[2] This is the space of literature – an imaginary space, for sure, but one rooted in real things, in houses, roads, graves. From these it draws all its strength. It could have been my mother's house I chose, in Wexford, in Ireland's south-east, a place somewhat more benign than the once impoverished west. That was the house of my remembered childhood. But the first house I was taken to was my father's house, in 1949. He died relatively young, when I was young. My mother lived longer. So it was to his house I went to find him after his death, and have sought him ever since.

The beautiful words of Novalis speak of much else, of course, for in going to the father's house one is on a road; one might not arrive, but one is travelling there anyhow. One may not get home, but the point might be that the going is enough. Nonetheless, there is a yearning there – what the Germans call *Sehnsucht*, an acute longing for something or someone who is intensely missed. Home is the father's house, the first one and the origin, the real father and the mythic-religious one. Home is in death, therefore, in the grave.

No place more than this 'west' – Galway and its islands – has been the locus of lost origins and hoped-for renewal. It has come to be fetishized in Irish culture, and in others, including British and German culture. The journey in search of God is the foundation myth of the west of Ireland. All space is political, too. Galway's imaginative and real spaces are for example distinguishable as the 'Tory landscape' of Yeats's east Galway, the plains, and the *Galvia deserta* of the west, including Joyce

Country, the highlands. There is the 'radial space' of the east, with the big house at the centre; and then the 'itinerant space' of the west, the space of the poor, rebellious, and disrespectful peasant. If I have anything as grand as a 'method' in this book, it is to transpose this first, Irish house, road, and grave onto the other ones I have encountered in my life, my London life, the lives of other immigrants, and those of the 'native' English, if I can use that term.

'Beginnings' is concerned with the sense of place, and the place that lingers most is the house of childhood. This is what shapes the sense of place most as life goes by, for good and ill, for the house may itself be a good house or a bad one. It need not be the first house, either; but if not it is usually some house, a place where childhood was, where we leave behind a past that we forever carry with us.

As I wrote this book, I realized that my parents' experience of war was intrinsic to who they were, and thus to who I became. Thinking about my father, who was wounded in the bombing, I was led into thinking that war was a matter of the silences as much as the noise of my generation. This war, the silences and the noise, has long continued to reverberate. Silence was the price of the noise, the silence of my father and so many like him, the silences that bolstered the nostalgic idea of the Second World War and the nation that followed it, and that have done so much damage in Britain.

I came upon another silence as I went along, one that echoed powerfully for me. The truly forgotten are the bombed civilian dead of the other side – the German dead, the children especially, for I was then as they were, a child, if only in the womb, that of a 'war worker' who made the airplanes that caused this vengeful annihilation. My subject in the second section is war, so I cannot exclude what went on in the so-called 'Troubles', which was in all truth a war too, one that has made Britain and has so often threatened to break it. So I went to Derry and its walls to find what this war was and where it had come from.

North and south are natural contrasts in England, part of the history. My life has been divided into two halves both temporally and geographically, the first in London, the second in the industrial north. So in the third section, titled 'North', I am concerned with the destruction of a whole way of life – one that had lasted a century and a half by the time I came upon it, at the moment of its ending: the fall of industrial Jerusalem. My subjects are what this old industrial way of life was and what it has become, the uprooting of a way of life and a unique way of dwelling. These consequences concern what it is to dwell peacefully in the state that is the United Kingdom and the nation that is England; to dwell peacefully in a Kingdom torn apart by an argument that is also about dwelling – the argument about Brexit. What the coronavirus pandemic will bring to this condition of discord, it is too early to say.

I think here of Walter Benjamin's words on history. Benjamin wrote at a time when his perception of the breakdown in the authority of the European cultural tradition was corroborated by the terrible events of his time. We might do well, at another time of danger, to listen to this strange, messianic German Jew, the 'little hunchback' as Hannah Arendt called him.[3] His 'Angel of history' is often quoted: the Angel's face is turned towards the past, but a storm is 'blowing from Paradise' which irresistibly propels him into the future. The storm is called 'progress', and its results are not what we perceive – namely, the chain of events of which progress is made up – but rather 'one single catastrophe which keeps piling wreckage upon wreckage and hurls it in front of his feet … while the pile of debris before him grows skyward'.[4] Against the weight of dead tradition and authority, for Benjamin 'the past spoke directly only through things that had not been handed down', by which he meant the untold stories of the numberless dead, and the paths history had not taken because the weight of tradition and authority had silenced these stories and blocked this path, all in the name of the great story of progress.

Here, I try to listen to these untold stories and to track these uncharted paths. If we listen, we will hear – or so there is reason to hope. The following are the words of the great Austrian novelist Hermann Broch, a Jew who later converted to Catholicism. Broch was helped to escape from Austria after the *Anschluss* by another Joyce: James, my very distant kinsman. Broch speaks thus through the mouth of a rabbi in *The Guiltless*:

> But what then is at once silence and voice? Truly, of all things known to me, it is time that warrants these two attributes. Yes, it is time, and although it encompasses us and flows through us, it does so in muteness and silence. But when we grow old and learn to listen back, we hear a soft murmur, and that is the time we have left behind. And the further back we listen and the better we learn to listen back, the more distinctly we hear the voice of the ages, the silence of time which He and His glory created for His sake but also for its sake, in order that it might complete the Creation for us. And the more time has elapsed, the mightier becomes the voice of time for us; we shall grow with it, and at the end of time we shall capture its beginning and hear the call to Creation.[5]

Benjamin wrote eighteen 'theses' on history. Less cited is the second of these. He writes of how

> our image of happiness is indissolubly bound up with the image of redemption. The same applies to our view of the past, which is the concern of history. The past carries with it a temporal index by which it is referred to redemption. There is a secret agreement between past generations and the present one. Our coming was expected on earth. Like every generation that preceded us, we have been endowed with a *weak* Messianic power, a power to which the past has a claim. That claim cannot be settled cheaply.[6]

To Benjamin, we are all weak Messiahs.

The critic David Lloyd also attests that this claim of the past upon us cannot be cheaply settled. He is concerned with 'Irish times', and how in Irish culture a ruined past, the ghosts of those who never achieved their proper potential, still haunt the present, so that memory continually becomes displaced into present times. This means that forgetting becomes difficult.[7] This is hardly so in English culture, forgetting being all too easy for those who have historically been on the dispensing not on the receiving end of power. The past here is power, not wreckage; Irish history hurts in a way British history does not.

What does this talk of salvation mean, of redemption, of our coming on earth being expected, and so involving a claim on us? In the context of most histories, these words are unfamiliar – like the word 'Messiah'. I do not mean by 'salvation' that we can repair the suffering of the past. Reparation, compensation, is impossible. No justice is possible, either, at least in the redistributive sense. But perhaps we can save the past by seeing that its sufferings and hopes are not lost; not wiping away the tears of the past, as John D. Caputo puts it, but just keeping them *safe*, and pleading on behalf of the dead and their unheard stories. Their silences may thus be made to speak.

The hope is that these dead may be given a voice in a future that will not be closed but, because their voice will be heard, made open. The child is the future. 'The historian writes in the time between the dead and the children, between irreparable suffering and hope for the unforeseeable to-come'.[8]

PART I
BEGINNINGS

Josef Koudelka, *Ireland 1972*. Croagh Patrick Pilgrimage.

1

The Journey West

The most blood-stained of the districts of Ireland.

Alexander Shand, 1885

Josef Koudelka, *Ireland 1972*. Croagh Patrick Pilgrimage. The three men in this image kneel at the summit of Croagh Patrick, which has been a place of Christian pilgrimage for over a millennium and a half. Before then it was a sacred place for perhaps twice that time. Below the summit, and in the background, is Clew Bay, the Atlantic Ocean speckled with islands, drowned drumlins marooned by geological time. Josef Koudelka called this photograph *Ireland 1972*. It is part of a collection of his work entitled *Exiles*. In the other photographs in the collection, Koudelka photographed the margins of Europe, margins that are both geographical – Croagh Patrick is at the outermost western limits of Europe – and social. He was drawn to images of gypsies, one of Europe's most powerful symbols of what it is to be at the margins of an acceptable social life.

Indeed, Koudelka was himself an exile, an in-between person, having fled from Prague after the Russian invasion of 1968 and then taken up a relentlessly peripatetic professional life as a photographer, much of it as a stateless person. A man sans state is without a home, and Koudelka's photographs probe time as well as space in the pursuit of the in-between. Just as the people in the photograph are caught in a precise moment of time, they are also outside time. All photographs negotiate time in similar fashion and produce this effect: one frozen, timeful moment endlessly prolonged, the timeful outside time. Reality itself seems in exile, outside space and time. Koudelka's photographs powerfully accentuate this double effect.

The three men in Koudelka's image are kneeling, their individuality caught in their faces and the attitudes of their bodies as each leans on his pilgrim's stick in a different way. One uses it as an oar to steady himself, another as a rest for his head, while the last leans into the stick's point that is firmly embedded in the rocky ground. The men are decidedly in time, and of this place, but they are also outside time. They are separated from the others around them not only by distance, but by the gravity of their demeanour. The other figures in the background seem to be admiring the view, while the three men look inward, into themselves, compelled by the power of this holy place. It is said that St Patrick appeared at this site. They are kneeling, the others stand. They may indeed have completed the final stage of the ascent on their knees, which was, and is still sometimes, the custom, just as it is to walk up barefoot.

This tableau, evoking the disciples at the foot of Christ's cross, gives the trio an epic, monumental quality, and this further exiles them, sets them apart, from those around them. These surrounding figures dress casually; the short skirt of the young woman in the background reminds us it is 1972. The men, on the other hand, are dressed in what must be for them the appropriate attire for pilgrimage: dark suits and white shirts. The formality and the monochrome tones enhance their separateness from the others – something also caught by the striking deep black of their hair. This blackness further expresses being apart, for it is a genetic trait often found in the far west of Ireland. I too carry this mark. I too am of this place. Their hands are big. These men work with their hands. The blackthorn sticks on which they lean were fashioned by these hands. They know hardship.

Two of these men are my kin. The younger man on the right is my first cousin, Seán Joyce (Seán Seoighe), the man on the left, Paddy Kenny (Pádraig Ó Cionnaith), the husband of Sean's sister Sally, and so in Ireland a 'friend', which means of my family, unlike the meaning of 'friend' in English English. The third man, in the middle, is a neighbour of Paddy's, Máirtín Maingín. The steadying oar of Paddy's stick was to aid his injured legs. Embedded in the rocky ground, Sean's stick is an emblem of a life lived embedded on a mountainside farm, all rock, and all slopes that might give way. All three men have now died. For them, Croagh Patrick was always known as 'the Reek'. Carrying their mark – the height of my kin, their black hair – I share these bodies, our genes, a collective deep history.

I first saw this photograph in 1984, on public display in an art gallery in Manchester. It had very quickly become something new. Sean and Paddy had been 'hung' in a gallery, an aesthetic execution that pleased and puzzled me then just as it does now, as I write this. Pleased because my kin had become 'high art', unsure as to what this translation meant, for my kin had become symbolically possessed by others. A copy had been given to the family shortly after it had been taken but put aside and forgotten, or at least regarded as of insufficient importance to be mentioned to visitors.

The three men come from Joyce Country, Dúiche Sheoighe, twenty miles south of Croagh Patrick and to the immediate north of Connemara. The three men would have walked to and from the Reek as well as climbing it, walking over the summits in between. Dúiche Sheoighe spans the territory between the mountain of Maamtrasna (the south Partry mountains) in the north to the isolated settlement of Maam Cross in the south, and runs east–west from the village of Clonbur to Leenane on the Atlantic coast. These points are identified in the map below.

My father was born in 1905 in the townland of Kilbride, on the northern shore of lower Lough Mask, where the lake forms almost a small lake of its own, known on maps as 'Maskeen'. Kilbride is in the extreme south of County Mayo, another in-between place, looking south to Connemara and north and

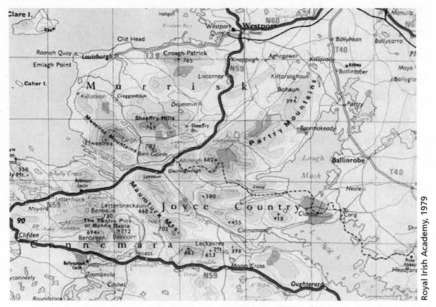

Royal Irish Academy, 1979

Joyce Country, north Connemara.

west outside the Gaeltacht, or Irish-speaking district, of which it is nonetheless firmly a part. Kilbride is near the tiny settlement of Finny, which leads into the mountains to the gaunt majesty of a separate lake, Nafooey, an unfortunate Anglicization of the Irish Loch na Fuaiche. This is a region of immense rain, and immense beauty, though as Seán Seoighe was quick to say, 'You can't eat a view.'

I, however, was not born here. I first made the journey west from London to Joyce Country in 1948, as a child of three. It was in those days such a taxing business that my parents did not repeat it for many years. There was the seemingly endless train journey from the city to the port, choked by rail smoke when the wind was not right, then the sea crossing on something not far from a cattle boat, and then another inexorable rail journey on the other side. Wexford, just across the sea from Wales, was easier, and there I spent the long, happy and yearning summers of childhood and adolescence. My mother, Catherine Bowe, always known as Kitty, was born three years later than my father in the settlement of Loughstown, in the townland of Great Island, in the parish of Kilmokea. The place lies on the river Barrow, near the confluence of the Barrow and the Suir, the Nore flowing into the Suir beforehand, the 'Three Sisters' as they are called – another place of rare beauty.

The names of places matter there, for townland and parish, village, town and county make up different layers of the deep preoccupation of the Irish with land, locality and origin. Dúiche Sheoighe is different again, and the same. *Dúchas* is an Irish noun that conveys the sense that the quality of a person or a way of life is innate in a native land or place, which themselves come down to one as an inheritance.[1] It conveys more than 'country' or 'birthright' in its English translations, more also than the sense that 'home' has, which it nonetheless embraces. Places inscribe *dúchas* and are inscribed by it – Croagh Patrick for instance, which embraces multiple times but also stabilizes time, as with our conceptions of the places we call 'home'.

For my emigrant mother and my father, the departed Irish places remained the guiding star of who they were and what they became, for it seems true that our sense of place becomes most active when we are 'out' of place. To the emigrant, who is by definition always out of place and denied home, this sense is always keen, and is often passed on to the second generation.

The concentration of similar names in one small area in my father's case, Joyce Country, compounds the force of the place as one of origins, though there are scores of Flynns, Lydons, Coynes and others who also have their claims. Besides, they are all intermarried over time anyway. In the burial ground local to Kilbride, Rosshill, just outside the village of Clonbur, some of the names and graves have in recent years been rescued from anonymity, recorded as they now are outside the cemetery walls. The Joyces preponderate. There are over 150 graves, though the Coynes (O'Cadhain) are a decent second. Even so, the ground here is studded by little stumps of stone for which there are no names, and its uneven ground betokens century upon century of the unmarked peasant dead below the stumps.

No names, but still the same names, unsaid but said, for these families have been here now so long.

My Joyces descend from Dúiche Sheoighe, the name Joyce deriving from the thirteenth-century Norman-Welsh Galway colonizers, who were rapidly either embourgeoisified as Galway city bigwigs (the Joyces are one of the seven 'tribes' of Galway city, each now with a traffic roundabout named after it) or Gaelicized, as with my lot, the great and mostly poor rural majority. My namesake James's family left Galway for east Cork in the late seventeenth century – there were 641 Joyce households on the Galway–Mayo borders in the mid nineteenth century immediately after the Great Famine, only eighty-three in east Cork. James, we are told, not differentiating Cork from Connemara, carried the Joyce coat of arms, 'with care', from home to home across Europe.[2]

'The soul is seen through its hardships', as the curator of Koudelka's *Exiles* puts it in describing his photographs. 'Hardship' can be defined as that which exacts physical or mental endurance, so that my parents' is also a story of endurance, and of the adaptation hardship necessitates if it is to be borne. The hardship of the peasant on the land and the peasant on foreign ground. The most emphatic example of this hardship was endurance of unimaginable catastrophe in the form of the Great Famine of the 1840s – or, as it was called in the Irish-speaking west of Ireland, in places like Joyce Country, *am an droch-shaoil*, the time of the bad life, or *am an ghorta*, the time of the hunger. Proportionate to population, this was the greatest catastrophe in nineteenth-century European history. During this period death and enforced emigration claimed a quarter of the population of around 8 million. In the western areas the toll was even greater.

One of the consequences of this death and scattering was the near-total eradication of the old Gaelic culture. Modern Ireland was 'spat out of the horror and squalor' of the Famine,[3] born in a form that eventually brought to pass the vision of the British governors: one of the small farmer operating on the model of the free market, replacing the unwanted remnants of the old subsistence agriculture of the rundale system and the *clachan*.[4] If the modern Irish state emerged from such horror – the 'curse of reason' as this highly effective form of state-building has been called – so too did the British one, for it was in the decades surrounding the 1840s that the modern bureaucratic state took the form we recognize today.[5] This form involved the routinization of suffering and deprivation in such a way that they became amenable to the operations of paperwork, whether locally or far away in the English capital. At the centre of this was Charles Trevelyan, not only the administrator of the famine but the inventor of state 'administration', and a father of the modern British Civil Service.[6]

But, at the same time as hunger and departure, enchantment. The famine cleared the landscape for a new gaze: that of the tourists who started to visit this region from the 1850s. This new tourist gaze was as callous as it was quick to find expression: these are the words of the historical geographer Kevin Whelan in his fine account of the making of the modern Irish rural landscape:

In pre-Famine Ireland one of the commonplaces of historical writing was that poverty spoiled the tourist's view, the contamination of the aesthetic by the visible, noisy, dirty poor … The post-Famine emptying of the west and the absence of poor people allowed the Irish landscape to be presented in appealing terms, just as its accessibility increased. The advent of reliable steamship passenger services between Britain and Ireland, allied to the spread of the railway system, ferried tourists into hitherto inaccessible areas. Trains carrying tourists into the west met those carrying emigrants out of it.[7]

In 1852 William Wakeman published in Dublin (not in London) *A Week in the West of Ireland*. The cover of the book shows a well-proportioned young man dressed in tight white trousers, a blue jacket, and a straw hat – the costume of the leisure classes at play. Fishing rod in hand, he scales a hill, his left foot planted on 'Joyce Country', his right, as he ascends a hill on his way to Galway, on 'Connemara'. The Joyces have played their assigned role in this depiction of the 'Western peasant', being both stood on and eulogized.[8] From one perspective, the people of Joyce Country represented the noble Irish savage. *Black's Picturesque Tourist of Ireland*, published in Edinburgh in 1872, for example, tells us: 'Much has been written about the Joyces, and the many marvels of their stateliness and strength are on record … Mr Inglis describes them as a magnificent race of men, the biggest, tallest and stoutest he has ever seen in Ireland, eclipsing even the peasantry of the Tyrol.'[9] In contrast, Alexander Shand's *Letters from the West of Ireland* (Edinburgh, 1885) portrays the local people as brutally ignorant: it is 'the most blood-stained of the districts of Ireland'.

Long before even the emergence of tourism, in the 1750s the Joyces had presented to those in authority a world that was felt to be strikingly different to their own. Lord Chief Justice Baron Edward Williams wrote to the earl of Warwick sometime around 1760 that the part of Connemara on the west side of the lakes, where the Joyces lived, was but little known 'to the gentleman even of Mayo … for the inhabitants are not reduced so as to be amenable to the laws, and have very little communication with what they call the continent of Ireland … They keep to the manners of the old Irish and are almost to a man bigoted papists.'[10]

The transformation of revulsion and contempt into enchantment is explained by Whelan:

Tourists were attracted to the West as an antidote to full-blooded industrial capitalism. The metropolitan centre redefined its rural periphery as unspoiled, and inhabited by uncorrupted and therefore noble peasants, living in harmony with their environment.

In Ireland, this conception of the west was also taken up by cultural nationalists, who presented its distinctive landscape as evidence of a unique, ancient and unchanging cultural identity. The west was constructed as the bearer of the authentic Irish identity in the rural, archaic and unspoilt landscape, an instructive contrast to modern, industrial and urbanized Britain. Escaping modernity and its brutalizing mass values, the western peasant became the timeless emblem of a pristine world, a precious ancient remnant on the remote rim of modern Europe.[11]

Does not Koudelka share in this 'enchantment of the West' in his depiction of the timeless, the epic, and the monumental? I think not, for in seeing the soul through its hardships he evokes the opposite of this version of a peasant Eden. Instead of his figures being frozen in time as the bearers of a changeless vision of authenticity, his images probe multiple times, and they encompass the 'in-between' of time, the interstices of different times, and the sense of being both in time and outside it. Nonetheless, he does depict a world that is on the edge, the rim – a world that is not 'ours', one exterior to the secular, developed Western economies and societies so many of us now inhabit.

As the historian Eric Hobsbawm recognized, this change – the death of the peasantry – is, in truth, perhaps the most fundamental one the contemporary modern world has seen. It is this that, as he writes, 'cuts us off forever from the world of the past', a rent in the garment of time more violent and complete than any other, though this violence upon the past has gone but little remarked in advanced societies. 'For since the neolithic era most human beings had lived off the land and its livestock or harvested the sea as fishers. With the exception of Britain, peasants and farmers remained a massive part of the occupied population even in industrialized countries until well into the twentieth century.'[12]

In Europe the Spanish peasantry, for example, was halved in the twenty years after 1950, the Portuguese in the two decades after 1960. In Spain agricultural workers formed just under half the population in 1950, and this was reduced to 14.5 per cent in 1980. In the 1960s, Italy was transformed by the vast movement of people from the rural south, the Mezziogiorno, to the rapidly industrializing north. Eastern Europe was slower to decline, but that peasant world too has now almost gone. The story is similar outside Europe: in Latin America; in Japan, where farmers were reduced from over 50 per cent of the population in 1947 to 9 per cent in 1985 – in fact, throughout the world except sub-Saharan Africa, India and Southeast Asia, and China.

This change has occurred in the space of my lifetime, since 1945, so that I have seen this world we have lost, and been part of its ending. The Joyces and the Bowes – both sides of my family – were part of this silently epochal transformation. In my family history I am the link between old and new, the firstborn of the new, and yet a carrier of the old. I feel myself deeply privileged to have seen the lost world. To adapt an English usage of my cousin Seán Seoighe, one surfacing from his own Irish, 'It was my glory' to have witnessed the old world. I witness it now in writing, and feel a responsibility so to do.

By 2010 almost two-thirds of Irish people were urbanized, and rural Ireland receded from people's daily awareness. Change in the nature of capitalist agriculture was complemented by immigration. Half a century earlier, around 500,000 out of a total population of 2.5 million in the Republic emigrated to Britain in the 1950s, the great majority of them leaving agricultural work. The encounter of the peasant with urban and industrial ways was in the Irish case particularly sharp for Britain was not only industrialized earlier than elsewhere, but had also been urbanized earlier and more completely than anywhere else.

Hobsbawm is right: this is a 'world we have lost', though this should not lead us to think of the old world as unchanging, so contributing to its mythologizing – something that seems both immune to historical knowledge and to go on relentlessly, in ever-novel forms but with the same delusion intact, that of Eden found again. What academics call 'tradition' and 'modernity' have for centuries sat side-by-side, sometimes in antagonism, sometimes as complements. This was especially so in Ireland, because of its closeness to Britain, and the geographical relationship of Ireland to the Atlantic world from the eighteenth century onwards. This was the case even on the 'remote rim' of Connemara. It was from there that the building workers who constructed industrial Britain were drawn. There was also centuries-old seasonal migration by agricultural labourers to Britain, and it is one of the ironies of the tragic history of the west that it was the remittances from abroad of those forced to migrate that enabled so much of the old culture to perpetuate itself, not least in places like Joyce Country.

My father's father, Patrick, does not appear on the census of 1911, nor does his son Patrick, the eldest boy. They had left thirteen-year-old Michael as de facto household head to help my grandmother Mary run the farm, aided or otherwise by my three-year-old father. The two Patricks were not absconders on census day, however, for they were far away in Pittsburgh, PA. My grandfather crossed over and back more than once in those days, to Pittsburgh and its steel mills, in search of work. His son Pat, on that day in 1911, with him as a young man of eighteen years, was to die in these mills, crushed to death in the railway yards of Carnegie's steelworks.

Many of the people from Joyce Country emigrated to other towns in industrial Pennsylvania than Pittsburgh (Pittsburgh abounded in Joyces, my aunt Mary marrying another Joyce on her arrival in the city, where she was to remain for the rest of her life). In particular, local people went to Scranton. Those who did so – people who might not own even an ass at home – rode the first completely electrified streetcar system in America, and lived in what liked to be called 'The Electric City'. There they held on to the Irish language with fierce determination, as many were monolingual Irish speakers.

Across the lake from my father's house lies Cloughbrack (An Clóch Breac). On the earliest nineteenth-century Ordnance Survey maps the area is marked 'America Village'. Baile Meiriceá was a cluster of houses forming in those days a clachan (*clochan*) – a small, nucleated settlement that was not a village in the English sense, but a place where people lived cheek-by-jowl, house upon house, going out each day to tend to lands they held in small and irregular 'strips', as in so many peasant settlements in Europe. This was how it was before the single family farm developed gradually before 1900 (as late as the 1880s rundale was common here). Baile Meiriceá is at the fork in the road where people said goodbye for the last time, the 'American Wake' now ended and departure inevitable. It is at this fork that Paddy Kenny and my cousin Sally lived and brought up a family of five children. It was hardship for those who went and for those who stayed; rural Ireland was a poor place to rear children until the years of the 'Celtic Tiger'.

My parents were part of this ceaseless movement of people. Through the 1930s and '40s they went backwards and forwards between England and Ireland before making a life together in London, where children anchored them, even though my mother would exit London for Ireland at every opportunity that presented itself. Indeed, like many others, emotionally and spiritually she never left it.

For all the coming and going, and for all the interpenetration of the modern and the traditional, my parents' world was radically unlike that of London and the English. They made sure we were aware of this other world, inducting us children into it with energy and enthusiasm. From childhood onwards, their difference from what was around us alerted me to what was being lost; as they lived their lives and met their deaths, they played out before my eyes a world that was indeed being lost forever. Emigration and life in London, if not sealing them off completely from the momentous changes that were going on in Ireland, nonetheless preserved the Ireland of their childhood and young lives as the present tense of their English ones.

In Ireland today, my still Irish-speaking kin in Joyce Country, the sons of Paddy Kenny in Koudelka's photograph, now refer sardonically to themselves as 'hobby farmers', their regret mixed with realism. In the booming Tiger years between 1993 and 2008, the number of Irish farms declined by over one-third. By 2015 only one-third of Irish farms were economically viable, while another third only remained sustainable by means of off-farm income. The remaining third face a precarious future, if any at all.[13] Of the viable, it is estimated that, in the near future, over three-quarters will be part-time in operation. The sons of Paddy Kenny and their like farm on regardless, and pass down to their children the same love and knowledge of the land. Some sons will take this knowledge on, others not. Paddy's daughters take the language on, and marriage to other farmers perpetuates knowledge of the land between families. There is still a tenacious attachment to the land, the language, and the old ways. Yet what for the most part is happening daily and inexorably is that all these things are now seen by conscious effort. The old ways are now viewed as the past, not lived as part of the present.

Instead, the urban bleeds into the rural. The housing boom of the 1970s laid the foundations for the later disintegration of rural Ireland. By the 2006 Irish census, records showed that 27 per cent of *all* housing had been built in the previous decade. Dublin now sprawls out into the rural hinterland. This is unparalleled globally, as was the increase in house prices over the same period. The countryside was no longer concerned with agricultural production, but with the consumption of lifestyle, leisure and the aesthetic.

Change has been evident in terms of language as well as land. Parallel to a two-thirds urbanized Ireland in 2010, the numbers of those in the Gaeltacht who used the Irish language as their primary means of carrying on their daily life could be measured in the low tens of thousands. Even if outside the Gaeltacht, the better-off sort of Irish are now educating their children in all-Irish schools, and there has been a language revival of sorts; the tie between the land and the language is almost broken. In my lifetime, Irish in the Joyce Country has gone from being the first to the second language, and if the pattern of its use is still complex, held together as it is by communal ties, inter- and intra-familial loyalties, and very uneven educational provision, then this is a pattern of what looks like inevitable decline and possible extinction. Certainly extinction when the language is understood as the unbroken inheritance of the generations who have worked the land and the seas for their livelihoods.

Endings and losses; beginnings and gains. These things are without measure. The life of the land has been eclipsed, the culture that went with it eroded. A threshold seems to have been passed, an ending reached. In an essay called 'Campo Santo', W. G. Sebald contemplates the Corsican dead and peasant death. In the graveyard of the village of Piana, he reflects:

> They are still around us, the dead, but there are times when I think that perhaps they will soon be gone. Now that we have reached a point where the number of those alive on Earth has doubled within just three decades, and will treble within the next generation, we need no longer fear the once overwhelming numbers of the dead. Their significance is visibly decreasing ... In the urban societies of the late twentieth century, on the other hand, where everyone is instantly replaceable and is really superfluous from birth, we have to keep throwing ballast overboard, forgetting everything that we might otherwise remember: youth, childhood, our origins, our forebears and ancestors.[14]

Now, when the living overawe the dead, when it is no longer necessary to hold on to their dwindling number, a strange reversal takes place. For with the coming of the Internet and what has been called 'web memory', which Sebald could not foresee, it now becomes conceivable to remember to an extent never previously possible. Just as the need to remember is eclipsed, so the possibility of remembering is enhanced. But this new mode of remembering is different to the old. It is subject to the algorithmic lottery; it is distanced, mediated, and marketized. It is a narcissistic remembering of ourselves rather than of the dead, so that it is likely to bring, as Sebald writes, 'a present without memory, in the face of a future that no individual mind can now envisage'.[15]

How might we remember, retain and preserve? With the tide of time against us, should we even try? Or can we, as Sebald suggests, do without the dead? This depends partly upon the view of time we have. We commonly think of it as linear. This is public time, the time of science, but also of common sense, in which the present succeeds the past to be followed by the future, in which only the 'now' of the present is real. But, as we know, 'now' evaporates as soon as we try to grasp it.

However, what may be called cultural time understands time as something that exists within the unfolding of human life. If the linear view of time privileges the present as real, this contrary view of time sees the past as real too, real in a different sense from the actuality of the present, but still having a reality the future does not share. After all, only the past has existed, and so only the past is real. Many cultures, if not our own, still have such nonlinear conceptions of time. We are odd. In fact cultural time – time that is relative – is nearer to the time of modern physics. Past and present seem in truth to be in coexistence, in mutual dependence, so that we might think of the past as always coiled within us. It is ever ready to unfurl, so that the past in this sense has not passed, and is constantly happening in all our presents. One answer to why we should retain and linger alongside the dead is that they linger in and retain us. Koudelka's photographs show this coexistence at work: being in different times, being between times, seeming to be outside time altogether.

2

The Journey East

They would have thrived on our necessities.
What they survived we could not even live.

Eavan Boland

When writing, we converse with ghosts it is difficult to hear back, even when they are benevolent ones. The experiences my parents encountered, as I think about the two of them now, so long after their deaths, seem to me akin to those of benevolent ghosts. Johnny died half a century ago, Kitty almost thirty. I listen hard after all these years and they are still there to guide me. Through them I have conversed with the world from which they came, and now I do so with the world that they made as emigrants when they came to London.

My father first made the journey east to England in 1929; my mother, one of fourteen children, was not far behind in 1932. They both came from and went to a world of hardship. In Boland's words, 'What they survived we could not even live.' I lived what they survived, at least a part of it. Numerically and historically the emigrant Irish have for most of British history been by far the most important immigrant group, though you would not know this from the discourse of British public life. They remain still 'an unconsidered people', their children even more unconsidered.[1]

The London world my parents made was also one they made for me, and my younger brother John, and they made it emphatically an Irish immigrant one. Being Irish and immigrant were bound deeply into being Catholic. Catholicism gave me a sense of what it was to live in a structure of meaning that embraced almost everything. And then I moved beyond this embrace into nonbelief at an early age. Nonetheless, I could still see the interconnectedness of faith and life, and how it all worked to make a single thing, a way of life I always felt a kinship with. Being Irish Catholic was to be in effect an ethnic Catholic, and so even without faith I remain an ethnic Catholic, a devout ex-Catholic.[2] Which is to be at the same time nationalist and universalist, at home in a church of the One True Faith anywhere, part of those who congregate to make a way of life.

The literary critic Terry Eagleton comes to mind here. Our backgrounds are similar, though he was from working-class Salford. He writes of how Catholicism as a body of ritual creates a mental constitution 'at odds with a social order which made a fetish out of interiority', so that for him there was no instinctive feel for a liberal sensibility.[3] Catholicism is about doing the proper things, building from the outside inwards. Rather than contingency and self-creation, both Catholicism and an Irish devotion to the tribe above the individual gave him, as it gave me, an appreciation of how the habitual, the inherited, 'the sheer inertia of history', govern our lives. The public, collective and symbolic dimensions of selfhood were what mattered. And so, as Eagleton noted, Catholicism, just like Judaism, is at bottom fundamentally un-English.[4]

This is how the writer John O'Callaghan describes being brought up Irish Catholic in England:

To be brought up as an Irish Catholic in England is to be nurtured as a schizophrenic ... History is the most obvious place to see the effect of being introduced to a background of which I was not the true inheritor ... the Irish – the native Irish-presence of my parents at home – brought reminders that the fair play, the self-control, the impartiality of the British is as skin deep as in any other race ... [T]hings in England are not always what

29

they seem. You are born outside furrows of thought that some pure natives never see over. It is worth risking the schizophrenia to be reared without blinkers.[5]

Schizophrenia? Not quite, perhaps, but decidedly born outside the furrows. Louis MacNeice's words catch it better, if out of a very different experience: 'I wish one could either *live* in Ireland or *feel oneself* in England' (the emphases are MacNeice's own). I could not live in Ireland because I was habituated into English-ness, and I could not feel fully at home here, in a 'background', a history, of which I was not the true inheritor. Standing in an English churchyard, the dead around me were not mine. But I was still born into the Englishness that surrounded the Irish-ness, the Englishness of the streets. There in the London of the 1950s, we were described by our parents as 'Irish descent', not English or British, not postcolonial 'hybrids', not 'diasporic', not Irish either but of the Irish. It was good enough.

In-betweeners, in fact, but of the Irish sort, *idir eatarthu*, between two things and yet of both at the same time, which had its comforts as well as the unease MacNeice's words suggest. Sounding English and feeling Irish conveyed a sort of liberat-ing invisibility, but might also sunder us from who we were. What hue of green one was depended on the generation one was born into, of course, but also on the presence or absence of the Irish childhood summer, family involvement in Irish and Catholic associational life, family size, and the number of Irish relations over here and over there – among many other factors. We were deep green on all these counts; others, the majority, were of a paler hue. For these and so many of the others who preceded them, there was in time nothing left but the bones of their names.

This in-between condition was informed by a deep sense of place that was located in the physical setting of the different 'homes' I experienced: those of west London's inner-city Pad-dington, where I spent my first eighteen years, and the other homes in Wexford and Dúiche Sheoighe. Anthropologists tell us that place is sensed, and in the process the senses are placed. This means that place is experienced as a meeting of space and time, so that lives and events are joined together as embodied memories. We are not only in places, but of them. This is especially so in childhood, when the senses are alert and the heart open, and where all memory is shaped.

Beyond the Church, the most important institution in my parents' lives was the British welfare state. The British state, for their generation as for mine, became indeed a sort of 'home', or at least a source of refuge. As regards us migrant families, there was what has been called a 'conspiracy of denial' on the part of the Irish government – about emigration in general, and in particular about the mass waves of emigration to England in the 1950s. It was the Catholic Church, for all its self-interest, that came to our aid, especially to the aid of women like my mother. Irish England remained ignored by the Irish state until relatively recently, when in Ireland, in trouble in the post-Tiger years, we went from being the 'diaspora' to the disbelieving targets of something called the 'Gathering'. The Irish embassy in London had little impact on our post-war communities, just as the middle-class Irish Club in fashionable Eaton Square could have been on Mars as far as we were concerned. As Boland's 'Emigrant Irish' begins (Boland was the daughter of the Irish ambassador in England, it might be noted):

> Like oil lamps, we put them out the back –
> of our houses, of our minds. We had lights
> better than, newer than and then
> a time came, this time and now
>
> we need them.

After his first journey east to England, my father then went back and forth between 1929 and 1944, when he married my

mother. Like most of his peers, he went to work in the building trade, and in the 1930s and through the Depression he led
the usual life of the itinerant Irish labourer, 'sleeping on the
job, and eating off the shovel', as the saying went.[6] When we
returned 'home' to the West just after his death, his fellow itinerants greeted us with remarks such as 'I slept with your father
in Harrow Weald in 1936.' This 'home' was populated by men
who told of their English labour and their unavoidably shared
berths as if they were battle honours, 'Stratford-upon-Avon',
'Rugby', 'Potters Bar'.[7]

Before their marriage, my father and mother lived in north-
west London, where they were part of the intense social life
of young Irish immigrants of their day, centred upon the pubs
and dancehalls of Willesden, Harlesden, Kilburn and Cricklewood, another 'north-west passage' alongside that of Jewish
London. This one ran from the Euston and Paddington railway
termini, instead of the East End. This was the world of pub
names that were exotic to me as a child: 'The Big Crown',
'The Little Crown', 'The Case Is Altered', 'The Skiddaw'. The
places where what seemed to me giant men gathered, always

My father, Sean Joyce, and me. Kilbride, 1949.

in their blue serge suits, fabled labourers among them ('The Steam Man', 'The Man and a Half'). The feared and respected 'Connemara Men'.

My father was the mildest of men. Above is a photograph of him if not quite in his early days then in 1949, when he was still a robust and healthy man. He holds me, smiling down, his arms enfolding me, his left hand showing the signs of the damage war had done as well as the signs of love. It is his hands I remember him by; as children we examined them closely as my mother, not he, told us what had happened. His hands – the means of his livelihood and the embodiment of his identity as a 'working man'. I am a big child, he a big man, beside is my tall cousin Seán, the man on the right in Koudelka's photograph of 1972. He is barefoot.

Behind is the wall up the long bohereen to the house, behind which Kilbride mountain stretches, the lake below. Johnny was the first to be born in the new house of 1905, in that same year, the four others in the old house even further up the hill. His mother, Mary Burke, raised her five children in the knowledge she would have to lose all but the one who inherited the small farm. Most other parents shared this terrible knowledge. As the historian David Fitzpatrick has observed, 'growing up in Ireland meant preparing oneself to leave it'.[8] More than Poland, even more than Sicily, more perhaps than anywhere else on earth.

It was in the old house that my father's grandfather was born around 1850, Liam na hAille – Liam of the Cliff, as Seán translated it. Where the house is sited a deep cleft cuts into the mountainside and marks the townland border. These old Irish are a hidden people, as the national census records were destroyed either by the deliberate action of the British government or in the fire at the Four Courts at the beginning of the Civil War in 1922.[9] The new republic was founded on the ashes of the *ancien régime*. The old house was there when the first Ordnance Survey was finished in 1842. We know the hidden

Irish through the political abstractions of maps, a vestige of what was.

The buildings took my father to Portsmouth in 1940. There he was buried alive in a German bombing raid. He was the only one of seven in the house to survive. The physical damage done to his hands and arms left him unable to do the hard but well-paid labour that would have earned us a better life. Of the mental scars we knew nothing, though I can read the signs better now. These in retrospect seem huge, both in my life as in his. I describe them later. Nonetheless, year after year, he was up each day at 5:30 a.m. and out to his job as a 'general labourer' for the municipal council. Then home at four o'clock in the afternoon. The wage of the 'Council labourer' was among the lowest in the country at that time. And so each evening he was out again at his shift in the kitchens of the Cumberland Hotel on the corner of Edgware Road and Oxford Street, then home at ten. In the 1950s the Irish had almost completely colonized the staff of the giant Cumberland. We saw too little of him as children, apart from the precious evening hours and the weekends. Hidden Ireland, hidden father.

Here is a photograph of my mother in the 1930s. She stands in the haggard, dressed in her best London wear, in front of the two-storey family house that was impossibly small for the many children. (A haggard is a farmyard, the local term of use, and there one was not out in the farmyard but in an old tongue "abroad in the haggard".) My grandmother is there in the middle, my aunt Stasia's young suitor Mick O'Shea on one side. This photograph was taken

My mother and grandmother, the Great Island, c. early 1930s.

on one of my mother's periodic visits back as she see-sawed between the two countries, between domestic service and home, before marriage. My grandmother was a striking woman; she 'holds herself' well, as it used to be said, and is well turned out in her farmwife's garb, her hair carefully parted, her glasses adding to the dignified bearing.

Her composure seems only temporary, as if she is ready to get back to work as soon as possible. This is the woman who by then had given birth to fourteen children, suffering the grief of four of them dying early. Three lived their lives in London while the others were scattered around Ireland. My grandmother was a Kent – a family that had prospered in her townland of 'the Island' (Great Island), where the land was good and money was to be made from wheat and barley; also from fishing in the Barrow, which all the local men did, often illegally, at night in their black-tarred 'prongs'.

Great Island, like Joyce Country, has a very strong sense of its own identity. My grandmother had chosen Patrick Bowe from the nearby village of Ramsgrange. Bowe is a west Wexford and east Kilkenny name, Anglo-Norman in origin, like so many in this corner of Ireland so near the Welsh coast and the Old English enclave of Pembrokeshire: Englishes, Butlers, Suttons, Wheelers and Whittys abound. My grandparents' wedding photograph hangs above me as I write. She is a beauty, he not her equal in looks. He was an only child, his mother having died giving birth to him. Again it is the hands that speak; both their hands are big and powerful. If the Kents had land they worked hard for it, and Patrick was a farmer too.

As it turned out the marriage was a rocky one, as he seems to have reduced the large farm to a small one by his drinking. ('Sure he drank three farms', reports his grandson.) I knew my grandparents as a child, and was taken back by my mother for my grandfather's wake and funeral when I was eleven, in 1956. His body was laid out in the back bedroom of his eldest son's new house. Dressed in splendour, in death he was got up in what seemed to me then the vestments of a priest, singularly inappropriate given the accounts of his life. The corpse and the decaying lilies in that back room overwhelmed my senses.

My mother, Kitty, was as outgoing as Johnny was quiet, and as tiny as he was tall, which did not prevent her absolute rule over the three men who loomed over her. She loved to talk, liked company, and told endless stories about 'the Island'. Like my father she was educated at the local National School, walking the seven miles there and back every day, without shoes in the summer, and taking the younger ones with her. There she was met by the impudence of petty authority so characteristic of the time: the local middle class, the priest, the doctor, and the teacher. My mother experienced a new form of authority when she came to work in domestic service in London. She met kindness too, and later a sort of liberation in well-paid wartime weapons manufacturing.

All the property my parents had was in us, their children. They left enough to bury themselves, a prized tea-set, a few letters sprinkled with the 'TGs and PGs' of a ritualized form of writing that had little or nothing to do with an interior life. It was the rituals that mattered: the Thank Gods and the Please Gods. Letter writing was to give news or transact family business rather than to convey states of mind and feeling, as among the educated middle class, whose epistolary legacies I envy. They were the same as peasant letters everywhere – those of Polish peasants for instance.[10] Theirs was still in good part an oral culture anyway, especially in the far west.

As their children were their only property, so are we their legacy, and our children too. I then am their 'document', as is the life they made in London a kind of 'document', the 'home' they made together and for us, the thing that proved they were there. The house is the cradle of the home, and it is the symbolic meaning and the physical reality of the house that most eloquently speak of who we are. The Irish house tells of who they were; but so does the English one, for it was made, as best

36

they could make it, in the image of what they had left. The English one made me, too, the old conjured into the new.

Our 'house' was in fact a flat, at 11 Ashmore Road in Paddington. My mother and father lived there for nineteen years, almost all of the span of their twenty years of marriage. It was there I spent the first eighteen years of my life, my brother sixteen of his. This place is ineradicably within me, organically. As the years pass, I remember No. 11 and its neighbourhood with more, not less, intensity. The place inhabits me. The words of the great sociologist Pierre Bourdieu come to mind: 'What is "learned by the body" is not something that one has, but something that one is.'

The French philosopher Gaston Bachelard, in his *Poetics of Space*, writes, 'The house ... is a group of organic habits. After twenty years, in spite of all the other anonymous stairways, we would recapture the reflexes of the "first stairway", we would not stumble on that rather high step ... The feel of the tiniest latch has remained in our hands.' He writes of how 'in its countless alveoli space contains time. That is what space is for.' Memories are housed, quite literally stored up, within the physicality of the rooms of the habitation. The house/habitation, according to Bachelard, is 'one of the greatest powers of integration for the thoughts, memories and dreams of mankind ... Its councils of continuity are unceasing. Without it man would be a dispersed being ... It maintains him through the storm of heavens and through those of life ... It is body and soul.'[11] It is the human being's 'first world'.

In Bachelard's understanding, we make our homes as we go through life; but the house goes with us always, as it is through this form that we most fully know what home is – the first house above all, but also the other subsequent ones of later years. These successive houses reverberate one with another, the new shaping the old and the old the new. In this sense we never really leave our houses, especially the first one. How does this 'reverberation' work, between the old and the new 'house'? First the old house, the Irish one, and then the London habitation.

In order to understand the Irish house, I turn to the remarkable work of the folklorist Henry Glassie. He writes of rural Fermanagh in the North, but what he says holds good elsewhere.[12] The Fermanagh house has the essentials of the houses in Kilbride and on 'the Island'. The central kitchen, where one entered the house, then the two rooms off to left and right, the hearth the centre of the centre that is the kitchen. At the middle of the hearth is the fire. Directions are 'set in motion around the fire', the sun around which everything is set into motion. As Glassie puts it, 'The hearth burns still in the centre of the mind'.[13] There should be nothing to impede the space between the fire and the door, the door being always kept ajar to welcome people, for it is bad manners to knock or to stop the visitor in the doorway. People should stay in the kitchen and not go into the two rooms, stay in the kitchen where they can be watched and helped, stopped from brooding. In the kitchen one was in 'company'. The rooms are for sleeping, where a limited privacy could be had if necessary.

The kitchen is intermediate between the rooms and outside. The outside is formed by what are in effect concentric circles radiating from the house, taking first the 'street' outside (the walkway in front of the house), then the outhouses, including the farmyard or haggard (into which, once the hay and turf are brought, they are said to be 'home'), then the fields of the holding, then the moss and the bog, then the world outside made up of the local, and only then the great world beyond. This is a culture of centres, according to Glassie, not margins.[14] 'Community' and 'society', just like the household, involve this creation of centres, the original of which is the house. No name marks limits, for the priority of the creation of centres means that these define social entities. As he says, 'The one becomes the all at the centre. This way to create order is not restricted to space. It is applied in the still more arbitrary realm of time.'[15]

The year is organized around centres more than beginnings and ends. Order is created not by demarcating a whole, then cutting it into parts, so that this culture is a matter of key occurrences, epiphanies, 'letting the whole take care of itself'. 'History is a cluster of powerful events, space a collection of landmarks', so that 'order is ceded to an endless reality that cannot be completely known', to 'the nature of things'. People's responsibility is not the shape of the whole, but 'the force of wholeness: continuity'.

Continuity is at bottom about survival, as John Berger's magnificent writing on French peasants reveals. Peasants are above all survivors, now for thousands of years, and now for not much longer. Life for the peasant is an 'interlude', one between inheriting and passing on the family holding. The peasant's ideal is in the past, in the dream of not being handicapped in the struggle to survive. His hope is in the future, in handing on the means of survival. After his death he will return to the past and not, he knows, be transposed into the future. 'Progress' means nothing, for the unknown assails everything, and as there is no secure arrival point in the future it is better for the dead to return to the past where they are not at risk. Life goes on in a circle. As Glassie says, continuity is all.[16]

In the house upon which Glassie meditates, the hearth is a point in the continuous whole, the 'crucible of continuity; here, at the centre of space, people work to unify time, keeping a fire alight that consumes the intervals between generations, between the great days and every day and night'. The house is said to be 'lonesome' without a fire. The fire must never go out. Travel from the hearth betokens potential danger; holy water is at hand, and one's view on leaving the house is of the cross and the Sacred Heart picture, the latter always with a light burning below it – the candle, and later the tiny electric cross. The fire protects the seams of space and time, stitching them safely together. Fire therefore burns away 'categorical distinction' by unifying women and men, inside and outside, setting the scene 'for the formation of society'.[17] Thus the community builds itself at the hearth, which is where 'fireside law', 'fireside lore', 'fireside stories', are made. Like the fire, if talk and stories flag they must be revived, continuity must be maintained.[18] What Glassie calls 'organic order' involves the growth of reason through 'an incompleteness, through the complexity and interpenetration of categories'. 'Nothing stops or starts exactly, things go on'. Continuity is established through the stories, including the histories, that are told, and through the homes that are made.

As regards the house in Ireland, one is aware nonetheless of the force of the margins that push in against the centre, constantly threatening it – the margin of the encroaching bog for instance, the curbing of which takes constant labour. Death itself, the grave, is only another margin, for in Irish rural culture the living and the dead mingle. In the past especially so, when a 'fairy' reality ran alongside and penetrated the everyday. My parents and my wife's parents believed in it still, after coming to England: the power of the lone bush in a field, the cry of the *bean sí* (banshee) foretelling a death. It was and still is in some places regarded as wrong to mock and belittle these versions of another supernatural; in the 1930s, long after my mother was a child, the bean sí was simply taken for granted in rural Ireland.[19] Seán Seoighe firmly believed in the powers of the bean sí and of the seventh son of a seventh son. Indeed, the local town of Ballinrobe in Mayo not so long ago had a shop premises given over to such healers.

Irish culture has for good reason been called funerary, and Irish Catholicism itself still has strong residues of this older reality. Those born before baptism entered the marginal state of Limbo – formal doctrine being reproduced at another level by believing Catholics as, under cover of darkness, infant bodies were buried at margins, by walls, between cultivated and uncultivated land. Sometimes burial took place in *cillíni*, children's graveyards; but these had to be located in the corners or on the edges of official graveyards, and sometimes further away if this was not possible, as in the one on the brow of the mountain between Kilbride and Maamtrasna, where good and bad land meet. Not only children were buried in such places, but also sometimes suicides, shipwrecked sailors, strangers, unrepentant murderers, all of whom were at a margin and of an ambiguous condition. The Irish *idir-eatarthu*, in-between, each and both, applies once again.[20]

My parents thus came to England with these ideas of what dwelling in this world was, and what a dwelling should be. They faced many a disappointment at 11 Ashmore Road. The house in which we lived was inhabited at cross-purposes to its design and intention. It was twice removed, once from the respectable classes for whom it was built around the 1870s, and once again from the house in Ireland. The neighbourhood was composed almost entirely of three-storey houses that, by the 1940s, as in so many other districts in this part of London, had for long been given over to individual tenancies. The area had one of the highest population densities in London. Invariably there was at least a single household to each level, so that the occupancy level had trebled from the original. This meant that we lived in a flat not meant for single habitation. The internal structure was simple, to the point of crudity. The kitchen was at the back, a large bedroom to the front, a smaller one in the middle, a passage, 'the hall', to the side, running between the front door and the kitchen at the back. Half way from the front door to the stairs the first part of the hall led to a separate flat upstairs, the remaining part bending on its way to the kitchen. This meant that access to the two bedrooms was through this semi-public no man's land of the hall. The bedroom doors were locked, so that to enter we had to bring the key with us each time.

As in so many Irish dwellings in post-war London, one of these rooms, the small 'back' room, was rented out for a period to an Irish family of four, not for profit but out of solidarity.

This, a strange echo of the conacre micro-division of land in an older, rural Ireland, seems incredible to me now; we were so short of space (albeit not as cramped as the large families of many of my school friends). No bathroom, no inside toilet, the outdoor privy reached through the apartment below. A stinking clump of grass formed the tiny, unattended front 'garden'; the larger back garden, part of downstairs' patrimony anyway, was a blasted wilderness.

Like everybody else, we rented from anonymous landlords, 'slum' or otherwise (the notorious Rachman held much property in adjacent north Kensington, where I went to school). However, our manor was a cut or two above the real slums that surrounded us and through which I walked to school every day. Most notably, those in the area around Golborne Road and Portobello Road, 'the Lane', which by the early sixties was already becoming 'trendy', itself a sixties coinage. This perambulation included Southam Street, thought by Brendan Behan to be the worst slum in Europe. As a consequence, and with some justification given our family size, we never thought of ourselves as 'poor'; they were in Southam Street.

Roger Mayne, Southam Street, London, 1957.

Mary Evans Picture Library

Our house in Paddington was nonetheless deeply connected to the ones left in Ireland, and the reverberations of the homes left behind were nonetheless strong and clear in the new one. If it is the first house that most fully helps us know what home is and how it can be made, then my parents transplanted the old into the new, despite the appalling obstacles. Peasants are survivors, and life the interlude when something must be passed on – the patrimony. For Johnny and Kitty this could not be land, but it was the passing on itself that mattered, 'the force of wholeness: continuity', as Glassie says. Life went in a circle, with the old places in Ireland always at its centre. The physical form of the London house was magicked into something else despite all the defeats.

We lived our life in the kitchen, as in the Irish house. There in London the welcoming path ran from the front door through the hall down to the kitchen, in which the fire was almost constantly lit. Directions were still 'set in motion around the fire'. Travel from the hearth betokened potential danger in England, too; as across the sea, holy water was at hand, and the perpetually lit Sacred Heart picture looked down on us, a picture on which was inscribed the dedication of the 'house' to this particular manifestation of the Faith. The fire was never lit in the bedrooms, which were for sleeping. People should indeed stay in the kitchen and not go up into 'the room', though illness often forced my father there. In the kitchen of No. 11 there was a stream of visitors from the west of Ireland and Wexford. These visitors would stay, crammed together, so that Ireland was reproduced in the talk that surrounded us, which included Irish when the westerners visited. Talk came incessantly from the kitchen, and my mother did most of it. I knew 'the Island' as well as if I had always lived there, her childhood memories and London stories mingling together.

My mother only had 'school Irish', and my father did not think to teach us his language, whether because it was thought useless in England; or because it was a badge of the hardship left behind, and so to be hidden; or simply because he did not have the time. Nevertheless, stories had to be told in full and in the correct way every time, so that experience and memory were passed on to us in forms that were designed to be remembered. Continuity was established through these stories and the home in which they were told; as Glassie puts it, 'Nothing stops or starts exactly, things go on', and in that London kitchen The Island seemed to have gone on forever.

This was also reflected in my parents' accents, which remained completely unchanged despite the decades in England. These stories and memories were rich in sound, observation and humour, and – like so much humour that came and comes out of rural Ireland – wickedly accurate in their delineation of character and circumstance. The linguistic resources of Hiberno-English were rich and extensive, and how things were said mattered to us as much as what was said, for even more than the music it was the talk that most enabled one to enter the world my parents brought with them.

The music mattered greatly, however, and matters more and more as I get older, until now the sound of the *uilleann* pipes dissolves all space and time for me, and I walk again by the Barrow as a child, my parents beside me. In his poem 'An Irishman in Coventry', John Hewitt writes, 'The jigging dances and the lilting fiddle/Stirred the old rage and pity in my heart'. I was spared the rage, much of it anyway, but kept the pity.

Seamus Deane has written of how Irish is intractably a spoken language, asking as regards translation into English, 'How can we "hear" in English a language which has been compelled, for its survival, to proclaim a kind of acoustic autarky?'[21] I nonetheless heard Irish, ventriloquized through the deeply Irish language-inflected English of both parents, especially on my father's side, and in Ireland especially through Seán Seoighe in Koudelka's photograph. I heard Irish full-throated at the great, tumultuous weddings we went to as children, my brother and I, pageboys to marrying cousins sometimes, always at the Quex

Road church in Kilburn, when the western crowd gathered and it was only Irish that was heard. Two decades later I was married in this church – the Church of the Sacred Heart.

Just like the photograph, language is absolutely of the moment yet carries within it multiple times. The past works its way silently through us in the present, shaping it and us in ways themselves not present, or even available, to its recipients. Language is the past silently working its way through us. These are words from John Montague's 'A Severed Head':

> Decades later
> that child's grandchild's
> speech stumbles over lost
> syllables of an old order.

The past, as the Irish in the English, flowed through us, and vice versa too, all tangled together; my father's people had by 1950 been bilingual for at least two generations. At what cost, as the Irish declined in this process, I do not know, and so I present more of Montague's words, dark ones:

> To grow
> a second tongue, as
> harsh a humiliation
> as twice to be born.

This notion of the past as language, as with the house in Bachelard's words, was and is a material thing, a 'group of organic habits', something in our bodies, 'what is learned by the body'.

Multiple times are at play here: the moment of listening and talking, the centuries in which language is made and remade, and the deep history of language made in material bodies over species time, the time of genes.[22] We change the past and language in the present, but my Catholic sensibility tells me that it is more a question of language and the past speaking us than we speaking them. The past is something that one is.

The talk of my parents connected the multiple times of language together, and presented them to us as their unknowing gift. Language and the house in which it was heard formed their own sort of Irish 'centre' in England. Language included the strange and wonderful English talk of Wexford, close to eighteenth-century pronunciation, full of words taken from an even older English and given a meaning now specific only to that Irish context.[23] Tea rhymed with tay and sea with say, and abroad in the haggard there might be 'na'ar – a one'; and thus some time would have to elapse before one might see 'ere a one'. My mother's language was agricultural, though na'ar a curse word passed her lips, her lullaby for us, for she was not a sentimental woman: 'There's a hole in me head you could ready roll a turnip in / Another in me arse you could ready roll it out again'. Blessed with a good appetite, one was said to have the capacity to eat the twelve apostles and the Holy Ghost.

Irishness was made outside the house as well as within it, and 'home' was formed not only by the concentric circles of the Irish homestead, but by the complex paths running through the local neighbourhood and connecting all things and places Irish and Catholic.[24] All things Irish and Catholic had a long history in the area, so close as it was to Paddington Station. The railway (to Ireland) and the Grand Junction Canal shaped the geography and political economy of the immediate area, and both were built by Irish labour long before we arrived (the canal was completed in 1801). After the work, much of this labour settled in the area.

Our social life in the street was almost entirely confined to the Irish families. We had no English callers except the odd English Catholic pal of us children, and the stream of rent men, book sellers, milkmen, knife sharpeners, coal men, postmen, hire-purchase men and French onion sellers who came to the door, with whom relations were always very cordial, some of them having been callers for years, above all 'Charlie the milkman'. Nonetheless, this was a city not a rural habitation, and it is here that regulations, metrics, inspectors played their part. Sanitary inspectors enforcing housing regulations, school inspectors school ones; meters for gas and electricity; and 'piped' TV and radio: our space was governed by forces beyond our ken, though not as much as later, in the 'council estate' housing we eventually moved to.

In Ashmore Road we children departed England most summer holidays for Ireland for the whole six weeks of the school holidays. The doctor was Irish, the dentist was Irish, a Wexford woman always served my mother in our local grocery, 'Pearkes Dairies', and if she patronized the 'Home

London Wexfordmen's Association children's party, late 1950s. The author, back right, is the only bespectacled child, surprisingly. He wears (proudly, because somehow to him gangsterish) a striped jacket sent by the Pittsburgh Joyces. His brother stands on his left. This photograph was taken by Paddy Fahey, and is present in the book *Irish Londoners: Photographs from the Paddy Fahey Collection* (Stroud: Sutton, 1997). My mother, however, bought this at the time of taking, from Fahey.

47

and Colonial' grocery she always sought out the Irish assistants. Men had their community at work or in the Irish pubs of Notting Hill, Paddington, Kilburn and all points north-west, although many Catholic parishes had men's clubs. There were also the various county associations, most prominent for us the London Wexfordmen's Association, much patronized by my Wexford uncle Michael, which organized parties and outings with the direct purpose of making us Irish. The outside margins were marked by the 'Protestants' that surrounded us, 'heathens' sometimes being the term of description chosen by my mother, only half-jokingly.

We went to Catholic cubs and scouts. I went to a Catholic primary school, run by nuns, most of whom were Irish. Religious-cum-social outings were organized by the Church, and more than once, and usually in protest, we went on 'pilgrimage' with my mother, never my father. She was a member of the Guild of Catholic Mothers, an organization founded in 1913 and still going strong. This aimed to infuse us with Catholic family values, and to encourage us to have a priestly vocation – its success rate in this being inauspicious, though it is true that I had the odd school friend who had mysteriously emerged from a seminary in Ireland

The author, aged seven, in First Communion regalia outside 11 Ashmore Road. He is ready for the event and anticipating the ice cream and jelly to follow. The horse-drawn milk cart is visible behind. The street contrasts with Southam Street in its order and cleanliness, even though the standard of the accommodation was poor.

or England, transparently unfit for the calling. This piety we experienced at home, too, as we were regular 'reciters' of the rosary, which for the uninitiated is a devotion to the Virgin Mary marked by the ritualized repetition of certain prayers, the ritual for us involving kneeling on hard floors and cold linoleum preparatory to bed. 'Oh no, do we have to say the rosary tonight?'

Life in the kitchen at No. 11 continued. The frequency of the family rosary declined as time went on and adolescent recalcitrance emerged. Memory now is still for me fixed in that room of the cold linoleum floor. The summers when we did not go to Ireland and there was time to be had with my father, the four of us packed together on Saturday night as the radio played: the schmaltz of 'If You're Irish Come into the Parlour' announcing the 'Irish Favourites Hour', the straining to catch a signal from Radio Eireann, the 'Adventures of Dan Dare' ('Pilot of the Future') on Radio Luxembourg on Monday night. Nostalgia. My father teaching me how to shave.

And the boredom and heat of August in London, not a past to be pined for, but for me forever remembered: it is things like the experience of seeing flypaper hanging down from the kitchen ceiling covered in dead and dying flies on an August Sunday afternoon that separate the past from the present, the small things as well as the big, the smell of the sticky insecticide from the flypaper on which the executions took place. High summer, and blacker and blacker the paper, until it was time to change to a new one. Flies everywhere then, especially in those houses; flies no more now, it seems, people never having even known houseflies. For me that past is ever-present and not separate from the present, moments in that summer room returning constantly, and incongruously: the repeated words 'Dien Bien Phu', the music of the syllables from another world, one far beyond that of the one in which I sat, a boy of nine. Dien Bien Phu (to me then one word, not three) was the climactic siege-battle of the First Indo-Chinese War. Only it was not in the summer of remembered kitchen time but the spring of the year of 1954 that it occurred.

My father's latter years were taken up with repeated illnesses. Intimations that he might die came to the child early, the first time never forgotten, that moment on the No. 36 bus as it rounded Marble Arch, my mother and us two boys returning home from visiting my father in what we knew as the 'Nervous Diseases' hospital in Soho's Dean Street. It was my task sometimes to guide him around the streets outside, for he was at times afflicted by a malady we were later told was something called 'tobacco blindness'. He chewed as well as smoked heavy pipe tobacco, 'Digger Plug', his knife skilfully paring it down from the hard tobacco block.[25] After his sudden death, my mother wore black for a year in the fashion of her countrywomen. Ironically, after this we were rehoused; as was the practice in those days, people were scattered around London in various Council tower-block dwellings, which, if they showed a higher degree of comfort and hygiene than Ashmore Road, were far less socially congenial and culturally engaging, for all the flypapers and flies.

The early death of my father in 1963 at the age of fifty-five was an experience shared with many of my generation of Irish immigrants' children. These were the men that truly 'died for Ireland', men forgotten, worn down by hardship and neglect – not least the neglect of the young state they had left and which was usually only too glad to see the back of them. The women were survivors. Like my mother. Twenty years stretched from my father's death to her own, as she slowly made her way back, if not quite completely to the Ashmore Road beginnings, then nearby, so that she could be nearer to the 'home' she had made and left, and to the pathways through the city that she and my father had made and known together. This twenty-year circular movement through West London – itself a kind of new emigration and return, a diaspora in the diaspora – ended with her burial beside my father in Saint Mary's Cemetery, Kensal Rise.

The cemetery is wedged beside the canal and the railway line that run towards the west, and so to Ireland. They lie facing the rising sun so that at the Resurrection they may rise and meet their Saviour as He comes from the east, ready to follow Him to the west and the setting sun, to Paradise. Then they will make the journey west.

As time has gone by, I have been better able to see my parents' experience as at one with that great change which was the death of the European peasantry.[26] They would not have called themselves 'peasants', of course – did not know what the word meant even; but they were of that vanishing world. So I see them now in a light that connects the houses from which they came to houses across the breadth of Europe. For 'the house' I have described thus far was the material and symbolic bodying forth of a peasant way of life that was at heart an *economy*, the family economy of the peasant. At its centre were not what we would understand as economic considerations, but social ones. The two were the same, are the same, and it is the family that makes them so. The collective took priority, not the individual. Profit only has meaning in terms of that which is handed down. This economy was thus an economy of desires, longings, resentments, attachments, and not only production – or, rather, production was inseparable from these other things.

This is what gave form to the ties that bound; ties that still bind me. 'The house' means more than the physical and symbolic habitation alone. It means what is handed down, the patrimony, which is also a birthright. And what is not so often understood is that what is handed down does not just concern those who stay, but also those who go, like Johnny and Kitty. It was this sense of still being part of the house that was at the centre of my parents' universe, in England as in Ireland. I and mine are part of this house, too, even at the remove of generations, even if dimly so as time multiplies generations (but then, what is dim may be lighted again as future generations join hands).

At the centre of peasant culture everywhere are the house and the land, *la maysou* in the Béarnese dialect of French, from *la maison* in standard French. The two things are meant in the one word 'house': the physical land and the house. Pierre Bourdieu was the son of a postmaster in the Béarn region, and grew up among peasants. He wrote one of the classic books on peasant culture, one that describes the 'house' in this sense of more than the physical house alone.[27] Were you to consult *The Polish Peasant in Europe and America*, Florian Znaniecki and William I. Thomas's great masterpiece of 1918, you would find the same house again, on the other side of Europe this time.

A third thing is meant by the word 'house', and that is the lineage – land, house and the integrity of the family present and past making up the totality of the patrimony. 'Lineage' does not do justice to the force of these attachments. If what my parents bore with them and passed on to their children could not be land and the house that stood upon it, and was what I have called the passing on itself, continuity, then this continuity lay in *la maysou*. The 'house' in this sense is the primordial cell of peasant life. It is the essence of what we like to call 'tradition'.

In France, in Ireland, in Poland, in almost all peasant worlds, the head of the household is the trustee of the name and the land. The name and the house live on together when the family that personifies and perpetuates them has gone. The house carries the name, even if uninhabited. The household must sacrifice for the good of the whole, for the continuation of the patrimony (the lineage system is what is called patrilineal, but patriarchy is an inadequate term to describe how this society works). Dúiche Sheoighe: *dúchas* overlaps with 'patrimony' in different ways, and conveys some of the complexities involved.

A hard price may have to be paid for the perpetuation of *la maysou*, and it is paid by those like Johnny and Kitty who emigrated. It is also paid by those who stay and do not inherit. By the sacrifice of all these people, the 'house' is able to be continued, the primordial cell reproduced once again, and so the peasant world itself. If a man stays, he may have little or no chance of a wife and wages. He may be a subject man in his brother's house, or else working for another and so without authority. As for the girls of Béarn, and of Ireland, they must be content with a dowry of sorts if they marry, or some sort of accommodation is made if they do not. If they emigrate they are forced to renounce these, like my aunts who were scattered around Ireland, England and America, gone in search of work and husbands: Bridgie Bowe to Dublin, Maggie to the wilds of west Cork, Mollie not far, over to Kilkenny, Kitty and Stasia to London – only Esther at home, the slow but loving youngest child. On the other side, Mary to Pittsburgh, two of her brothers gone before her. Then the next generations on that more impoverished western side.

Those who suffer the sacrifice of emigration (or dispersal) still remain part of the house, however, and reproduce the force of wholeness and continuity as best they can in new worlds, as Johnny and Kitty did. Or not. Some may reject the old ties. Some may be only too glad to move away. But, even with those who reject what they have left, a price is often paid, paid in guilt, in the pain of a separation never accomplished, in longing for past days. For underneath is a deep attachment to the 'home place', to the land and what is on it, and respect for the family and the name. Without these attachments the entire peasant world would die. So I think of my mother and father, born to leave as they were, and of how they sacrificed so that the home place could be renewed. They were therefore conjoined with it by this sacrifice, after decades in London part of a household that extended over many miles and across seas and oceans. Part reciprocally of two households, in fact, the Joyces and the Bowes, both houses strengthened by the bond of marriage. My mother kept firmly with the Joyce connection after my father's death.

La maysou is a matter always of reciprocities, for the one who inherits is what I have called a trustee – one therefore with obligation as well as rights. The patrimony is a shared birthright. Reciprocity within houses: within the one at home, for 'father' and 'son' are emotional symbols of great power in peasant society and there is a solidarity between the sons, an obedience to the father, even though all but one must eventually relinquish rights to the farm in the interests of the family and its identification with the land. But the new head of the family has obligations to those who stay, and must assure their well-being. For the daughters there may be long years of waiting ahead if a marriage is not made and independence made possible, or if emigration is not the recourse. Even after the parent dies, there is tardiness about leaving. No one wants to be the first to go.

Reciprocity within houses: within the one that is dispersed and away as well as the one at home. The new head of the household has obligations to those who leave as well as stay. Those who leave have certain rights of return, in my case my mother encamping with us children each summer for the Wexford home place, crowding in a house too small, four to a bed. Rights of return in Mayo, too. The departed had an obligation to be remembered by those who stayed, to be enquired after if contact were lost, for matters to be arranged so that an eye was kept out and help given by people from the home area in the vicinity of the one who strayed. I remember vividly cases of men who had left Ireland and had lost contact with home, men that seemed to me to be drifting, lost, itinerants by occupation, itinerants in the head. Often the drink, and the loneliness, had marred their lives. We kept an eye on them. They came to the house in Ashmore Road, always generous with their money to us children, just as they were ruinously generous with their money in the pubs.

But men like this would sometimes save up enough to be buried in Ireland, and I recall as a child the glimpse of coffins in the goods wagons of trains bound for the Fishguard ferry to Ireland. The dead fellow passengers on the long six-hour journey to the coast. But the house that meant most for those who, like Johnny and Kitty, remained in England could only be the one they had made in England. That house was made in the form of the life they had created for their children. And in England they were buried, so that they might be where those who survived them lived on.

3

Time Thickens, Takes on Flesh:
The Other West

In my Father's house are many mansions: if it were not so, I would have told you. I go to prepare a place for you.

John 14:2

Reproduced below is a photograph of St Mary's Catholic Cemetery, in west London's Kensal Green. It is here that my parents await the resurrection of the body promised by their faith. They wait alongside some 170,000 others, mostly Irish peasants in origin, buried since it was established in 1858. Crowded together in life, they are crowded together in death, for the cemetery is only twenty-nine acres. In life they and their like were little regarded, and they are in death, too: in 1992 the ground level of the southern part of the cemetery was raised, the dead now piled upon the dead, the older, untended graves removed. Kitty and Johnny Joyce survived this turmoil, but this fate will no doubt come in time.

This expectation is not for those in the mausolea and cat-acombs of the socially exclusive north-east quadrant of the cemetery; inequality in death, as in life. The cemetery is a desolate place, trammelled by the unloved Harrow Road on one side and the Grand Junction Canal on the other, a giant gasworks looming in the distance, factories and apartment blocks abutting on its different sides. The Great Western Railway runs close by. No one digs a friend's grave in St Mary's, as is the tradition still in rural Ireland. The burial places in London are mostly untended, the children of the dead these days scattered

Wikimedia Commons

St Mary's Roman Catholic Cemetery, Kensal Green, West London.

to the great reaches of outer West London and beyond. It is too far to make the journey; kin are not forgotten, but lingering with them is difficult.

St Mary's was opened in 1858 as part of one of the first great municipal cemeteries in Britain, and put into the hands of the Reverend Francis J. Kirk. In the first eight years, Kirk claimed to have personally officiated at most of the 14,000 or so Catholic burials here. His claim was probably correct. The number of burials is substantiated in the cemetery records, and there were precious few Roman Catholic clergy in 1858 to do the job if he did not. In 1850 there was only one Catholic church proper in the nine miles between almost West End Bayswater and far-flung Harrow-on-the Hill. This colossal total of the dead was largely made up of those who had fled the recent famine in Ireland.

Writing almost half a century later, Kirk reported that what he called the better class of funerals occurred in the morning, whereas the afternoon saw a rush. It was then that 'order and decency' were not so easily maintained.[1] On Saturday he might have taken between eighteen and two dozen funerals. He wrote as follows: 'A very large number of the poorer class of funerals at that time were those of emigrants from the West of Ireland, all speaking the Irish language.' Money for burials was collected on the day of the funeral itself, when the streets heard nothing but Irish. Because, as Kirk put it, 'grief is dry', public houses such as the Case Is Altered and the King William – fabled names – on the Harrow Road, were regular stops along the Via Dolorosa of the mourning Irish.

I recall the words of Walter Benjamin: 'Our coming was expected on earth ... There is a secret agreement between past generations and the present one.' Our road was mapped, our coming expected, our sins prepared for. It was men like Kirk who had prepared the way for my Irish London. In 1858 he began his labours in the church of Our Lady of the Holy Souls on Bosworth Road, in Kensal's New Town. It was from this location, on a bitter day in January 1963, that my father's funeral procession left for its destination, St Mary's. Kirk was a man who, before his conversion, had first forged his considerable ministerial will as a Church of Ireland cleric in County Wexford.[2]

From its opening, Holy Souls established a special relationship with the cemetery, and so with the dead. In the early days the revenues gained from officiating at the cemetery came back to Holy Souls. The dead souls funded the souls of the living, ultimately ours. There was, however, a class system at the Holy Souls, as everywhere else in London. Kirk wrote in 1902 that all Catholics in the country could share in the devotions of our Lady of the Holy Souls, as the mortuary lists are open to all, funds permitting. For four shillings one could go on the permanent list; for the yearly list it was a shilling; and £25 bought you a marble tablet in the church. And thus, eternal rest was open only to those who could afford it.

Kirk had been appointed by Cardinal Manning, the founder of the Oblates of St Charles, in St Charles Square. Kirk too was an Oblate – one who offers.[3] Booth's late-nineteenth-century survey of the London poor describes what those like Kirk offered:

> The priests live as poor men among the poor. Their food is simple, their clothes are threadbare; they take few holidays. They live from day to day; if they have a shilling in their pocket no one in want will ask in vain. Abstemious and self-restrained themselves, they are yet lenient judges of the frailties that are not sins, and of the disorder that is not crime. This kindly gentleness is all the more uncompromising in denunciation or more prompt in interference. It is said that the voice of the priest or the presence of the Sister will quell any disorder; but the trouble recurs.[4]

The Oblates proper were in fact usually socially superior products of the English public schools and Oxbridge – though Kirk took his degree in Dublin, at Trinity. Then, as later, the higher reaches of British society were drawn as bees to the flower by this area of London. We worshipped first at St Vincent's Church in the Harrow Road, across the canal from the Holy Souls. There, before our time, Father Douglas Hope, Eton and Christchurch, and a cousin of the Marquess of Queensberry, had worked himself into an early grave on behalf of our forbears. Booth's *Life and Labour of the People in London* records in 1902: 'On the further side of Harrow Road there is an intensely crowded population of the poorest description', mostly Irish Catholics (this side was my side). There Hope practised 'a remarkable self surrender' in what Booth called 'the unromantic monotony of the Harrow Road'. He is buried alongside my parents somewhere in Kensal Green, unremembered.

Kirk was enjoined by Manning to care for the 'straggling flock' of Irish Catholics, many of whom had been displaced from their lodgings nearer the centre of the city by the building of the Great Western Railway. The Harrow Road, which ran from Marylebone westwards, and the Grand Junction Canal – all built by Irish labour – configured the psychogeography and the political economy of west London, especially my enclave of Paddington and adjacent north Kensington and Notting Hill.

Next door to St Mary's is the Protestant All Souls Cemetery, opened in 1832, and modelled upon Père Lachaise in Paris. The dead here are less crowded together. The city of the dead reflects the city of the living, for here a quarter of a million dead luxuriate in the open spaces of seventy-two acres. In All Souls 550 lives of the buried were recorded in Britain's *Dictionary of National Biography*, and no less than 500 'members of the British nobility'. The Catholics in St Mary's could not hope to compete, and while they have their notables they are few and idiosyncratic: Feargus O'Connor, 'The Lion of Freedom'; the notable female impersonator of his time, Danny La Rue; two Cardinals, Manning and Wiseman. What is left of Sax Rohmer, the creator of Dr Fu Manchu, can be sought, and of Prince Louis Lucien Bonaparte. However, the dead in both places share a similar destiny: the graves are untended and mostly unvisited. Once on the pastoral edge of the city, the cemetery has now been absorbed by the urban sprawl.

As Bachelard says, time and space are in truth not two things but one, and if space contains time ('that is what space is for'), then time 'takes on flesh', as the great Russian literary scholar Mikhail Bakhtin put it: 'Time thickens, takes on flesh. Space … becomes charged and responsive to the movements of time.'[5] For Bakhtin, time and space were 'forms of the most immediate reality' and not simply the transcendental conditions for the possibility of perception which they were to the philosophers. He wrote of what he called the 'chronotopes' to be found in literature, more simply 'timeplaces', and he is clear that these are drawn from life itself.

These timeplaces are the organizing principles for the narratives of our lives. He writes of roads and houses, of rooms, of thresholds.[6] It is our bodies through which the stories speak.

To recall again the words of Pierre Bourdieu, himself the child of a peasant culture, what is 'learned by the body is not something that one has, but something that one is'.[7] This charging and thickening of time and space is above all the case in childhood, but occurs throughout life, too: the times of our lives are rooted in places, spaces that carry time 'forever'.

As well as the house, it was through the streets of my 'other west' that my body learned who I was and where I became what I am. Time was thickened by those streets, the paths we follow form the tiny universe of the child – and they form too the universe of most city inhabitants. They make up the tiny parcels of territory, the small worlds, that are the real city for most of its people. Adults, no less than children, occupy tiny corners of the universe for the majority of their lives, and it is in these corners that we become habituated to life. The same can be said for places of burial, little pathways leading us to known graves, little corners in what, for city dwellers, have now become like cities themselves, big places in which we can easily get lost. The times of childhood and adolescence are forever rooted in those pathways that make up the abstraction 'city', and it is in and by these roads, ones like Ashmore Road and Southam Street, that for me time thickens, takes on flesh.

To the east of St Mary's and All Souls cemeteries lay poor Paddington, my cloth-cap respectable Paddington of Ashmore Road and the main westward conduit of the Harrow Road, of which the novelist Colin MacInnes wrote: 'You'd hurry through even if you were in a car', also noticing 'a canal ... that nothing floats on except cats and contraceptives'. Over this canal from the Harrow Road was 'North Ken', now claimed by the estate agents as 'Notting Hill'. Road and canal witnessed my walk to the first school, the school walk the most deeply etched in memory of all the city's pathways, except the road of living itself, Ashmore. Ashmore ran down to the shops in Harrow Road, the walk with my mother in earliest childhood.

Along the Harrow Road and similar streets throughout the city, the ownership and style of the shops, pubs, cinemas and services (medical, legal and so on) changed little between pre-war days and the 1970s. These shops catered to almost every conceivable need, so that one rarely had to leave the area.[8] This represents a degree of lived and densely textured continuity unimaginable today, when shops change so much and so often and provide so little, and when local services have been cut so much. My memory is structured by this seemingly changeless succession of way stations on the roads of our west, the same shops and offices always returned to, the same people always in these offices and shops. The shops; Pearkes the grocers, the 'Home and Colonial' where the 'rations' of post-war London were to be had; Holtoms, the corner shop; the cobbler on the corner next door, framed by the window and seemingly always at his last, his fingers deformed by his trade; 'Dolly, The People's Florist'. The offices: the rent office, the post office, the office of the 'poor man's lawyer' my parents spoke of. Memory is scaffolded thus, by the incredible force of things.[9]

The way to my first school led over the Harrow Road by way of the 'Ha'penny Steps' to Kensal New Town, where the native poor and the immigrants then as now found a haven of sorts between the canal and the railway. The Steps were in effect a path over the Grand Junction Canal, a roadway in the air, one nonetheless heavy with the mass of its iron construction, its high elevated sides overwhelming the child. A magic place, too, for on one side of the Steps a newspaper seller plied his open-air trade all day and in all weathers, set back a little from the pavement, his livelihood stored in a cleft in the wall behind him. From this he brought forth 'the comics' at the appointed time each week, *The Beano* the most beloved of all of them to me. The force of things overwhelms me again when I see these images.

In the photograph above is a woman shopping in the Harrow Road in 1952. Six years earlier, my mother and I might have

Woman shopping, Harrow Road, 1952.

B. Green, Portrait of a London Borough, Westminster City Archives

presented a picture similar to this one, the prams and push-chairs the same; the same clothes; the same things. It looks like summer, for the woman has her sandals on. The child turns to the mother, as I might have done. The reader can see something of the world of shops, so remarkable to the child then, so memorable now, so different to the Ireland left by my mother. The shopfront is decidedly grand, the goods on display prolific, china and glassware displayed beside peat fibre and flower bulbs. The shopping street puts its best foot forward.

The second image is a photograph of The 'Ha'penny' Steps' taken sometime in the 1950s. Both are from the album of an anonymous photographer donated to Westminster City Archives, called 'Portrait of a London Borough'. These photographs express ordinariness; they are of mundane places, then disregarded and now mostly forgotten, if they even physically exist any longer. For me, they magic the past into new existence. I walked these steps, passed this corner, thousands of times. They were a threshold, different worlds on each side; and even if the differences were in reality not great to the people living then, and to this child especially, they meant everything.

The man sitting on the right is a hawker-cum-beggar, likely a casualty of the not-so-distant war. Can this be him, the one for

B. Green, *Portrait of a London Borough, Westminster City Archives*

The Ha'penny Steps, c. 1953.

whom I felt pity and fear, his legs amputated below the knees? His clothes were filthy, though he affected dignity as best he could, selling matches and shoelaces to passers-by. The father of one of my fellow scholars, a blind man, an Irishman, sung street ballads in the streets not so far away from here. One could in this timeplace have been in Victorian London.

The man here leans on the wall of Wedlake Public Baths, an institution that, in the absence of bathrooms, was much patronized. I and my father were patrons on Saturday mornings – a chance to be with him, just the two of us. There the waiting on long wooden benches, moving along as your turn came – the same in hospital waiting rooms, the working classes sharing our lot, keeping order, being ordered. The waiting over, and then into the baths, great rows of open-topped cast-iron cubicles, each superintended by the attendant who ran the water not you, for there were no taps, but a spigot that could only be turned by the attendant's special device. The Victorian cubicle, one's special public–private space for cleaning the body and cleaning the soul in the solitary prison cell. The *lieux de mémoire* of the common people.

Over the Steps my primary school, St Mary's, was located. Situated a couple of hundred yards across from it, on the far side of a tiny park, is the church of Our Lady of the Holy Souls. Around the corner from the church lay notorious Southam Street; though so circumscribed was the world of the child that I only knew the street from the age of eleven, when, a thousand times again, like the Ha'penny Steps, I walked it between home and secondary school. On this bad side of the Harrow Road the future British Labour Home Secretary Alan Johnson lived. His hugely popular memoirs give a revealing picture of the Southam Street he lived in up to the sixties. And yet he scarcely mentions us Irish, except for seeing us as interlopers at the end of his street, kids not from around his neighbourhood and recognizable by our freckles and red hair.[10] Not one in my class had red hair.

Earlier on, the Catholic Irish had thronged Kensal New Town. Kensal first grew up between 1835 and 1850. In 1851, only half the inhabitants were London-born, many of its people making the trek from another west, this time from the agricultural west of England – from Somerset, Dorset and Wiltshire.[11] Employment was to be found for men in the gasworks and women in the laundries. 'Soapsuds Island' was the name given to the place then, and 'to marry an ironer was as good as a fortune'.[12] Kirk, the first Bosworth Road parish priest, reported that in the late nineteenth century the population of Catholics there and in its surrounding area was 10,000, many of them dislodged from Marylebone by the building of the Great Central Railway, the tracks coming into London from the north this time.[13] The dispossessed made their own journey west, the regime of the railway dictating all. The reportedly mile-long Catholic procession on St Patrick's Day in the town attested to the faith and to Irish identity. According to Booth's Survey, the Catholics were the only ones locally who went to church.

My second *via scholostica* led through Southam Street. The street photographer Roger Mayne took around 1,500 pictures of Notting Hill's Southam Street. For all the brilliance of his presentation of the squalor and vibrancy of that street and area, his is still a view from outside, another bourgeois drawn to the imagined exoticism of that place. Nonetheless his presentation of the street and that of the insider Alan Johnson between them present a compelling picture of the old London. Mayne was a great photographer by any measure. His Southam Street photographs remain his most celebrated works. They have been exhibited worldwide, and were a highlight of Tate Britain's blockbuster exhibition, *How We Are: Photographing Britain* (2007), for which his *Jiving Girl* (1957) was the show's poster image. The entire series of his photographs is now held by the V&A, part of the 'historical record', how we 'the British' were, who 'we' are supposed to be now.[14]

The photograph below shows people in the street, this time not so many as is usual in Mayne's vast number of Southam St images. In a lousy street, this was one of the lousiest corners. In a street that stank, this corner stank the most. It is one of my ineradicable timeplaces. To the child's memory, manifest now but made in my body then, the rotting windows and doors and

Corner, Southam Street, 1961.

Mary Evans Picture Library/Roger Mayne

the makeshift curtains, and the even more than usual awfulness of the disrepair of the buildings, all these convey the sadness and the destructiveness of the place with a force that corroborates memory more than Mayne's others. The brother of my best friend and his young family lived for a time in the decaying building on the opposite side of the street. A school friend lived in the street. Edenham Street, to the right, was just as bad as Southam. Going along Edenham, the Church of the Holy Souls was in a short distance to be found, the Faith of our Fathers standing proudly amidst the alien core of the extreme poverty and decay around it.

Photographs by their nature exclude as well as include – for instance the insides of the houses, figures of order in the streets, the other streets adjacent, all similar, but all different for those who lived there, like Edenham. As a child and much later I dreamt of being lost forever in these same streets, trapped in their squalor, alone in the dreamt ruins between Edenham and the Kensal Road. Aside from dreams there is no weather in the pictures, no seasons, which existed even here. There is no colour. And there is no sound. Mayne mostly photographed at certain times of the day, when children were playing and young people out. We do not usually see the street at other times. Like Colin MacInnes, Mayne emphasized children and youth, for the child in post-war Britain was a symbol of hope and of what was new, contrasting here with the battered street itself.

Mayne said he photographed Southam Street because he thought it was 'beautiful'. 'My reason for photographing poor streets is that I love them', he stated in the late 1950s. 'The streets have their own kind of beauty, a kind of decaying splendour.'[15] The houses in his photographs form a sort of frieze in front of which people move. The photographs are an example of the contemporary current of 'street photography', and so part of the 'documentary' tradition. Twentieth-century truth became located in this tradition, and it is by photographs like these that we know, or think we know, the truth.

But we do not, for the photograph as document buys into the fantasy that photographic images are not so much statements about the world as 'miniatures of reality'. Photos are also possessive, acquisitive; to photograph people is indeed to 'capture' them, to see people as they never see themselves, to present them in ways they have no or little control over. Nonetheless, they have their own truth if not the truth, as they are tokens of absence as well as presence, suggesting in this first guise an awareness of the unattainable, 'conferring on each moment the character of a mystery', as Susan Sontag put it.[16] I write from behind the photograph, in the mystery – not that I claim the truth in doing so.

What the photograph cannot convey is of course the other senses beyond sight. The sense of hearing: the fraught arguments emerging from basements and front doors in Southam Street, the sounds conveying the sheer sense of people's helplessness I felt even as a child, the barely suppressed violence in people's behaviour. The street was riddled with petty crime and youth gangs were numerous and vicious.[17] The sounds of street life, the smells. The smell of the bubble gum factory at one end of the street and mingling with it the stench of the Robin Hood and Little John pub across the road both announcing the beginning of my morning walk down the street. Here, in a cleaning job that was far too much for her health, my mother was forced to work during one of the prolonged periods of my father's ill-health. In memory, the smell of dirt and decay lingers most, dirt and decay being an altogether different matter to the lived senses from their presentation through the photographic eye.

Neither is there in these photographs the touch of the street to my feet as I walked it morning and night, through all weathers, or as I felt my way through it in the midst of London's smogs, the handkerchief around my mouth black by the time I reached my destination. It was then I tasted the street, the smog given added strength by smoke from the steam trains that ran at the back of one side of the street (to Fishguard and thence to Ireland, some of them). Malcolm X and Brendan Behan, who both saw the neighbourhood, and probably the street, and who both knew a thing or two about slums, were taken aback by the awfulness of the place, an abomination that ruined people's lives.

Before my time matters were even worse, people brutalized by extreme poverty and terrorized by the various manifestations of Victorian philanthropy that were still manifest almost halfway through the twentieth century. Ten minutes' walk or so from Southam Street you are in Notting Dale, just around the corner from my secondary school, as was the primary school around the corner from Southam. There the writ of the monitorial Improved Tenants Association and the Harrow Mission ran unchallenged for a good proportion of the twentieth century. The Mission was an offshoot of Harrow School, as was the Rugby Club of Rugby School, the club letting the old school down when, in 1958, it became an epicentre of the race riots of that year. Notting Dale was also a home to the 'Cruelty Society' whose ever-present threat was to take away one's children; home also to a 'Tuppeny Leanover', where men who could not afford a bed slept upright (attached by ropes to a pole). Present behind all of these was the spectre of the Workhouse, where for a day spent breaking stones a night's lodging was to be had. Old England, my inheritance.

Yet even here, the heart of the home – the kitchen, and the hearth at its centre – could serve as the point around which decency could be wrung from that life. The testimony of those who knew the twenties and thirties as well as the fifties and sixties in Notting Dale and North Kensington shows us this, and takes us into the houses.[18] The fire range in the Improved Tenants Association flat became a version of the hearth around which things turned, 'as we did everything in one room'. Later on, Pearl Jephcott, a scrupulous observer, recorded how the 'one room flat' of the West Indian migrant was better kept than many a white habitation, one Jamaican women's room being furnished 'by the most lush of Edwardian tastes'.[19] What was wrung from this life was nonetheless missed by many when they were rehoused, so disturbing might be what came after, even if it was materially better.

There is a poem called 'Southam Street' by Gavin Selerie in which one of the former inhabitants explains:

> I'm not complaining mind
> I've got my own place-
> one family one place
> that's what you get
> with the modern.[20]

And in Trellick Tower, now a Grade II government-listed building, which was at once a salvation and a new kind of scourge:

> the lift section, with ten bridges
> four funnels and lifts like a castle
> it's called the 'Psychiatric Wing'
> because when the lift breaks down
> you don't want to come out
> the best view of London
> she said.

The cover of the first edition of MacInnes's novel, *Absolute Beginners*, carries a photograph of Southam Street, and in the near background is Ernő Goldfinger's newly built Trellick Tower, for a time the largest single-building residential block in Europe.[21] The crumbling old and the super-modernist new. The old way of life was in the end completely obliterated; Southam and the neighbourhoods around were demolished. The people of the other west moved on, to their own houses if they were very lucky. Chiefly, however, they moved to the new council estates of the 1960s and later, often far-flung, as in Alan Johnson's case. These are the words of Kit Roper in the 1980s – an old inhabitant of the area: 'It doesn't seem possible what they've done. You thought you wouldn't ever forget it, but you did. That's how it's gone. Unless you had a photo of it to show people. Otherwise you have forgotten how actually it was.'[22]

It is difficult to find a printed map that conveys the micro-georaphies that are composed out of the body's memories, the psychogeography. The one shown below helps somewhat. It is a section of a commercial London city guide map of 1894. It has the virtues of visual clarity and benevolent anachronism, being not of my time but of my times.

The railway, the canal and the Harrow Road are clearly marked, cutting east-to-west. Kensal Green is there in the top left-hand corner, and on the opposite side the squarish presence of 'the Rec', where we played as children. Paddington Work-house is well marked near the centre – the birth-site of the author, the workhouse being transformed into a hospital by my time. Marylebone Infirmary is visible in the middle left, and below it lies the Catholic Kremlin of St Charles Square. On this can be found St Charles College, later my Cardinal Manning Secondary Modern. The script 'Kensal New Town' (Bb) almost directly overlays my primary school, St Mary's School, and

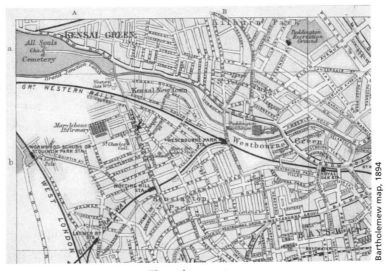

The other west.

the Bosworth Road Church. The jewel in the crown, Ashmore Road, runs into Harrow Road near to the left of 'B' at the top of the map. Just as Harrow Road cuts diagonally east to west, Ladbroke Grove is another large arterial road going north to south, and parallel to it runs the Portobello Road. Notting Dale begins in the extreme bottom left, around Latimer Road Station on the map, which unfortunately does not reveal the Dale's true lineaments.

The Dale lies on one side of Holland Park Avenue, the avenue just out of view at the bottom of the map. This is the border between North and South Ken, and (roughly) that between the fabulous riches of the latter and the poverty of the former, then as now. Only now the wealth is Russian and Arab as well as native (native-imperial in earlier times, in fact, South Kensington having been a favoured retreat after the spoils of empire had been accumulated in the Deccan or Jamaica). The Dale was the most notorious and the earliest of all the slumlets of the area, known in the mid nineteenth century for its potteries and its piggeries. It had been flooded with people displaced by inner-city railway building, many of them Irish. Crime was another occupation, not least in my time, when the area had become pretty solidly poor white English.

The area was the cradle of the Notting Hill race riots of 1958.[23] This was Colin MacInnes's 'Little Napoli' in *Absolute Beginners*, published in 1959. He describes the Latimer Road that went south into the Dale, 'which I particularly want you to remember, because out of this road, like horrible tits dangling from a lean old sow, there are a whole festoon of what I think must be the sinisterest highways in our city'. Despite his breathless veneration of youth and denigration of age, MacInnes is correct in his description:

This was the residential doss-house of our city. In plain words, you do not live in our Napoli if you could live anywhere else. And that is why there are, to the square yard, more boys fresh from the nick, and national refugee minorities, and out of business whores, than anywhere else, I should expect, in London town. The kids live in the streets – I mean they have *charge* of them, you have to ask permission to get along even in a car … and there are piles and piles of these dreadful, wasted, negative, shop-soiled kind of *old people* that make you feel it really is a tragedy to grow grey.[24]

In 1963 – ironically just after my father's death – we had rejoiced in moving out of Ashmore Road to an 'estate' in Fulham-cum-Wandsworth, but like many others rapidly missed the old connections. Alan Johnson went to a house in Slough on his way to the top via the job of postman. Londoners were arbitrarily sent to all corners of the city and beyond, happy to be out of what they had, yet fearful of the new. My mother moved back to a partly reinvented Notting Dale in 1970 – the 'council estate' version – and then to the Portobello Road itself before her death in 1982, living for a time in what was called Portobello Court, in a small two-bedroom flat, now on the market for not much less than a million pounds. I and my brother moved with her, of necessity, as I was either an impecunious young worker or a student.

In the middle of Notting Dale is Portland Road, the subject of a BBC television programme of 2013, which asked, 'Is this the UK's most gentrified street?' and answered in the affirmative.[25] Dale and Hill after the 1960s became not only 'gentrified' but 'super-gentrified', among the most sought-after parts of a bloated, unequal city. From the *Rotting Hill* of Wyndham Lewis in 1952 to the *Notting Hell* of Boris Johnson's sister Rachel in 2006, so went the times. The first described the post-war desolation of the place, the second the trials of selling a 'rare-to-market' mid-Victorian house, and tending to little Posy, Mirabel and Casimir – names that had displaced the Freds, Dorises and Alberts of an earlier day.[26] People were, as always in London, ejected from their own city.

My own Ashmore Road, the north star of my streetwalking, was part of an original development called St Peter's Park (it is marked on the map). The censuses of 1901 and 1911 show considerable crowding in Ashmore Road even then, worse than in my time in fact.[27] The developers of St Peter's comprised the usual mix of new and old money invested in land and titles. The story of the park is fairly typical of London as a whole.[28] One family dominated, the Neelds – members of parliament, speculators in East India and Bank of England stocks, governors of Harrow School, students of Cambridge University, lords of several rural manors, and masters of houses the size of which would have contained whole streets of us heirs of old England.[29] St Peters' developers worked in parallel to the Anglican landlord interest in Paddington – holy money; Oxbridge money, too, at a time when the two were conjoined twins.

For in Paddington, All Souls' College, Oxford, and the Ecclesiastical Commissioners (later the Church Commissioners) were big property owners. The Commissioners managed land held by Westminster Abbey and the Bishop of London. Absentee landlordism, the curse of old Ireland, but of old England too. Trinity College Dublin, Protestant alma mater of the Anglo-Irish aristocracy, was the ground landlord of the land my father's family house stood on, and much more of rural Ireland besides.

The Ecclesiastical Commissioners were widely criticized for drawing revenues from slum properties. In letting these they certainly laid down housing regulations – but these concerned the regulation of 'vice', not roofs, pipes and walls. It was as late as the 1960s that the commissioners escaped the embarrassment of being slum landlords by selling much of the south Paddington part of their estates. But the great secular developers had themselves come well into the picture earlier, after 1850 when the streets of London (for example Bayswater) exploded in number with the astonishing growth of the city.

In 1921, Bayswater's prosperous Lancaster Gate East Ward was inhabited by sixty-one people per acre (inner London had about seventy per acre). Harrow Road Ward (the end towards Paddington station), on the other hand, had 180 people per acre, and much the same number in 1931. Infant mortality was very high at this time in North Kensington, and the worst parts of Paddington were designated areas of 'housing stress'. In 1951, with ninety-three persons per acre, Paddington had the highest living density of all the metropolitan areas of London. In 1961, the figure was eighty-six, still the highest. In 1967, Westminster City Council, which included Paddington, surveyed 16,500 households (it owned 10,000 dwellings), finding that 86 per cent of them were still without their own lavatory or bath.[30] It was worse still in North Kensington. Golborne Ward, which took in Kensal, had the highest population density of any ward in London – seven times higher than wards in South Kensington. An enormous number of these people were children. By 1961, 26 per cent of North Kensington's population had been born outside the borough.[31]

The other west from above, North Kensington section, Kensal/north Golborne quarter, 1962. The Grand Junction Canal is visible in the top-left corner.

London Metropolitan Archives, City of London

And then came public housing. Pevsner and Cherry wrote of Kensington that it was

[a] microcosmic representation of all public housing develop-ments in London ... Here one can trace the whole history of changing positions in urban improvement from the piecemeal philanthropy of the late nineteenth century, through the radical slum clearance schemes, planned in the 1930s but not carried out until the 1950s, and later to the realization, from the 1970s onwards, in favour of rehabilitation and more homely contex-tual infilling.[32]

Homely? Certainly better, though the space people had to breathe in was still very limited, and when a home was made, it was tenant make-do-and-mend that did the making, working always in the face of the poor build quality and the restricted space that the planners thought adequate for the lower orders. British living space per person is still among the smallest in Europe. 'Contextual infilling'? The astonishing growth of London after the deregulation of the financial sector and the effective destruc-tion of public housing in the 1980s are well known.

London ebbed and flowed around the little but populous ter-ritory I describe. If we mark St Mary's Cemetery as the western border of my manor, and Paddington Railway Station as the east, then to the east roughly speaking lay Paddington's Maida Vale bedsit area and the considerable wealth and chic of 'Little Venice'. There the canal turned decidedly more posh, and no longer stank. As always in London, neighbouring but divided worlds, bad houses and good, were within sight of each other.

To the north of my enclave were Irish Kilburn and Camden Town. To the west beyond the cemeteries lay the vast expanse of outer west London. There were the interwar suburbs of Willesden, Harlesden, Cricklewood. The great architectural historian Nikolaus Pevsner was characteristically unkind and accurate about this less salubrious side of suburbia, the antithesis of John Betjeman's 'Metroland': Willesden was 'a dismally incoherent muddle'; Harlesden 'unremarkable'; Dollis Hill, north of Willesden Green, an 'indifferent array of industry and offices'; and as for Kilburn, to the north, 'there is very little to single out here'.[33]

And yet, for the emigrant young of rural Ireland who imagined, and who came to inhabit, outer west London, it was a singular place, one not only of work and church, but of dance halls, of sexual license, and of storied pubs. It was upon such places that the great wave of young immigrant Irish in the 1950s broke, including my cousins on both sides. Their aunts and uncles had preceded them. Camden Town, Islington, Hammersmith too, as well as the capital of Kilburn – the Irish seemed to be everywhere in those days, and there was indeed a sort of a shorthand psychogeography of the place, one not for the refined ears of such as my mother:

> Hammersmith for poverty,
> Kilburn for pride,
> Camden Town for the rough lie-down,
> And Hyde Park for the ride.

Those and their like who stayed in the inner west are now a spectral presence there, though most were driven out long ago, along with their families, including my generation, displaced by rising house prices and gentrification.

By the time of my adolescence, my other west had become one of the epicentres of 'the 1960s', the place where swinging London swung. Notting Hill now became a new version of what it had been before in other guises: the exotic slum. This was also a time when the 'working class' was being rediscovered, as was 'blackness'. The West Indian population of Britain, most of it settling initially in Notting Hill and Brixton, increased dramatically from a few tens of thousands in 1951 to almost half a million in 1971.[34] The rediscovery of blackness and of the working class came as one in Notting Hill. It was to there the so-called 'counterculture' drew the disaffected in their tens of thousands. Here was what Jonathan Raban in 1974 called 'The Magical City'.[35] This was 'a ruined Eden, tangled, exotic and overgrown, where people see signs in scraps of junk and motley'. Here people could explore a kind of hyper-privacy, a place purpose-built for the unrestrained exploration and expression of the liberated self.

Film made its own realities out of the place. Nicholas Roeg's *Performance* (1970), with Mick Jagger and Anita Pallenberg, was filmed in Notting Hill's Powis Square. This was a study of the excesses of the new freedom and its curious links to the old violence and an old London – that of gangs and their ter-ritories, or 'manors'. The contradictions of the time are caught in it, as they are in Michelangelo Antonioni's *Blow Up* (1966), a hard-eyed study of a new kind of bourgeois urban alien-ation emerging in the midst of our manor's plebeian *ancien régime*. The filmmakers did one job on the sixties, the novelists another.[36] The other west was the stage set of both.

All this attention was puzzling to us natives, me especially, struggling as I was to get out of the place. On the one hand, it was very pleasing to discover that one was at the centre of the turning universe. The sense of liberation, of something new, was tangible and exciting. Despite my paltry inheritance as a Londoner, I have been proud of the place, proud at the time in that familiar parochial way of Londoners, who usually know next to nothing about England.

Much of what went on in the fabled sixties was somehow out there, not quite part of what was real, even though with the vast talking up of the place it became difficult at times to be sure about what reality was. Can this really be 'swinging London', stinking Tavistock Crescent and the Portobello immured in the stench of decay, the usually advanced physical decay of the buildings themselves, a smell then found almost everywhere in the other west? While what seemed like universal attention was being lavished upon the place, it was between 1964 and 1970 being noisily torn to pieces, local objections disregarded, by the building of the massive overhead roadway, the Westway. I laboured upon the construction of this for a short while, for the money was great and the pace of work slow, as the dates of its construction suggest.

Reality was to be found for us in terms of what came out from within the area rather than what came in, particularly in the shape of music and the fashion that went with it. Long before reggae became popular, ska and blue beat were pounding out on the streets of much of the other west. The Who were originally denizens of nearby Shepherd's Bush; and in the 1970s, a later generation than mine, Harrow Road made claims to immortality as a birthplace of punk. The Clash came out of the Warwick Estate, built on the ruins of a section of the Harrow Road, not so long before a scene of gut-wrenching poverty.

The Road has indeed its own chronicler, the perfectly pseudonymed Tom Vague, self-styled post-punk Situationist, indefatigable local historian, 'psychogeographer' and political activist, the living embodiment of the counterculture of the time, still punching away decades later. His works include *Bash the Rich: The Radical History Tour of Notting Hill* (2007), and *Getting It Straight in Notting Hill Gate* (2012).

Instead, with the 1990s, and reflecting the times perfectly, came the bromide version of Notting Hill in the film of the same name. This, as Tory and New Labour boys and girls flooded into the area, expensive dress shops proliferated, and supergentrification moved relentlessly north up the lane. But only so far, for the wrong end has remained the destination of the immigrant waves that followed the Irish and the West Indian: the Spanish, the Portuguese, the Moroccans, the Filipinos, then those from the Horn of Africa. Ashmore itself has slowly become partly gentrified, but still remains fairly intact, grimmer in fact because the old life of the streets has gone. The immigrants remain.

4

Other Houses

To know the soul I have to know the home.
Warren Oster, 66, West Indian immigrant (1978)

'Exile Is Not a Word' is the title of the poem by Peter Woods that opens the lyrical novel by Timothy O'Grady and Steve Pyke, *I Could Read the Sky*. The novel concerns an itinerant labourer, not unlike my father, except this protagonist is without children, and thus without that consolation and without a home. I think of the poem's words as I remember my father: 'Exile is not a word / It is shaving against / A photograph not a mirror.' And also my mother: 'Exile is not a word / It is hands joined in supplication in an empty cathedral.' These lines speak for immigrants everywhere:

> Exile is not a word ...
> It is the purgatorial
> Triumph of memory
> over topography.

The triumph of memory over topography, yes, in the way the immigrant bears the old world into the new. But topography can be said to be the winner in another sense, for the topography of that which is left behind informs that which is found, the remembered house in Ireland shaping the new 'house' in England. So it was with my parents at Ashmore Road. Not with them alone, of course, for there were and are a multitude of other immigrant experiences of London. I think of the house of the anthropologist Janet Carsten's parents. Janet herself is a great explorer of house, home and family. She writes of her highly educated, middle-class German parents, who in the 1930s recreated in their north London house the *Mitteleuropa* Jewish kitchen they had left behind, as well as the cosmopolitan space of the inviolable parental 'study'.[1]

She informs us of the deep significance of the house for all of us. Kinship and the roots of belonging are formed by the repetitive bodily practices that can only occur in a place of home – houseworking, sleeping, eating arrangements, and so on. Through house practices the whole nature of social life is encoded and laid down in us: the social of family and kin, of age, gender, generation and their hierarchies, but also the social of the community and ultimately of the state.[2] In short, the political is encoded for us there. Our term 'economy' derives from the idea of household management, from Latin *oeconomia* and Greek *oikonomia* , and *oikonomos*, 'manager, steward', from *oikos*, 'house, abode, dwelling'. And so, inevitably, the house encodes the religious as well as the political, for in the Christian faith it is the house of the Father that promises to embrace all, redeem all. In the King James Bible, in John 14:2, we read, 'In my Father's house are many mansions: if it were not so, I would have told you. I go to prepare a place for you.'

In *The Suffering of the Immigrant*, the Algerian sociologist Abdelmalek Sayad relates how the immigrant lives along the fault-lines of the state.[3] These fault lines are at the core of our identity: not to have a state, nation-state or otherwise, is not to have a home, at least in the modern West. The immigrant is always anomalous, and therefore out of place, a 'displaced person' in the language of a devastated post-war Europe.

Place therefore seems to be central to our identity, and place in this sense is ultimately in the gift of the state. Because the immigrant is out of place, Sayad writes that she or he is always 'at fault'. So strong is our state-given understanding that being in place means to be accepted, someone who is not 'at fault'.

As well as at fault, the immigrant is always 'on trial', waiting at the door for entry, even when he or she is already within. As I write, Europe is convulsed once again by the question of the immigrant, so that it is as well not to forget these old stories, and that, contrary to many accounts of 'immigrant experience' today, things did not in the end turn out 'alright'. O'Grady and Pike quote a line of George Seferis: 'I whispered: memory hurts wherever you touch it.'

In my other west it was the immigrant Caribbeans who figured most, alongside ourselves. Unlike for the Irish, to many West Indian emigrants Britain was already 'home'. Schooling systems and the culture they implanted were 'British'. They were British subjects until this was taken away from them in the 1960s. On arrival in Britain, however, they became indiscriminately 'black'. To come home, and then to be rejected, was a hard road to walk. The title of Barbadian Austin Clarke's book conveys something of the realization involved in this abrupt stigmatization: *Growing Up Stupid under the Union Jack*. While the Irish had the advantage of whiteness, it also took their arrival in Britain to finish off the business of making them Irish. Britain, especially England, was in no sense 'home', but it might be made something of, especially with children.

The complex racial hierarchies inherited from slavery and empire in the Caribbean had differentiated shades of blackness at home and given each its place, but in Britain these were set at nothing, as were the distinct cultural differences between islands. Paradoxically, not having an identity, being anomalous, created an identity for the immigrant anyway. Given the history of the British Empire, being black was at the highest pitch of being anomalous. And being out of place was also a product of coming to England with the expectations of someone who was skilled or educated at home. Many black immigrants came with a level of training higher than the whites they encountered in daily life, and often with a respect for education not paralleled by the working-class English.

'No Irish, no blacks, no dogs' is now thought of by many to be the title of Johnny Rotten's first excursion into autobiography, rather than the parlance of Britain's advertising boards, brazenly apparent in shop and house windows.[4] It is easy now to forget that, as recently as 1965, racial discrimination was perfectly legal in Britain, and that it was not until 1968 that it was outlawed in housing. My generation grew up with the idea that skin colour denoted a form of existence not only different but inferior to ours. Some of us did not buy into this idea, but all of us were marked by it, for how could you be anything else when inhumanity was naturalised, made normal, skin colour 'natural,' like the cracked pavements you walked on and the polluted air you breathed? Generations since then have paid the price for those times; making blackness natural then meant making whiteness invisible, so hiding for many decades what is now called 'white privilege'. A Gallup poll of 1958 reported that over 70 per cent of respondents were against 'mixed marriages'.

The long history of slavery and empire was played out on the streets of Notting Hill in the summer of 1958 when I was thirteen. Violent attacks on black people had increased that summer, given gang form and so rudimentary organization by the 'Teddy Boys' or 'Teds' of the time. Oswald Mosley's Union Movement and the White Defence League were a more sinister presence. There was serious street rioting that summer in Nottingham, too, extending over a fortnight.

One of the key flashpoints in London was a public altercation between a mixed-race couple. A white woman and a black man together always invoked the greatest tension and possibility of violence. Three or four hundred white youths attacked the houses of black residents in late August, and the tumult went on until 5 September. Latimer Road was the Dale epicentre of the trouble. Black people fought back: iron bars, butcher's knives, bicycle chains, weighted leather belts, choppers and open razors were employed on both sides.

The familiar tale: they come over here and take our jobs yet they live on the dole, or else on 'immoral earnings', as in the parlance of that time. They eat tins of pet food, Kit-e-Kat being the favourite. The alliterative venom of 'black bastard' still rings in my ears, the hatred in 'black cunts' – both at the time seeming far worse than 'nigger' and 'coon'. I heard the Union Movement speak in the area at the time, and we thought them insane. As I look back now, I think Catholicism helped save us from the worst of the prejudice, as the avowed 'respectability' of our parents, reinforced by our schools, kept us apart from the worst.

This Catholic-Irish respectability was different to the English working-class forms, carrying I think something of the soft-ness and gentleness of country natures into the hardness and roughness of the city. 'Respectability' also carried with it what I can only call refinement, a certain dignity of comportment and attire that set our mothers apart, however poor they were, from rough city ways and people. The West Indian women who came not long after the men had arrived bore a similar dignity of bearing to these Irish women, especially the older women; matrons across the ocean, Irish and West Indians, both dressed for Sunday service in their treasured best, mindful of the virtue implanted by religious upbringings as strong on the one side of the Atlantic as on the other.

Of course, Catholicism and Irishness also carried an inev-itable sense of distance from Britishness and Englishness. Growing up, I heard volubly and frequently from my mother about the prejudice directed against the Irish during her time in England, especially in the employment practices of the thir-ties. 'No Irish need apply' outside works' buildings was there decades before the more famous 'No blacks, no dogs, no Irish' of the house rental signs of the fifties and sixties. 'No Irish need apply' until Britain came to need the Irish in the war effort and its aftermath. Then it went on bended knee.

The British and English variants of identity were in fact being redefined at this time in terms less of empire than of nation per se. But as this new nation was white anyway, empire and colony were there in the wings, and Ireland was of course the ur-colony of the English. Other empires also mattered at the time, if these are now forgotten, including the Russian and the Austro-Hungarian, out of which issued the rampant antisemitism of the time and the ill feeling towards eastern and central European immigrants, for a time after the war white immigration being numerically superior to non-white. Poles and Ukrainians were especially marked out.

Not that the immigrant Irish were immune from these tensions and sometimes hatreds, especially when pubs were taken over by a black clientele, as was true of the Frankfurt Arms, at the bottom of my Ashmore Road (the white English children standing outside for hours on Saturday nights, lemonades in hand, their parents inside getting blootered – how respectable we were as we scurried past in disapproval!). My secondary school, 'the Manning', had feeder Catholic primary schools, of which one, St Francis, was near the origin of the troubles in the poverty-stricken and unrespectable Dale: boys from there notably outranked us on the 'hard nut' scale, but were full of teen bluster, too, sometimes riding on the back of the reputation of Dale well-'ard non-Catholic friends, the shock troops of the riots.

But it was not as if school could be an incubator of hatred, anyway, at least in terms of racial propinquity, for at that time immigrants usually came without children, and Catholicism was not anyway a big presence in the Caribbean. We had only one black boy in the whole of the Manning, a much-adored mascot called Locksley Booth. My school friends went down to have a look, certainly; but we were boys of twelve and thirteen then – not that children younger than this were not caught up in the trouble.

I missed the riots altogether, having made the annual pilgrimage to County Wexford that year. But a year later, on the corner of Southam Street and the Golborne Road, where I went back and forth to school, the Antiguan carpenter Kelso Cochrane was brutally murdered by a gang of young whites. I turned this corner on the morning following the killing. Returning from Paddington General Hospital shortly after midnight on 17 May 1959, the thirty-two-year-old Cochrane was assaulted by a gang of white youths, and stabbed with a stiletto knife. He died an hour later.

The police denied it was a racist killing, and the press followed suit. Police investigation of the murder came under much scrutiny at the time, but what was known locally as 'the worst kept secret in Notting Hill' remained a secret. Local white *omertà* won out, with the collusion of the authorities. Preserving stable 'race relations' took precedence over justice. 'Rab' Butler, the Home Secretary of the time, was regularly kept abreast of developments, as there was governmental concern that organizations campaigning against racism would make a martyr of Cochrane. This black life did not matter.

Cochrane's funeral procession to Kensal Green Cemetery in June 1959 departed from a church not far up the road from the schoolroom I was sitting in that same day. What is striking in the cinema newsreel coverage of the event is the large number of white as well as black people who congregated outside the church, and then together formed the long funeral cortege that followed the hearse all the way up to the cemetery.[5] It was the same route, part of the way, as my father's funeral four years later. In the Pathé film, one sees the Jewish faces in the crowd, glimpses a white woman holding a black child in her arms, perhaps minding the infant for a black mother while she attends the service; black and white together, a black life mattering there and then.

The history of the aftermath of the riots is almost as shameful as the riots themselves: the local publicans, the local authorities, the local MPs (especially the Labour one, to us 'Georgie' Rogers),[6] the press, the police, the Church, parliament – all brought this shame upon them by directing blame away from their own overt or covert racism and towards the 'hooligan' elements on both sides.[7]

Although most West Indian immigrants did not come directly from rural or farming backgrounds, their story is also, like that of the Irish, part of the greater story of the death of the world peasantry in the second half of the twentieth century. Plenty of those with the experience of labour in agriculture and of owning small farming properties became migrants. In the 1948 census, 50 per cent of men and 17 per cent of women worked in agriculture. A very large number of people were scarcely more than a generation away from the land. Furthermore, people still lived in the shadow of slavery. In the plantation economy of Jamaica in 1950, farms of over 100 acres were only 1 per cent of the total number, but represented 51 per cent of the total acreage, while 70 per cent of farms held only 14 per cent of the land.[8]

In Caribbean culture the house, unlike the Irish farmhouse, was more a sort of congeries of spaces – the yard (or plot, garden) and the house together; the house by itself was of less significance. Culturally, coherence is given through the deep significance of the 'yard', which signals the unity of the space that is one's own and can be called 'home', and that above all represents the continuity of the kinship group.[9] Yard is a synonym for home, especially in Jamaica.[10] The yard is also a place of social exchange; and there are specialized yards for medicine, healing and religion, say. The yard is particularly important as a place for growing things and supporting life – a kind of garden, in fact. There seems a deep connection between the kitchen, and within it the hearth, in the Irish house and the yard in the West Indian one (the garden is markedly less significant in Irish culture than in the British Caribbean). And these connections are profoundly historical in both cases. Both can be taken to be chronotopes, real places where time and space are most deeply sedimented.

The transplanted Caribbean house has been considered by several scholars. The West Indian 'front room', for example, in some accounts exemplifies elements of what has been left behind.[11] Others argue that the front room is less a matter of transplantation and more one of adaptation to the forms of respectability immigrants found around them in England.[12] But surely it is both, and in a curious and circular way, because the respectable, Victorian English bourgeois interior (like the working-class 'parlour' that copied it) was first exported via the colonial process to the British Caribbean before it was brought back in altered form.

So, the story of how the old house is transplanted in the new is both similar to and different from the Irish story, just as is the material nature of the house itself.[13] Again, it is a story of loss as well as adaptation. It does not do to romanticize the old dwellings. Sometimes the original house was what the immigrant wanted to lose, not hold on to – something that had become inadequate or even repellent to them. Coming to the new house in Britain may have been a liberation – though very often more in expectation than reality, the new abode a desperate disappointment. In a sense, however, this is beside the point, for the Irish rural house and its Caribbean cognate were the type of what 'home' meant, and what it *should* be, so that this is what people struggled against the odds to make. The yard in the head.

Therefore, I consider the struggle to find and make a house that might be home, and so to the suffering of the immigrant, for things did not in the end always turn out 'alright'. The suffering not only of the immigrant, but of the immigrant's child too. I draw on the testimony of West Indian immigrants and their children, my own thoughts at times interspersed among their stories.

In my mind while doing so is Donald Rodney's photograph *In the House of My Father*, a close-up image of his own hand, in which sits a minute sculpture of a house constructed from pieces of Rodney's skin removed during one of the many operations he underwent to combat sickle cell anaemia – an inherited disease that affects people of African and Caribbean descent. The exhibition from which the photograph is taken was dedicated to his father, who had died in 1995. The house is fragile. It is two-storey, more like the English house than the Caribbean one perhaps. It is made of a skin that is itself, however, not English, or at least not made first within the shores the father who conceived him had come to. The black skin makes the new house in the new land, just as the old house makes the new. Rodney is always going to his father's house, always going home.

The 'testimony' comes from a remarkable and it seems largely forgotten work by a white American sociologist called Thomas J. Cottle, on West Indian immigrants to south London in the mid 1970s.[14] Cottle, also a trained clinical psychiatrist, is rightly famed for his extraordinary writing about, and sensitivity to, the experience of children. This London work is remarkable because Cottle listened hard over a period of years to a few people so that he got to hear stories not usually told.

Stories of houses; stories of the old, as well as the young. Warren Oster is sixty-six. His is the usual narrative of poor rented housing followed by the passage from one council flat to another – one only slightly less inadequate than the previous one – especially as the family grows. Energy wanes, hope fades, resignation comes as he fights what he calls 'the battle of the house'. Because he is black, the battle is especially hard. As Cottle writes, the 'single most effective cause of segregation' for the black immigrant in London is housing.[15]

Throughout his life, Warren told anyone that employment and education were the vital aspects of living, but to himself he admits that it is the home which above all determines whether a man is happy or not: Cottle reports of Warren, 'Take a happy man, he would always say, and put him in an unhappy house and you will see a change in that man. Overnight, you will see that the spirit of that man has left him.' Warren ponders, 'People think that men do not take an interest in their house, only women, but they are wrong: a person is judged by the house, because the poor flat means the poor life.' If a person wants to reveal his or her success, it must be done through the home. 'Clothes are like beauty; only skin deep. To know the soul I have to know the home.' Cottle is welcomed in this home, 'but never am I there without him looking about his reception room or kitchen, his eyes getting smaller, his face showing a familiar sadness. He looks because the presence of a visitor reminds him to look again, to take stock again.'

His home always seems to remind him of where he is in the world, and where he meant to be:

> It pulls me so far down, my home. I come back from work …
> and I reach the corner, the turning even into the street where I
> can see the building, that's all, just see it, and it's like I've just
> remembered something that I was supposed to get, but it's too

A man on the doorstep of a house in the vicinity of Ladbroke Road Underground Station, 1961.

late now to get it. So I must go home, every night of my life with this feeling that something important hasn't been taken care of ... It's like some men receive their sad news in the post. My sad news is the house.

He is surrounded by

people, good people, but living so close together like animals, not like people, and every single one of them, just like me, old, young, in between, men, women, all of them doing the best they can do to fight off the feeling that the building, their homes, are making them feel. They don't want to feel what they feel, you know it isn't something that they like to do.[16]

But it is how they cannot avoid feeling.[17] He is consumed by a sense of waste: 'Strange how it goes. You come here, an immigrant, life starts again, it really does. You, and all these people, but you're special, they're special, it's like maybe you can be reborn ... But you're not, we are all together again, just the way we were when we came, just the way we've always been.' He lies to himself the most in spring, when the weather is warm for the first time.[18]

On the other hand, Beatrice Waters, of a similar age, has not given up, although in Warren Oster's world she may be deluding herself. She will move 'till the day I die', and life is filled by the pursuit of a better place, for she will not flag from, as she puts it, always 'settling up'. It is the same story, shared by her, Oster and the others: the relentless search to find comfort in the city that is to be their new 'home'. Beatrice keeps moving until 'I'm happy in this country'. Yet comfort, pleasure and happiness prove elusive in an England that shows them little welcome. Her sense of worth rises as she secures the top floor in a council house, but there is a price to pay, as her husband Henry has heart trouble. Perhaps the relentless search is something to do with the fact that she has no children – children would slow her down, although she may have found a kind of rest with children that the ideal home, perhaps instead, still holds out for her.[19]

Few, perhaps, have Beatrice's seemingly boundless energy and hope, and many do not share Warren's bitter sense of waste. Sheila Cooperton is thirteen years old. She has rarely slept in her own bed, never mind had her own room. Sheila's family has never known anything but economic hardship, and its anxieties are always on display. Anxiety for Sheila was multiplied because movement in the small flat was so difficult, people always on display to one another. 'Nothing anybody in the family does ... can be done free of evaluation and a display of all the family problems, anxieties, despair.' The habitation itself is 'a symbolic representation of precisely how far they have gotten, and how far they are going to get.' 'It is a monument to nothing,' her father says.[20]

Anxiety was our lot, too: anxiety on display in Ashmore Road, most of all the worrying of my mother as she tried to keep us (anyway well-instructed) children ever quieter for fear of the gales of abuse that would blow from below, three families stacked in a row, one on top of another. A state of barely interrupted civil war existed for eighteen years between my mother and 'downstairs', the sovereign territory of an appropriately named English tyrant called Mrs King, christened 'Banty' by my mother in recognition of her indestructible will to fight and – none too obliquely – her diminutive stature and bandy legs.

Anxiety is transmitted from one generation to another – my brother's anxiety more than my own. He feared 'the hall', the connecting corridor from kitchen to front door shared by 'above', for then you left the home, you crossed a threshold. I took it in my stride, for the upstairs neighbours were benign. But there was anxiety for my parents, for my war-damaged father; their anxiety for me, hospitalized regularly as a very young child with a defective eye; and my anxiety at separation,

Chippenham Road, London W9, ca. 1952. The houses behind are almost exactly similar to those on Ashmore Road, though in better repair, and the lamp is a double of the one of my dreams, except for the shiny (Coronation?) paint. The lamppost was also an item in the furniture of street play – a goalpost, a gathering place, a tree to climb, a swing (the ladder support is slightly buckled).

at a time when, with great but unwitting cruelty, parents were not allowed to visit their children in hospital.

Anxiety, being always on display, eats the soul. The hidden injuries of class are to be numbered among life's burdens, part of what Samuel Beckett called 'life without tears, as it is wept'. The toll of all this on the immigrant's health and on their children is great, as medical statistics show. Nonetheless, it was at No. 11 that I learned intimacy with the world, being at home in it as well as anxious in it, learned what space and time might be, lying in the big bed of my parents in the dark night before sleep, waiting for my father to come home, and watching the few and so at that time still mysterious car lights from outside, slow and steady, climbing up and along the walls and ceiling of the room. I loved the 'back room', too, where I slept, always in a separate bed, my brother across from me in another.

The 'front room' was where memory was more sharply made. This was the room that all night received the pale yellow light from the gas lamp immediately outside the house. Gaston Bachelard's 'poetics of space' again speaks to this experience of dwelling, of being housed, enclosed, sheltered, safe – the experience of rooms, but also of intimate objects within them, boxes within boxes, cupboards in rooms. For me, the furniture made up familiar and happy ghosts in the shadows seen from the bed; for others, places where unhappy ghosts might dwell. Boxes in rooms, the cigar box in which my treasure was kept. I heard the sound of the shunting and whistling trains from the lines going into Paddington, blessed music.

The thirteen-year-old Sheila Cooperton imagined a room somewhere in London, 'which she wants to believe does exist, and is what she calls heaven. You spell that', she adds, 'with a capital H.'[21] The child daydreams about paradise, and the house is reduced to a sort of essence that is the room, the shelter: she does not even see what the inside of the room is like – it is a room just by itself: 'I imagine a little block that a child plays with, you know. And it's just there, in the middle of nothing. If you see what I mean. That block is my room … I'm afraid to imagine what it looks like because then it will go away.' She has dolls and toys, not a lot, but what she loves above all is the place 'where all these things go' to be contained and thus safe. There was an old chest her mother had, an old doll's house the girl once had, but the room that counts is the room that comprehends these other little rooms: 'If you have a real room that you like, then you can play with a doll's house better.' Then you can 'make up anything'. There you can be alone, and yourself, be creative and therefore fulfilled.

What she is expressing goes to the heart of human experience, for as young children we learn about the world by what are known as 'schemas' of behaviour. One of these basic schemas involves enclosing, and being enclosed. Children will form enclosures either around themselves or around their play areas. They may enclose items in boxes or other containers. Through this schema they learn about ordering things and spaces, so that we see how deep is the desire for shelter, for habitation, and how this desire for order in and over things is about creating the safety of the self.

Sheila loves the family and wants to be close to them. However, she feels like she is 'living in a tube station. Everybody is always coming and going. I don't even know who I am, half the time.' When you live so close to people, you feel you're all becoming one another, 'so you start thinking and acting like them, until you think you really are them'. This is highly disturbing for the child, as her sense of self is obliterated. She dreams that she is her sister, and that the sister was still herself, too, which means that 'nobody was me anymore, even though I wasn't really dead'. She has lots of dreams where she either disappears or turns into somebody else. She says that sleeping in the same bed as others doesn't mean you aren't afraid: she lies there in the dark afraid that something is going to happen 'in the bed, I mean, I don't know what it is, but I start to shiver'. To have one's own room is to have one's own world. Even to share a room with one other is to have a world.

Hope, regret, resignation are a matter of the spaces of the house, but also of time, of fate and of history. These narratives of these spaces are just that, narratives, stories always set in time, and stories about time as well. For example, Cottle talks to and of Doreen Grainger, and we are still in the same south London housing estate of the late 1970s. Doreen is a bright eleven-year-old, but she does not know what it is to feel eleven. 'Well, I feel old lots of the time … More than anybody believes. People think children only think about getting old, but never that they're old.' She goes on, 'You know what I think? I think families that don't have a lot of money always feel older than they really are.' She explains what children are really like around here: 'Actually like us, we're afraid too many things are going to happen that are going to make it bad for us.'

The etymology of 'education' tells us that the Latin *educatio*, a bringing up, a rearing, is related to *educo*, combining the sense of 'from, out of', and 'bring out, lead forth', *ducere*. This is so for Doreen, as for me. For her, if only for a time, education leads her out of herself, out of familial anxieties, and out of the sense of an unending sameness that stifles her. Her favourite way out is reading history, as it was one of mine. The conundrum of what being a child is, which this astonishing child confronts in her life every day, she explores through this reading, and her thinking about it. Will things get better? Will they stay the same? What does it mean to grow up, to be an adult? Does it have any meaning at all – and so does making a progress through life have any purpose? She is drawn to history because she already partly feels an adult, and therefore that things may always be the same for her and her like. She wants to understand the origins and have some kind of explanation of this seeming sameness.[22]

She wants to find out about West Indian history and about people like her, not kings and queens. Nobody writes about those who were not rich, and she is sad about this, for these are the people who made her as she is. 'Maybe things that happened long, long ago to people you've never even heard of is the reason why things are the way they are for your parents and you. People say, well, that's the way it's always been, which is what you study history to find out about, the way it's always been.' But then she works out a way forward that is other than an awareness of things always having been the same:

But nobody knows if it's *always* been like that. How could they know if they were not alive? See, that's what's important about history; that you can sort of be alive when you were not really alive. That's why teachers should tell you about the people who were alive then, and not just the things that happened ... That way, learning about history is like making believe you could live three different lives instead of just one life: the life you have, the life people had before you were born, and the life people are going to have after you die … Maybe things have always been the same; I don't think so, but maybe for some people they are. But people don't look like they did millions of years ago, so how could other things be the same? I was thinking, maybe what I want to know about history is whether everything will be for my family like it is now. Nobody can see the future, but they can see what history was like, only not the kings.

Doreen is a social historian without knowing it. I became one. She knows that the history books are mostly written about the rich people, so that it is unlikely 'somebody will write a history book about me … this for sure is never going to happen'.

The house is a material and cultural form that permeates all of life. But there is more than one house. We talk about schoolhouses, courthouses, houses of God, the Houses of Parliament, for a reason. The schoolhouse is my subject here. There is, as we have seen, a profound connection between houses – the first, domestic house, the *domus*, and subsequent ones. In academic historical work, I have explored this in terms of the state and the British public schools.[23] In these the most crucial element was indeed the 'house', in which most of school life was lived, and where boys were best taught to govern themselves so they could govern others. This amounted to a grand larceny of the domestic, bourgeois home: a translation of the first, family home and all its great symbolic and emotional charge into the subsequent experience of the child in the public school. This involved not only the schools, but also the Oxbridge college, which like all colleges including religious ones also functioned as a house and a home. Perhaps the most traditional of Oxford colleges, Christ Church, is called 'The House'.

Educatio? It was my way of leading out, out of Paddington, out of life on a 'council estate' like the ones Warren, Sheila and Doreen struggled against. Out of that suffocation. It was the Tory politician Robert Lowe who coined the term 'educating our masters', during debates on the Second Reform Act of 1867, knowing that, if reform had to come, it was necessary to educate 'the democracy' he so feared. The state in Britain still educates the democracy, the political elites of one day replacing those of another. Lowe's attitude is still there in one of the most highly governed and highly centralized education systems in the world, in which a secretary of state has only to lift up their hand, and all changes. It was Lowe who invented 'payment by results', forms of which have in recent decades been reborn in British education.

But if our masters were to be educated, what model was needed? The one ready to hand was that of the new and reformed 'public' (independent) schools of later Victorian Britain, where our real masters were, and still are, educated. The state and the independent systems grew up together, the former in the latter's image, one trinitarian hierarchy following and aping another: Greek, Latin, modern languages in the independent schools themselves; the public, grammar and elementary hierarchy from 1870 to the 1944 Education Act; then, in my time and until comprehensive education, public, grammar and secondary modern. The whole thing was an image of Britain – had in fact made Britain what it was, and what it still is.

Many of the essential techniques of British education were pioneered by the public schools in the nineteenth century and then transplanted into the system at large. Even in my own lowly secondary modern school we had houses, housemasters and weekly house meetings to exhort us to greater achievements, including sporting ones that were organized on a house basis (Alban, Beckett, Fisher, More – good English, Catholic saints). We had a headmaster, the reign of whom was set in the pattern of the original Victorian invention. We had a prefectorial system, a praetorian guard chosen only from the 'A stream', of which I was one.

One's fate in the 1950s was pretty much decided at the age of eleven, when the eleven-plus examination sorted the educational worthy from the unworthy. Only four out of thirty in my junior school class passed the eleven-plus (the preparation for this supposed intelligence test was woeful). I passed the examination; but because there were not enough Catholic grammar schools went to the Cardinal Manning Secondary Modern School for Boys to give it its full title, in St Charles Square, in what is now called Notting Hill. Going to a non-Catholic grammar was possible, but did not for a moment enter into considerations of either my parents or my teachers.

Almost to a boy at 'the Manning', we were Irish-born or first-generation children, and taught by those of similar shades of green. Our teachers were Nolans, O'Donnells, Lynches, Maloneys, Cosgraves – the list went the length of Ireland. If not of Irish history, nor of the language, we Manning Boys knew much of Roman Catholicism, and the Roman Church in England was its familiar self-interested self in seeing to it that we turned out dutiful sons of the temporal power, unburdened by inconvenient Irish histories such as that of Oliver Cromwell in Ireland. Nonetheless, the Irishness flowed through unabated. I joined a Catholic youth club, Stonyhurst and Barrett (named after the prominent Jesuit public school, which gave us its patronage – although precious few Jesuits or public school boys were to be seen on the premises). This was the nearest we got to public school, at the receiving end of this peculiar expression of upper-class paternalism.

Rugby School and Harrow School patronized the equivalent and eponymous 'Protestant' (and thus not Irish) youth clubs of the adjacent locality of low Notting Dale. The local state schools of a non-Catholic sort were by common consent awful. The nearby and inappropriately named Isaac Newton School was sensationally publicized at the time as a 'blackboard jungle' in the *News of the World* (then the largest circulation newspaper in the world). The desperate violence produced by poverty and the poor education of the white English working class around us was all too real, as the 1958 riots in Notting

Hill illustrated. On our margins then lay 'rough' Protestants, not least those of Southam Street.

The Catholic Kremlin of Charles Square was made up of land and properties donated to the Church by the family of author G. K. Chesterton. It comprised, in addition to my school, the Cardinal Manning Girl's School; a Catholic primary school; the Crusade of Rescue hostel for fallen girls and their offspring; the parish church, Pius X; and a very large convent housing an enclosed community of the Discalced (barefoot) Order of Carmelite Nuns.

Most of us, and indeed most of our parents, did not know what a university was. This was a time when only a tiny proportion of young people went on to university anyway. 'The big school in the country', my mother called it, when I later attended one. I was the first and for years after the only one from the school to go. Most left the Cardinal Manning at fifteen, and by the time today's students are pondering their futures at eighteen we were already long in paid work. If you were not in the 'A Stream' you headed for a life of manual work; and if you were, perhaps for the lowliest ranks of the professions and business.

Riddled by class without, education was for us also riddled by class within: 'without' in terms of the distinction between us and the local Catholic grammar schools, class distinctions also being accompanied by those of gender. We were educated to be boys, the Cardinal Manning girls to be girls, separated from us and down the road, and to our displeasure released from school at a different hour than us. Girls did needlework, domestic science, and if they were lucky or in the non-academic stream at a grammar school, shorthand, typing and bookkeeping. The Sec. Mod. Boys, in contrast, did woodwork or metalwork, and not a syllable of a foreign language passed our lips. But the teachers were good, often devoted; to them the idea of having a 'vocation' touched upon teaching as well as the priesthood. We studied and practised, if sometimes in a fairly desultory way, music, art, and something called 'speech and drama'.

The author, far left, returns to his school at the age of seventeen, shortly after leaving at the relatively advanced age of sixteen and a half. His lack of sartorial elegance contrasts with his fellows. How adult the young ex-scholars seem, propelled by circumstances into adulthood as they were. However, the boy kneeling at the front corrects this impression somewhat.

We were riddled with class 'within' by the system of 'streaming', which was organized by 'intelligence'. The British class system was actively taught in the schools, as much by the physical experience of being classed at school as by the subjects taught. The classroom itself did the teaching – in fact the class*room* itself, which with its emphasis on classifying and ranking was, in significant measure, a result of the reformed nineteenth-century public schools, including their obsession with competition and hierarchy. Even though we might have brothers and sisters (in the Manning Girls) in other 'streams', the 'A' team was a team apart – the people who did the exams, the prefects who exercised petty authority. The humiliations and other hurts of streaming, of going 'up' and 'down' and adjusting, of being in the 'C' or 'D' stream for good, were perhaps as hurtful as the negative experiences of grammar school for many who went there – those who did less well in them or faced their snobbishness.

Not only were decisions about a child's future arbitrary, but it now turns out they were fake, for the whole system was based on the now-discredited idea of intelligence testing. Discredited especially in the case of Sir Cyril Burt, one of its foremost advocates and a major architect of British education. Burt in fact experimented directly on us specimens of my other west. He was keen to apply his principles to 'backward' children, and those he lighted upon were from Kensal New Town, in the school next to my own primary one (on East Row), a notoriously bad 'Protestant' one (on Middle Row).[24]

The grammars were a different world; however bright many of us were, they lay beyond us. The London County Council published a list of secondary schools in West London in 1953, aiming to inform parents about choosing schools.[25] This publication never crossed the threshold of our house, and our parents were poorly informed about the choices available – something compounded by their own limited education and lack of acquaintance with English ways. They were, however, fanatically devoted to the education of their children in so far as they understood it.

If my compatriots, at least most of them, do not feel robbed, and do not feel bitter looking back, then I do not forget, for I progressed further through the class structure than they did, and so I saw what was on the other side. Being able to see both sides at once brings both release and anger. God help the poor man's son whom, as Adam Smith once observed, 'heaven in its anger has visited with ambition'.[26]

As John Lydon – previously Johnny Rotten – put it in a somewhat different context, 'anger is an energy'.[27] Lydon's father came from Galway, and there are plenty of Lydons in Joyce Country. I have a family relation to Lydons. I share some of this anger of John's, and with it the urge to express oneself that anger brings with it. I did not share the awfulness of Lydon's upbringing in north London, a decade later than mine. Above all, I did not share his insulting experience of rejection and failure at school, although I know about it and about the other things he experienced in the city's north. I have seen families ripped apart by drugs, prison and alcohol on the outside, and on the inside by the withering experience of poverty and of insecurity of the self. The big family, the lost father, the help-less mother, and what these brought in their train: lives ended decades too soon.

I took these feelings into the adult life that awaited. I was an angry young man, my anger fuelled further by my own father's early death. University at twenty, after the grind of A levels by correspondence course while working all day, so that I count among my honours graduation from a 'correspondence college': 'Wolsey Hall', no less. Institutions like Wolsey Hall, now forgotten, thrived at the time for us relatively few autodidact children, its green cyclostyled sheets the source of the wisdom that would get me through. *King Lear*, Gerard Manley Hopkins, 'The Age of Discovery' – nothing but discoveries.

I was educated by London in these years, too, by having its wealth of resources to hand and learning to make use of them. One of my teachers, I realized later, was the CIA, for at the age of sixteen I discovered and frequented the United States Information Service Library near the US Embassy in Berkeley Square. They just let you in! The American Dream was around me in the reading room itself – at least my version of it, dream furniture now real, dream books real, and dream magazines, *Colliers*, the *Saturday Evening Post*, *Life*: images of what I was missing once I knew it was there. Enormous and comfortable armchairs, gigantic table lights with tasselled shades, and the smell of polished tables whose enormity matched the chairs and lights, so that all America must be like this around me. Mayfair educated me in other ways, too, as an adolescent, as I wandered alone there on Saturday mornings discovering a city I both loved and despised. The objects of my ire were evident, standing outside the opulent Park Lane hotels where I saw the well-heeled being grovelled to by doormen, both partners in this dance of power being the object of the uncharitable anger of sixteen years.

I had only the haziest idea what a university was, and thought that my only way out of eternal clerkship was to train as a teacher. The 'New Universities' were then just beginning, and in 1965 it had not been long since grants were available to aspirants such as me (not long either since the need to have a classical language had been waived). Keele University took me in – a new, democratic and happily experimental place of learning at the time. The institution's motto was and remains 'Thanke God for All'. The labourer's son and the admiral's daughter got on famously in this place where we hoped a new and better Britain was being made. The founder of Keele had been the master of Balliol College, Oxford – Lord Lindsay, a radical, Nonconformist Scot. The bright boy whom heaven in its anger had visited with ambition had been sent along the train to first class, and I found myself after Keele on the way to Balliol as a postgraduate. I saw there how the flummery of Oxbridge was meat and drink to those – the very great majority – who were there by birthright, left or right politically.

The master of Balliol in my time was the Marxist historian Christopher Hill, and Balliol was the radical college (and historically the brainy and politically savvy one). Hill presided happily over the neo-feudal hierarchy of bedmakers, porters and disciplinary 'bulldogs', willing and obedient lackeys as then I saw them, though my anger was I fear compromised by the seductive powers of the place, powers well known. 'Masters' of colleges, radical or otherwise, continue to preside happily over a situation remarkably unchanged from those days, for all the corporatization of the universities. The self-conceit of the place is still remarkable, as are its self-deluded efforts to reach outside the charmed circles of the privately educated, a few token efforts apart. From Southam Street to Balliol, but pulled back always to the other west, a London only ever half left.

PART II

WAR

5

The Death of Myles Joyce

Memory is framed by forgetting in the same way as the contours
of the shoreline are framed by the sea.

Marc Augé

Myles Joyce/Maolra Seoighe.

Reproduced below is a photograph of Myles Joyce, *Maolra
Seoighe* in Irish. He stares out at us intensely, and is slightly
out of focus in the image, as if he had moved his head as the
photograph was being taken. His eyes cannot be clearly seen,
yet they seem to be fixed on the camera, and perhaps too by
then they were also fixed on his fate. In the yard of Galway
prison in December 1882, three men – Myles Joyce, Patrick
Joyce and Patrick Casey – were executed by hanging for the
horrendous murder of five members of a Joyce family in the
vicinity of Maamtrasna townland, County Mayo. The murders
had occurred in the August of that same year. Myles Joyce was
innocent of the crime for which he was executed – the two
others executed very likely not. Eight men in total were convicted on perjured evidence, the perjured guilty and innocent

alike. Five of those convicted were sentenced to penal servi-
tude for life. It is generally accepted that at least four of those
imprisoned were innocent, having changed their pleas to guilty
in the hope of avoiding execution. The instigators and main
perpetrators were allowed to go free.

Maamtrasna is at the northern edge of Joyce Country. My
father's townland, Kilbride, is immediately to the south, at the
other side of the mountain that also bears the name Kilbride.
His house and that of the murders were less than a mile apart.
My Joyces shared the same townland as the wife of Thomas
Joyce, one of the falsely imprisoned, to which she returned
after he was jailed. My father's father was born around the
time of the murders, and his father, my great-grandfather Liam,
would have had a good idea of what went on. This knowledge
was not shared with outsiders. The bodies of the murdered
Joyces were buried in the ancient graveyard of Kilbride, itself
now long gone to ruin. The bodies were carried over the mountain, from one side to the other.

At the time, cooperation with the authorities was forbidden by popular fiat. The townland, and those adjacent, were
after the murders studded with 'police huts', rudimentary tin
structures set on the bleak uplands and in the beautiful valleys,
erected to observe the local people during this time of the Land
War in the West. In these huts the police roasted in the summer
and froze in the winter. After the trial of Myles Joyce, the huts
served to provide protection for those who had informed on
the convicted. This was a time of war: the so-called Land War
was a period of intense agrarian agitation that took both political and violent forms. At its peak, between 1879 and 1882, it
had its origin and epicentre in my father's 'bloodstained' Mayo.
The movement aimed to secure fair rents and security of tenure
for tenant farmers.

Silence was everything in the face of the authorities, and it
was everything for long after these events, as people learned
to live with the aftermath. The awfulness of this was a mirror

to the murders themselves: some of the guilty and those who gave perjured evidence were well known, and went on to live in the community after the trials, among the kin of the innocent and of the murdered. But the innocent eventually returned after long imprisonment, and had no option but to enter this impenetrable mesh of silences.

Most of the men involved in what came to be called the 'Maamtrasna Murders' did not speak English, including Myles Joyce. Myles was represented at his trial by a defence lawyer who knew no Irish – a callow twenty-four-year-old recent graduate of then Protestant Trinity College, Dublin. The court interpreters used were either unwilling or unable to convey the impassioned stories of the accused. In 1881 the barony of Ross, in which Myles Joyce lived, had a population of 8,260, of which 7,350 people were Irish speakers, over half of those (3,714) speaking Irish only. The jury in Myles's case was composed of ten Protestants and two Roman Catholics. Not only was the evidence perjured – it was paid for. The move to pay the witnesses, and to press for the death penalty, bore the signature of the lord-lieutenant of Ireland, the Earl Spencer, great-grand uncle to the later Princess of Wales. He seems to have paid well

Maamtrasna townland, north side of Kilbride mountain, showing the road leading down to the site of the murders of the Joyce family. My father's house is on the other side of the hill to the right of the photograph – Kilbride Mountain, so called.

over the going rate: a sum totalling £1,250, enormous for that time, went to the three perjuring witnesses.

'Perfidious Albion': this is how an appalled James Joyce (Seamus Seoighe) described the fate of our namesake at his trial:

> The magistrate, 'Ask him if he was in the vicinity at the time'. The old man [sic] began speaking once again, protesting, shouting, almost beside himself with the distress of not understanding or making himself understood, weeping with rage and terror. And the interpreter once again replied drily: 'He says no, your worship' ... The figure of this bewildered old man, left over from a culture which is not ours ... is a symbol of the Irish nation at the bar of public opinion.[1]

The *Irish Times* described Joyce's execution. 'At a quarter-past eight o'clock the prison doors were thrown open', the paper's correspondent noted, 'with startled looks they marked the wild, hollow eyes, sunken cheeks, and shrunken forms of each other, but not a word passed between them. Myles Joyce came first, between two warders, bareheaded, repeating in Irish the responses to the prayers which were being read by the Rev Mr Grevan. Then came Pat Casey, pinioned, silent, and with a look of great agony on his features. Last appeared Pat Joyce, taller than the others, wearing his hat, silent, too, and walking with firm and steady step.'

The executioner, William Marwood, then placed them with the tallest man in the centre, and began pinioning their knees. Myles Joyce continued to speak in an 'excited way', the *Irish Times* correspondent noted, and continued:

> It was impossible to gather the meaning of much that fell from him, even by Irish-speaking persons who were present; but the following sentences have been interpreted for me by one who understands and speaks the language thoroughly, and who was close enough to hear the greater part of what he said. These

sentences were: 'I am going before my God. I was not there at all. I had no hand or part in it. I am as innocent as a child in the cradle. It is a poor thing to take this life away on a stage; but I have my priest with me.' ... Two of the ropes remained perfectly motionless, but the third, that by which Myles Joyce was hanged, could be seen by those who watched it closely to vibrate, and swing slightly backwards and forwards ... It soon became evident, from the hangman Marwood's behaviour, that there had been a hitch of some kind or other, and he muttered, 'bother the fellow', sat down on the scaffold, laid hold of the rope, and moved it backwards and forwards.

Myles Joyce's death was an awful one: he protested his innocence to the end. His terrified movements in his last moments dislodged the noose from around his neck, and he was strangled to death after two minutes of the utmost agony. The violence of the state was duly registered and recorded in complete bureaucratic detail; ten different documents were needed in order for the inquest jury to identify the bodies of the executed.[2]

The reasons for the violence of the crimes themselves are still opaque. The authorities hinted that the head of the murdered family, John Joyce, was treasurer of one of the local secret societies who opposed the landlords, and suggested the household was attacked because he was alleged to have misappropriated money belonging to the association. Others suggested that his mother was the principal target because she had allegedly informed the authorities about the location in Lough Mask (almost opposite my father's house in Maskeen), where the bodies of the Huddy family had been dumped – two men, the agent of the local landlord, and the agent's grandson. This landlord was Arthur Guinness, 1st Baron Ardilaun. The Huddys were held to be 'informers', reported spies for Dublin Castle, the hated centre of colonial British governance in much of rural Ireland.

However, the murdered John Joyce was reputed to have stolen his neighbours' sheep, and years before there was already trouble over land and stock between these Joyces and other Joyce families and the Casey clan. 'Big John' Casey may have been the leader of a murderous gang, but no one can be sure of anything now. The bitterness of the feud was in the air. This was a place not just geographically at the edge – the Atlantic was over the hills – but physically so, too: a place of constant struggle for a livelihood, a sort of battlefield, a place at war to survive. In the mountain uplands of Maamtrasna, sheep were the means of life itself, and there the landlord system drove a genial and generous people to violent rebellion, and in the end to awful crime. The landlord of those involved in these events, an evicting one, was known to push his tenants to the limit, leaving families to eke out a living from the unforgiving snipe grass of the uplands and 'living in crazy congestion at one another's back doors'.[3]

As well as Ardilaun's agent and his grandson, Lord Mount-morres, who was another local aristocrat and absentee local landowner, had also recently been assassinated, less than a mile from my father's local village of Clonbur. He had been shot by the side of the road on his way back to Ebor Hall, the family residence overlooking magnificent upper Lough Corrib. He was returning from the village where he had called for coercive measures against the rebellious people that surrounded him.

The area had a history of agrarian protest. It was the original home of the 'boycott', directed against a land agent of that name. The military and Orangemen had to be drafted in to harvest the crops of targeted landlords in the boycott area of the Neale, as it is called. Joyce Country was considered a centre of 'Ribbonmen Fenianism'.[4]

Only memories of memories of memories remain – for instance, those of Michael Anthony Seoighe, once the local postman, and the son of the man who went to labour in England with my father when they were both young men in the 1930s. From Michael I learn that, for these people, what happened in that territory stayed in that territory when it came

The Death of Myles Joyce

Prison portrait of Myles Joyce. The large
hands of the peasant are evident.

to outsiders, especially official ones. He tells me nonetheless
that it was the uncle of his grandfather who found the bodies
of the murdered Joyce family.

This is a world of a very ancient form of silence, peasant
silence, something enmeshed in cultures that are largely oral in
nature. Agreements might often be concluded without resort
to writing, or even speech. To be taciturn was itself a form of
speech. Silence involved what was implicit, employing other
codes than those that governed speech. Silence in peasant
worlds is a strategy, one of protection, within and without.
Family secrets must be guarded, and any attack on the family
repulsed, for the family and the family holding are everything
in this world where survival is key. Survival might demand
revenge and reprisal; it certainly demanded patience, so that
ambition and vengeance were slow to come to an issue. The
right time had to be found. When it was found, violence might
be unrestrained, as in Maamtrasna and the Land War, as in the
age-old tradition of peasant revolt.

Peasants are people of few words, speech often seeming
pointless, even in the act of prayer. Alain Corbin writes in his
history of silence of a French peasant looking at the Eucharist

silently: 'I perceive him, and he perceives me.'[5] No words need be uttered. There are many forms of peasant silence. When a peasant wishes to be credible, there is often a long preliminary silence, the better to point up the boldness of speaking. Boldness is needed when the great world outside is encountered. Silence directed without the community is stronger than within, where there is usually ample talk. Silence is directed at the tax official, the policeman, the soldier – all the outsiders – and the priest sometimes. Fear and silence might go together, the fear of saying too much, the distrust of those who ask questions. Silence out of fear and distrust of one's own capacities as a speaker. And there was the great silence of incomprehension, of the disjuncture between codes of the utmost difference one from the other.

In effect these men were silenced, state silence versus peasant silence being an uneven match. The history of silence and forgetting is a tangled thing.[6] In Maamtrasna the layers of silence were seemingly without end; as soon as one layer is revealed another one is visible below it. In May 2019 I met Johnny Joyce, the great-grandson of John Joyce, one of the murdered in 1882. He knew nothing of the events until his adult life, the family remaining silent all those years, the forgetting strictly policed. On a visit to the West as a child, he recalled his father looking long and hard into the distance from time to time. He wondered about this then. Now he feels he knows why. When we met he embraced me warmly, the embers of some long-ago kinship rekindled in that Galway room. Forgetting was banished for a moment, silence broken.

The afterlife of memory here has gone through a resurrection of sorts in recent years. The historians and the literary scholars have rediscovered the case, doing Myles Joyce a long-postponed posthumous service.[7] Indeed, he has gone through a second coming, now with his own Wikipedia entry, his execution acted out in an Irish TV film, hoods, rope and all, so that via the television screen one may voyeuristically suffer the

Prison portrait of Maolra Seoighe II. James Joyce's 'old man' is another person in this other prison portrait, presumably taken earlier than the previous one. He looks calm and hopeful. He was only in his early thirties when he died.

'reality' of what he suffered. Nonetheless, for all his second-returning fame, he long lay buried unmarked and forgotten under the tarmac of Galway Cathedral's car park, itself atop the old prison yard of Galway Gaol and his place of execution.

Maolra Seoighe died long ago. Is it not time to 'move on' – indeed, in the words of some, 'get over it'? While all this seems to have something to do with me, a Joyce, what can it have to do with others and with our day, and with you? People such as the dead and calumnied Myles, and all the others, do concern us still, because they have a claim on us, and a claim on the present, even if this is the claim of only one person among the millions that might also have a claim. As weak Messiahs, we have a duty to try and save them, remembering our loss too. For we have lost not only them but all the unborn that might have come from them, the lives never lived, all the songs that would not be sung. And the half-lived lives, the lives lived without hope, of those who survived.

If we cannot wipe away the tears of the past, we can attempt to remember them, while not forgetting the ease with which we can all become accomplices in amnesia. None of us is immune to forgetting. None of us is beyond betrayal – one that, as Seamus Deane writes, 'will always make us foreign, especially to ourselves and to a past that is ours but to which we only weakly belong, since it asks more questions of us than we do of it'.[8] So then it is that we owe a debt to ourselves at odds with a present that was shaped by what destroyed them – those whose images come weakly to us now. I recall again Walter Benjamin, who thought that 'the past spoke directly only through things that had not been handed down' – *not* been handed down: the silences that needed telling in the teeth of the opposition of authority. The past is *not* a foreign country.

That inveterate city man James Joyce wrote that Myles Joyce came from 'a culture which is not ours'. What culture, then? And, more to the point here, what history? And whose history? Not just mine, and not just Ireland's, but Britain's too – and not only because this was once part of the British state. To *have* a history is to establish who we are, and by most reckonings we ought be responsible for who we are. Today we hear much in Britain of the history of empire and colony, and of the need to recognize the crimes that marked that history, and for restitution. But there is far less recognition that this is all nearer to home than we think, across a narrow sea, among us in the lives of so many settled in that near and other island.

The image of the ruin in Irish culture has often been taken as a symbol of Irish history itself: the ruin of the big house of the Ascendency, and of the small one of the peasant. The fields of my father's Kilbride are in ruin now, the houses ruined too, the fields gone wild, the houses now buried in ferns and young woods, each year ever more hidden on that side of the lake, from where so many have left. Subsequent generations are often loath to pull the old houses down, as they might shelter ghosts – the ghosts of those unborn to the Famine dead, and of those who emigrated, as well as those who stayed. This means that forgetting becomes difficult, much more so than in Britain.

Silence is the steward of ruin, just as it is the accomplice of atrocity: a silenced landscape, a silenced history, a history silenced by its own resistance to that silence (in the 1922 Civil

War many of the public records of Ireland perished in the gutted Four Courts). England, Britain, unhidden, powerful, noisy, the cause of ruin, and of powerlessness. Hidden Ireland, as one historian terms it,[9] the old townland or *baile* culture of the clachan, mortally wounded by the famine, surviving here around Maamtrasna and Kilbride later than perhaps anywhere else. It was hidden from the colonial authority around it, hidden by custom, by geography, by language, by its oral nature, and by its limited access to conventional powers to resist subjection. So it took up the means found in Joyce Country in the Land Wars – namely the secret, the silent, the coming-by-night, political as well as feuding murder in Ireland's collective affairs: sociable murder.

There was no legal or political recognition for the clachan/townland culture in Ireland; but this culture was the means by which, below the official level of private property and the law, land and livelihood were ordered by the vast majority of rural people until well into the nineteenth century. This being outside, being hidden and silenced, is at the heart of colonial experience. So too is the fragility, the scarcity, the impermanence of a subsistence culture (the famine was only a few decades distant at the time of Maamtrasna). The tenacity of collective social bonds, which had subsisted for centuries, had by the time of Maamtrasna been stretched almost to the limit, the bonds turned in upon themselves, a damaged and exhausted culture unable to see itself because to do so was to weaken the ties that bound.

In the case of Myles Joyce, memory still hurts, just as British forgetting goes on in the familiar way, even if things are slowly changing – sometimes also changing for the worse in a land torn apart by Brexit and its proponents' fantasies of the past. British Forgetting: in 2011 David Alton, a British Liberal MP and a crossbencher in the House of Lords, whose mother was from near Maamtrasna, joined with others to seek a review of the case of Maolra Seoighe.[10] Crispin Blunt (Wellington and

Sandhurst), parliamentary undersecretary at the Ministry of Justice, while conceding that while Myles Joyce was 'probably an innocent man', said he would not seek a posthumous apology unless there were 'compelling new reasons or sufficient public interest'.

Public interest, of the sort thought suitable by Blunt, did not arrive. On 4 April 2018 the Irish president issued a posthumous pardon for Myles, but he was the wrong head of state. One twist in history's tail in this case is that the two sons of the two survivors of the murders, one my namesake Patrick Joyce, played in the Croke Park Gaelic football game of November 1920, at which the British security forces fired into the crowd, killing eleven and wounding over sixty spectators. Their father, Maírtín, had been away from home when the murders took place, and both surviving sons were afterwards sent to the notorious Christian Brothers' Artane Industrial School in Dublin – a finishing school for the indigent poor.

We are not free to choose our inheritances, to choose our pasts, for these are given to us by history. They inhere in us. If we are not free to choose our pasts, neither are we free to choose our 'identities'. This is not to say that people are not free and do not have the right to determine what they think is their identity. It is to say that you do not really, in the end, choose your identity; rather, it chooses you.

The German political philosopher Jürgen Habermas gives eloquent expression to the urgency of understanding that we are implicit, and complicit, in our shared past, this sharing having, historically, most to do with the nation-state. In connection with the German guilt for Auschwitz, Habermas writes:

Our form of life is connected with that of our parents and grandparents through a web of familial, local, political, and intellectual traditions that it is difficult to disentangle, that is, through a historical milieu that made us what and who we are today. None of us can escape this milieu, because our identities, both as individuals and as Germans, are indissolubly interwoven with it. This holds true for mimicry and physical gestures to language and into the capillary ramifications of one's intellectual stance ... We have to stand by our traditions then, if we do not want to disavow ourselves.[11]

The past is a 'form of life' itself, including the 'national' past – a form of life that is 'ours', something which extends into the body as well as the mind; greatly into the body – a factor we neglect: into deportment say, into gesture, into language, into all the characteristics that mark our ordinary unthinking presence in the world: English 'reserve', Irish talk, with its own evasions, the way they/we hold our bodies, our habits of thought, genetic dispositions. In his autobiography, *Familiar Stranger: A Life between Two Islands*, Stuart Hall is keenly aware of these differences, the keenness sharpened to an edge by his black West Indian skin.[12] Between two islands in a different way to me, his middle passage like mine only intensified, child of his own people's original middle passage.

This all makes national identity the elusive and complex thing it is, partly willed, but partly unconscious too – the 'capillary ramifications', the 'web' of our traditions. As Paul Connerton avers, the past itself is reproduced through its bodily re-enactment, through its daily *performance*, so that 'tradition' is less a conversation with the past than its corporeal presence in us.[13] Seamus Deane writes in his poem 'Return' thus: 'In this Irish past I dwell / Like sound implicit in a bell.' This is true also for Britain, for England.

For the immigrant and the immigrant's children, things are different, since more than one past takes corporeal presence in us, and the different pasts that dwell implicitly within may be at war, or in a very uncertain peace. This is especially true of the pasts of empire, continually recomposed as they are within Britain's present. This warfare and uncertainty in Britain in recent times are accentuated, for the idea of being true to one's traditions has taken increasingly reactionary forms (not that immigrants and their children may not themselves sometimes be complicit in this). 'National identity' is the prize of the conflicts that take place – national identity in a political sense, at least, which is to say the narratives mobilized in the games of power, the stories that are supposed to hold us together as a society.

But what is the national identity that may emerge when, as Habermas indicates, we truthfully stick to 'our traditions' and do not disavow 'ourselves'? These traditions are almost always written in blood – the blood and the shame of slavery, empire and colony; and the blood of nation, which always is the blood of war. This blood is something that the majority of the British have yet to acknowledge.

On the reverse side of forgetting is remembering. Every remembering means a forgetting; something is always lost in order for something else to be found. My themes in what follows are the silences and forgetting that were essential for other things to be remembered – namely a national past. As the French anthropologist Marc Augé writes, in the words of my epigraph, 'Memory is framed by forgetting in the same way as the contours of the shoreline are framed by the sea'; Maurice Blanchot notes: 'To be silent is still to speak'. Both formulations are memorable. It is not the case that silence means forgetting and speech remembering. I attend in the next chapter to some of the silences that have most been part of my life: after the silences of emigration and class, the silences of war and its aftermath. What it is to have a history, especially a national one, is something deeply connected with having a home, and having shelter, so I turn to a world in which shelter was scarce.

6

Grave Births

The only defence is offence, which means that you have got to kill more women and children more quickly than the enemy if you want to save yourselves.
Stanley Baldwin, 11 November 1932

According to the belief my parents lived by to the end of their days, the soul enters the world at the moment of conception. Following the necessarily inexact computation involved, this occurred on the night of the devastation by bombing of the German city of Darmstadt. I was therefore born into a world of ruins, of ruined buildings, ruined homes above all. Ruin upon ruin, Irish, English, German. In the photograph of Darmstadt in September 1944 following allied bombing raids, only the walls stand, some of them anyway, mute reminders of all that had been lost. If my soul as conceived by my parents did enter the world that night then it was one close by, for it was all the same, as one German city after another was relentlessly bombed; bloody murder wreaked upon them all. On that night of 11–12 September 1944, over 12,000 were killed, and 66,000 made homeless. The population of the city not long before the bombing had been 115,211. On 1 March 1945 it was 51,750.

By one count, almost certainly an underestimate, 2,179 children were obliterated on that September night of the coming of my soul.[1] The air war on Germany killed about 75,000 children under fourteen, the number of the dead children exceeding that of persons *of all ages* killed by the German bombing raids on Britain in the Second World War. These German children died

The Luisenplatz in Darmstadt after the bombing raid of September 1944.

in the proportion of three boys to two girls. The injured children numbered around 116,000. The historian Jörg Friedrich reports that, in the devastation of the cities, the children lacked any shyness around the corpses.[2] They saw their friends and siblings without heads, the charred corpses of adults shrunk to the size of three-year-olds. The charred corpses were turned into dolls, almost. 'All day long', Friedrich tells us of the day after the raid, 'the people of Darmstadt brought their dead in old pails. A family in a washtub.'[3]

The Darmstadt 'area' bombing was focused on a quarter-circle of intense, concentrated bombing. The vertex of this area was the parade ground. The left edge of the fan formed a line that, by some demonic coincidence, continued to the city slaughterhouse. Bombing followed the path of the three sides of the triangle, with three waves of bombers operating along the three sides. The destruction of everything within the triangle was complete, the firestorm consuming almost all inside the fan. Incredibly, 300,000 incendiary bombs are said to have been dropped on this small place, including phosphor bombs.

A young girl of seven remembered how the phosphor stuck to her legs as she ran. She thought it was wire cutting into her, the streets turning to fire as she ran. She had several operations afterwards, but after a year the phosphor wounds were still open. She married an English serviceman and moved to London, telling nothing of this afterwards (you stick it away 'for all posterity', she says) until the fires of 9/11 brought it all to the surface.[4] In the raid she was at first entranced by what she calls the Christmas trees in the sky – the flares that marked the paths of the bombers coming to kill her.

Before my birth my mother worked in the Handley Page factory in Cricklewood. There, in industrial north-west London, the immigrant Irish had clustered, drawn by the relatively high wartime wages in factories – in her case wages in some excess of what was to be had as a domestic maid in the houses of the city's middle classes. She helped make the bombers that destroyed the German cities – the Halifax bombers though, not the Lancasters of the Darmstadt raid.[5] Perhaps there in her womb the homunculus was a mute witness to the work that enabled such destruction, connected to its mother now as part of the movements of her body, conjoined in what was now one single motion of hand to lathe and eye to drill.

As if in a distorted mirror-image of my mother's experience, my father was nearly killed by German bombers when, during one of the Luftwaffe air raids on Portsmouth in 1941, he was buried alive for the best part of a day. Several others

Bombed houses, St Paul's Square, Portsmouth, after a raid. Perhaps my father's house?

were buried under the same pile of rubble; they died, he lived. Out of the aftermath of one storm of disaster, the famine, my father was driven into the eye of another storm, the greatest storm of the twentieth century. A literal grave opened, but he defied it and I was made possible. Portsmouth dockyards were a key German target. There, the earliest raids in 1940–41 took most of the lives – 170 in January 1941, when 25,000 incendiary bombs were dropped, the water mains were fractured, and the city became a huge inferno, said to be visible from France. In all the Portsmouth raids up to 1944, 930 died and 2,837 were injured.

It has been estimated that perhaps over 15 per cent of Ireland's eligible population came to Britain to work in war production. Perhaps as many as 80,000 Irish fought for Britain, a good half from the South, mostly Catholics, and plenty of Catholics from the North too. If we scale this figure up in proportion to population, it is quite astonishing. Most of the Southerners enlisting seem, however, to have been perfectly happy with official Irish neutrality, while themselves fighting on. The first RAF bomber pilot to be shot down and killed in 1939 was Willie Murphy, from Cork. The co-pilot of the last RAF bomber to be shot down over Germany, in May 1945, was Sgt W. Mackay, another Irishman. He was killed. It was not until recent times that these people were recognized in Ireland.[6]

W. G. Sebald writes that he is a child of the horrors of a war he did not experience but which nevertheless cast a shadow over him.[7] I feel this too. Born after the end of the German war – on the day Okinawa was effectively taken by the Americans after eighty-two days of fighting and as many as a quarter of a million dead – 'the war' was always somehow at my back. And in the course of my life I have glimpsed the devastation in backward glances, yet so often turned away, too. I turn now to view it again, a man of over seventy years. The 'history' which I purport to write must include those times, for they are my times, too.

The great British silence about the bombing of the German cities demands attention. It is said that forgetting makes a nation as much as remembering, and this particular forgetting made me. Furthermore, with every year we learn more of the atrocities that accompanied the dying of the Empire. We hear of its calamitous legacy over the centuries before. We need to hear – even though so many of us do not listen, do not know how to listen, our inherited whiteness natural to us, like having skin in the first place. Of this other enormity, however, a homely enormity as it were, only some hundreds of miles away, there is barely a distant hum of responding sound.

There is public awareness, of course, but it is limited. For the vast majority of people, knowledge is scant or nonexistent, and with this ignorance goes the sense that there is nothing that should be answered for. In his *A History of Bombing*, Sven Lindqvist reports that, in 1998, he travelled around Britain to see how the 160 museums and collections, great and small, that covered the air war accounted for the results of the offensive for the German populations. As he put it, 'None of them, as it turns out, wanted to acknowledge that the British had actually bombed.'[8] The great national museum of British aggression, the Imperial War Museum, also fails to tell the story. The noise of war in British life has in recent years been deafening – but that of the First World War, and not the bombing war on civilians of 1943–45.

I am part of the generation who experience the paradox that we had no direct experience – no recollection – of that which shaped our reality the most, namely the war. For us, in the twenty years after the conflict, official and popular culture were still overshadowed by those events. The noise of war was the noise of victory and of challenge overcome, of national mettle tested and not found wanting. The noble war. This version of war and the war we children read about in our 'comic books' were pretty much indistinguishable – childhood memory, and thus images of what war was, being shaped by the endless stream of 'comics' we devoured. This version of war was peopled by sturdy, invincible 'Tommy' on our side and 'Gerry' on the other, who was usually more stupid than malevolent, at least in the lower ranks, though the malevolence of the officers was strictly pantomime ('Ve haf vayze of making you talk'). Square-headed German soldiers invariably exclaimed *Donner und Blitzen* as they were surprised from behind by Tommy. Kids' German ran to *Hande Hoch, Schnell!* and *Achtung!* Italians were operatically ludicrous. The Japanese, on the other hand, were deeply malevolent, bug-eyed monsters, the real evil ones, rather than 'Jerry' (the spelling was flexible).

These war-ghosts peopled the imagination of our playground games. In the primary school playground in west London, it was 'Japs and Germans', which in memory seems to have consisted of much pointless running about in two large swarms, which then in equally pointless fashion collided with each other in the corners of a playground surrounded on three sides by the high brick walls of the local bus garage. That the two 'enemies' were incongruously fighting each other did not seem to matter.

After the arrival of black-and-white television for me and many boys of my age, there was the BBC series *The War in the Air* of 1954–55. The child thrilled to the excitement of images of aerial warfare as Luftwaffe fighters disintegrated in mid-air, and beheld with wonder the tiny blobs of light that coalesced on the ground to make a fabulous technological spectacle out of what he did not know at the time was the annihilation of the German cities below – the annihilation of the people, the roads, the houses, the playgrounds and their children, of the cities that had now become graves. This is the 'technological sublime' as it has been called: that which overwhelms the imagination of the human observer, and in so doing lends self-evident moral authority to the bombing. In this Manichean spectacle, on 'our side' of the camera (aerial photography was being perfected then, as well as area bombing), we behold the anonymized evil below in a landscape voided of human presence by the magic of war's new technologies.[9]

I now learn with horror that the spectacle was a product of calculated design and not just of circumstance, so that I and my like, our parents too, were worked on, duped. The bombing campaign was 'marketed', a product co-produced by the press, the Ministry of Information, the military, even the manufacturer who made the bombers. Tom Allbeson writes of war photography: 'Coverage of the bombing campaign', for example, in the mass publication *Picture Post*,

> reduced the campaign to the sorts of spectacular imagery that was the staple of the commercial photo-magazine. There were frequent invocations to readers to take forms of enjoyment in looking at photographs that depicted the bombing war. A host of articles aestheticized the air war, repeating the templates from the interwar period of revelling in unusual and arresting views provided by means of the airborne camera. For instance, 'What the bomb-aimer sees' offered seven aerial photographs depicting 'Patterns of strange delicacy and beauty [that] meet the eye of the bomb-aimer, as he waits the moment to make terrifying changes in the shapes he sees below.' ... Knowledge of what was happening is evident, but understanding is foreclosed through striking imagery of tangential subjects like cloud formations. When images of the impact on German streets were rarely shown, even these were marked by a lack of revelation.[10]

He then goes on to show how this Great Lie worked.

The war was all around the post-war child but, also not there. National Service was mandatory from 1939 to 1960, the last such recruit not departing the army until 1963. I missed the 'Call Up' only by a couple of years. The war was not there in the hushed remarks about those who had had 'a bad war', who, mysteriously, suffered from something called their 'nerves'. And it was strangely both there and not there in the disregarded, crippled beggars-cum-peddlers one still saw in the streets, like the man by The Ha'penny Steps off Harrow Road on my way to school in London's Kensal New Town. The image of the London child playing among the ruins of the bombed city is familiar, a cliché even, though the bombed-out house across our road was forbidden to this child, and yet perennially populated by the more daring and disobedient. Amidst the world of play there was danger and death, intimations of the silences of war amidst the noise.

For me in Ashmore Road, the greatest noise of the good war echoed within the pages of the six volumes of *The War in Pictures*, published by Odhams Press in 1946.[11] This was one of the few books that made its way into households such as mine: it was sold door-to-door by travelling salesmen, alongside encyclopaedias for children, the 'Medical Book' my mother swore by, and inevitably Catholic books. For me, *The War in Pictures* was *the war* – the war in black-and-white images, pored over and stored away in the mind for a lifetime, churning there, the words forgotten. This was the war in a guise in which it is still understood in British political and popular culture: the epic struggle of good against evil, for the nation, for the people – for, at the time, the Empire.

The War in Pictures reduced the destruction to a matter of fronts, campaigns, strategies, logistics, machines and technologies. The books echoed the official narrative of the lived war, the epic story now told in terms of the popular techno-conflict, one in which suffering was absent. Or at least, if it was present, suffering was inflicted elsewhere, not in Britain or against the Tommy. The suffering of the German cities and their civilian populations had no place in this narrative. There were, however, maimed bodies and death to be seen in the books, the soldier bodies of 'the enemy' mostly, and sometimes his putative victims. The images are relatively few of these victims, but the horror of them real enough: some photographs of the

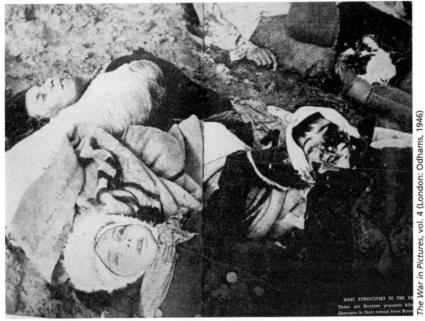

The War in Pictures, vol. 4 (London: Odhams, 1946)

NAZI ATROCITIES IN THE U...
These are Russian peasants kill...
Germans in their retreat from Ros...

Nazi atrocities in the Ukraine.

mounds of naked human corpses from the camps,[12] some of
the shooting pits on the Russian Front and of executed Russian
partisans, and one of a dead Russian peasant family as they
lay on the ground, massacred in the retreat of the Germans
from Rostov-on-Don ('Nazi atrocities in the Ukraine', reads
the caption).[13] These told the child another story, one only
amplified by the many war-silences around him.

The image above, more than any other, has stayed with me.
For the child, then eight or nine, it was the three children in
the foreground of the photograph that disturbed him, intimat-
ing that war was something other than the drama of strategy,
and that it killed children. The face of the dead boy, perhaps
just a bit younger than me when I looked upon him first, has
been half eaten away. Yet the purity and loveliness of that face
remains. How could he be dead, one eye still open, looking
at me? Children were not supposed to be dead. Beside him,
perfectly preserved and seeming to look quietly at the sky, is,
one assumes, his sister, even more beautiful and innocent than

him – almost doll-like in death. What must be their dead father lies behind, on his chest, as if laid carefully to rest, the corpse of a baby, perfectly swaddled in white. Behind the four figures are the outlines of another corpse, the view of the man or woman's right hand being the only sign of their identity.

What was war? The adult knows now that the image may have been made by the photographers of the advancing Soviet army, and so may not be as innocent as the children. Perhaps the bodies have been arranged, a *tableau mort*. If it was taken by the Germans, perhaps it was the aesthetics of death that appealed. The adult can be distrustful of the image; but perhaps it gives us this family as they were. They appear to be frozen. It was a winter advance, February 1943. Perhaps better to leave the truth to the child, insofar as I can be true to him after sixty and more years. Horror, death, innocence, beauty – all came together in a rush for the child who looked upon the faces of the dead, a small, perturbed *voyeur*. It seems to have been the juxtaposition of the seeming calm of death with the awfulness of the half-eaten face of the boy, in which his eye is gouged out, that opened up another door on the war, a door that enabled entry into a past that was at variance with the great story of the six volumes.

Certainly atrocity seemed to happen out there, but not here, out there in the East, the barbarous East, the Russian East, and the East of Japan. Atrocity was not to be found in the bombing of the German cities; *The War in Pictures* depicted the air war on Germany like the TV series did. The bombing was exclusively a matter of attacking only military or industrial targets, the photographs showing attacks on 'supply towns', on factories and on goods trains. The destruction wreaked upon the German cities is evident in some very early photographs of the gaunt remains of the cities, but the ruins are aestheticized, as in the famous photographs of what was left of Cologne Cathedral rising above the ruined city (St Paul's in London, defiant amidst the flames, was similarly aestheticized).

The noise and silences of the war enveloped my childhood. My father never spoke of his ordeal, only of the doctor who saved his hands, the labourer's means of a livelihood. I realize now that that the silent father was probably suffering the mental as well as physical effects of war, a soldier in the army of the silently afflicted. One did not then have any understanding of 'depression'. The army of the silently afflicted extended across the continent, and so did the insult given them: in Germany the medical profession rejected psychological interpretations of suffering for almost twenty years after the war ended.[14] What was needed was 'hardening', and blame was placed on the personality structure and the 'intelligence' of the affected person. Mothers were blamed, the children themselves even, who were often held to be 'abnormal'. Only in 1960 did a federal court allow compensation for psychological damage. Things were no better in Britain.

Paul Connerton tells us of an earlier army of the silently afflicted – of the silence surrounding these mute armies, which was a culpable silence, a deliberate act of state-making:

The International Labour Organisation estimated in 1923 that about 10 million soldiers from the German, Austro-Hungarian, French and English [*sic*] armies walked the streets of their countries. These were some 10 million mutilated men: half or totally blinded, or with gross facial disfigurements, or with a hand or arm or leg missing, hobbling around the streets like ghosts. They were badly cared for ... The war dead were annually remembered at memorial sites ... but 10 million mutilated survivors still haunted the streets of Europe. They were dismembered – not remembered – men; many were subject to chronic depression, frequently succumbed to alcoholism, begged in the street in order to be able to eat, and a considerable number of them ended their days in suicide. All sorts of institutional provisions were put in place to keep those mutilated soldiers out of public sight. Every year, the war dead were ceremonially remembered and the words 'lest we forget' ritually intoned; but these words, uttered in a pitch of ecclesiastical solemnity, referred to those who were now safely dead.[15]

My father's absence has been a foundation of my life, and I share this experience of absence and silence with millions. But only in small part, for I do so at one remove, and I do not share the bitterness of utter loss that many in Britain and elsewhere knew. Absence is a strange foundation for lives: the dreamt father. Before, as a child, and for years after his death, I dreamt about the 'man in the room', sick and absent from the life of the kitchen. I dreamt so much I could sometimes not tell reality from dream. When the father is absent but still in the room, the child is confused, and searches for him, tries to be him when he cannot be found. The son tries too early to find comfort in this kind of personhood, in this room where there is only silence. The personhood of being a man. And so to be somehow out of place, in the wrong room, but also finding a place after his death in his place, in Ireland and its west.

I read *The War in Pictures* in our front room at No. 11, my parents' bedroom, released there into its relative calm from the intensity of life in the kitchen. A large room with a bay window in which sat a dressing table, the amount of floor space a marvel after the kitchen, though the space was shared with the looming presence of large second-hand Victorian and new 'utility' furniture (post-war cheap standard-issue, the latter). I live there still. This was the room my father took possession of in his long illnesses, the one in which he was, it seemed, almost forever away. As a child, when he was well, I sometimes slept with him in the 'big bed', my feet against his warm calves in the cold night, after he came home from his second job, dog tired. In this room he died on a cold day in January 1963, more than half a century ago, 'the war' then still pervading memory but soon to retreat. It was a hard-fought death: blood in the bucket, blood everywhere – an aortic aneurysm. I poured the blood away after, the 'man of the house' now.

Post-war England: still no phones; I ran twice to the phone boxes in the Harrow Road, five minutes away, begging an ambulance to come; twice home, each time the dying man helpless beside my desperate mother and younger brother John; 'poor gorsoon' she called him then, I remember. Then, in my despair, to the hospital to beg them to come. Home again, and him dead. Then up in the ambulance with his body to the same hospital, for the dead must not be left alone, my grief already married to anger.

The Irish way of death bound me further into my parents' world: The flood of people to the house, so often with food. The invariable 'I'm sorry for your trouble'. The money collections made for us, a ritual of the London Irish that sustained us. And after the burial, silence, for grief stopped my mother's mouth, and we suffered her silence alongside our own.

I searched the silence once again for him in the records of the German bombing of Portsmouth. Without a date, time or location of the bombing, it is hard to be sure of what happened. He may have used Sean Joyce, even perhaps Seán Seoighe. He does not answer to these names either. He does not appear in the Air Raid Precautions ('airwarden') records, nor in the hospital, street directory, or newspaper records of the casualties. Perhaps his absence is no surprise, for his life was that of the makeshift existence of the building trades the Irish colonized in Britain. You moved on in that world, kept your contact with officialdom to a minimum.[16]

The most well-known, and the most contentious, of the historians of the air war, Jörg Friedrich, helps tell me something of the story of my father's Portsmouth experience, and connects me more closely with the victims of the air war on both sides. He writes: 'The self in conventional war was active. It showed strength, skill, and courage, but transferred to the group. The *corps* was not a body, and it asserted itself not physically but in cohesion and solidarity.' On the other hand, 'The target of the bombardment was the individual corporeality. The war was not fought, it was absorbed: the senses withstood it with each individual's own constitution.'[17] War got into the senses and did not leave.[18] He writes of how the body absorbs war. The air attack is anticipated internally, fear turns to dread, and dread draws a membrane over the human being. The membrane is that which then constantly picks up the frequencies of danger.

Friedrich tells of how, in such moments, experience is switched off. The bomb is anticipated, and expands into a continuous present. The self loses its sense of the passage of time; it remains spellbound in the 'now', and before and after cease to exist. Real time was compressed; it was always later than it seemed. Was it so for my father in Portsmouth? Twenty-four hours compressed into a few minutes? Did he feel the terrible blast of the bomb do its work on his body? Did he have time also to see the walls around him vaporized by the blast of the high-explosive device? This 'now' is the absence of fear, a kind of resignation, and represents what Friedrich calls 'the most intense exchange between the weapon and its addressee'.

The fear of the bombed was there in the memory of my mother, too. Above all the sound of the V1 flying bombs, so-called 'Doodlebugs'; when the noise of the engine cut out you knew the bomb was near you. For her also fear turned to dread, and she was spellbound in the timeless region of the bombed where war was absorbed by the helpless and resigned body. But, once in the senses, war did not leave, and she would constantly come back to this experience as she talked to us children. But we hardly listened then, so often had we heard the same tale, from her and so many others. When silence was broken, we did not listen, nor did we know how to listen. Now one can listen, when it does not matter anymore. Just as it is possible to plot on the Internet the site of every bomb that fell on London, so can one hear the V1: the still-terrifying sound of the preceding warning sirens, the laboured grumble of the V1 rocket engine, the silence that follows, and then the sound of the explosion.[19]

During the bombing raid itself, as Friedrich puts it, the inner realities of the self are reordered. This results in what he calls a 'psychological immunity shield'. Even the mentally ill conducted themselves with deportment. He also reports how sound predominated, above all the transition from silence to shattering noise. Perhaps in the womb I too heard and felt this fearful transition from silence to noise? Between June 1944 and March 1945, over 3,000 V2 rockets hit London and its suburbs; almost 9,000 people were killed, and 24,000 seriously injured.[20]

Numbness, the lack of sensation, is seen by Friedrich as helping when dealing with memories of the bombing war later on. At the time in Germany, it helped in coping with horror: body parts were assembled and taken for burial, often by family members. 'I saw a man dragging a sack with five or six bulges in it, as if he were carrying heads of cabbage. It was the heads of his family, a whole family, that he had found in the cellar.'[21]

It seems that this numbness did not later give way, but continued into people's experience. It was much reported on in Germany as well as Britain after the war. Beneath its surface, however, lay demons that were later released. As Friedrich writes, 'The knots let go of each other again, the bombers left, but the war has worked its way into the senses and will not leave. Not for the children or the children's children.'[22] 'Numbing does not eliminate the pain, it only blocks the perception of it. But it exists nonetheless. The remembered scenes hand down a torture that will not always remain unspeakable.'[23] That was the hope: that the horror would be not understood, but at least spoken.

What was the purpose of the air war? In 1942 Bomber Command shifted its focus to area bombing.[24] In Germany, as a consequence, and by a conservative estimate, 410,000 German civilians died thereafter, along with 70,000 prisoners of war and foreign, usually forced, workers. The great majority of all these were the working classes, the poor. Around half a million people were seriously injured, another half a million less so. On the night of 27 July 1943, 37,000 people died in Hamburg, and a total of 49,000 were killed through the course of the whole bombing war. In Dresden, 25,000 were killed in a few hours. In Germany's major cities and towns, 50 per cent of the built-up area was destroyed. These figures are supposedly 'well known', but they seem also to need repeating, mere numbers being the only epitaph many had.

On the British side, in contrast to the German civilian casualties of at least 1.5 million, the more precise UK figures are of 61,000 British civilians dead, with around 150,000 injured. Some 43,000 of the dead perished between September 1940 and May 1941, the majority in the London Blitz. An astonishing 55,573 Bomber Command personnel died – an enormous attrition rate.[25] My city of London suffered grievously, particularly the East End around the Royal Docks. My immediate manor in west London got off relatively lightly, although the areas near train tracks and around factories (including my mother's one in Cricklewood) were less fortunate.[26] Nonetheless, Kensington, for example, suffered a total of over 12,000 bombs, mostly incendiary ones. In the borough as a whole, 2,718 people were injured, 412 fatally. There were over 3,000 seriously damaged houses, and over 1,000 had to be demolished.

St Charles Square, the site of my secondary school, was heavily bombed, and our predecessor, St Charles College, a Catholic teacher's training college, was destroyed by incendiaries. Vast tracts of the centre of the Square were subsequently razed by the demolition of what was left, and our brand new schools were raised on the rubble of the levelled ground. I did not know at the time that we were learning and playing on the site of this great destruction. The Carmelite Convent beside us was spared, prayer obviously doing its work.

Outside London, Birmingham and Liverpool suffered most,[27] with 2,241 and 2,716 dead respectively over the course of the

war. Coventry suffered 1,250 deaths. More were killed in Darmstadt in one night than in the whole of the air war in Britain
outside London. By the end of the war, Bomber Command
had, in one twenty-four-hour period, dropped more bombs on
Germany than the tonnage dropped on London during all the
months of the Blitz. One of the tenets of the doctrine of just
war is that retributive violence be proportionate to the injuries
suffered. The disproportion is obvious when the two air wars
are compared.

Richard Overy is among the most eminent British historians
of the air war.[28] By his judgment, the air war did not greatly
retard German war production. It also had only a limited effect
on civilian morale. The argument about the detrimental effect
on the German war effort by the diversion of resources to air
defence holds up better, though many of these resources had
already been sent to the Eastern Front.[29] What mattered was
fighter dominance (US fighters, that is, especially the long-range
Mustangs), so that bomber forces could now concentrate on
the relevant targets – for example, the very successful attacks
on the German oil industry. And so, by the criteria of those who
prosecuted the air war, it was a failure. It may even have been a
wasteful diversion of resources that could have been used elsewhere (at peak production, 1.7 million people were employed
in air-war activity). The bombing of the German cities does not
seem to have brought the war to a quicker conclusion.

Further, as the eminent historian of Second World War
destruction Donald Bloxham observes of the case of Dresden:

Whatever the rhetoric of the generally beneficent effects of an
earlier end to the conflict, the real concern seems to have been
limiting the loss of Allied soldiers rather than of human life in
general, just as was the case with the decision to use the atomic
bomb on Hiroshima. The real ethical question here, therefore, is
not whether we accept the argument of utility, but whether that
is an acceptable argument to put forward in the first place in the

terms in which it has been made. Overall, the principle of the 'lesser evil' was not just breached in Dresden and elsewhere by the Allied bombers, but was entirely ignored as moral restraint gave way to the untrammelled pursuit of a military doctrine. Not only was there no convincing ethical or legal justification for the bombing, such contextual, historical mitigations as exist are nowhere near as far-reaching as we are sometimes told.[30]

Another tenet of just war doctrine is that civilians are not permissible targets of war, unless they are the unavoidable victims of a deliberate attack on a military target. Bloxham notes, 'As the state-sponsored killing of tens of thousands of people who could only be described as combatants if we allow the high priests of "total war" a free hand to determine our terms and obligations, "Dresden" is a black spot on the British conscience, and this irrespective of its relationship to the laws of war.'

The high priests dictate that vast numbers can be killed, so they will be killed. War is war: these things happen in total war, and it is part of the inevitability of the scientific and technological advance that goes with it. But there was nothing inevitable about total war. It was planned, and it was as much an invention of the British as anyone else. For the first time in history, civilians on a hitherto unimaginable scale could now *systematically* be part of the killing of war – that is, they could be targets, for there now existed the technology to destroy civilians en masse and with the utmost efficiency.[31]

Dresden is 'a black spot' indeed, but the point at issue here is much more than Dresden alone – namely the scores and indeed hundreds of other Dresdens about which the British know exceedingly little today, just as they knew very little in the days of the slaughter. The Pforzheims, the Darmstadts, the Nordhausens of the air war; these lesser 'black spots' merge into a vast stain. Dresden and Hamburg, London and Coventry on the other side – they have been the showpieces, the other pieces forgotten or never in mind.

Bomber Command was running out of targets in 1944 and 1945, so German towns without any significant industry or adequate air defences were chosen for destruction. These were often medieval towns, selected for their combustibility. Nordhausen was such a town, and lost 20 per cent of its population in one raid, Pforzheim an incredible 22 per cent, so that Darmstadt's awful 11 per cent population loss pales in comparison. Darmstadt was the rehearsal for Dresden, where the masters of area bombing came close to scientific perfection.[32] It was called the 'reference raid' of Number Five Squadron of Bomber Command, the elite group. The 'Dambusters' – 617 Squadron – were part of Number Five.[33] The rate of annihilation in Darmstadt was twice that of Dresden.[34]

Clearly, historical and ethical issues, as well as legal questions, surround the bombings. But there is also the question of what, if anything, we are to do with all these issues today. Now, so long after the event, why do I dwell on the bombing of German civilians? We now live in a world not only distant in time from these events, but also in a Britain that is peopled by those who seem to have little to do with them. Only seem, however, because it was the Empire that also fought the war, though this is sometimes forgotten. It was the war of the colonized parents and grandparents, and so of their children, too – its memory their responsibility if they are to be their true inheritors.

In whose name is this war spoken of? This is not a matter of guilt – a mostly inappropriate concept. But it is a matter of shame, for just as one may take pride in a shared past, so one should feel shamed when shame is what that past is due. In this way we may refuse to be amnesia's accomplices, and so avoid being strangers to ourselves and 'to a past that is ours but to which we only weakly belong, since it asks more questions of us than we do of it'.[35]

However, one silence enables another's speech. The silence on the bombings solidified both the official and popular accounts of the war as the Good War. The air war here, as I write, is for me a kind of glass in which to see more clearly the effect of the war upon the nation's self-understanding. The older generation of which I speak has recently decided the fate of the British nation in the most decisive of ways, those over the age of sixty voting overwhelmingly to leave the European Union. These are the people for whom, mostly, the war is still a great presence, and who still cleave to the idea of the Good War.

Most UK cities were not bombed after 1941, so that the immediacy of the bombing experience receded. And yet it was real enough, so ingrained in the public mind as to aid the authorities as they cultivated the idea that 'total war', as it came to be called, inevitably meant civilian sacrifice. The 'home front' became, as never before, an integral part of the war effort. The war had come home, into the houses of the people, who would now be defended by the 'Home Guard'. Thus it was possible to kill huge numbers of civilians 'with little public criticism', as Dietmar Süss puts it. The authorities colluded to produce this indifference, taking every opportunity to avoid any appearance of choice in the matter. The continued bombing of Germany (80 per cent of all the tonnage dropped by the Allies fell in the last ten months of the war) was seen by them as critical to maintaining popular support for the war.[36]

Killing on this vast scale also seems to have little agitated the press immediately after the war. I have searched the *Daily Mirror* and *The Times* for 1945–50, and while there is considerable discussion of the parlous state of contemporary Germany, there is no sense of the suffering undergone in the bombing itself, least of all of complicity in that suffering.[37] Nonetheless, what surveys of wartime public opinion there were indicated that there was no broad demand for revenge for the bombing of Britain – nor, curiously, was there much sign of hatred for Germans, particularly in areas that had experienced heavy bombing.[38] 'Total war', however, did not mean revenge; it simply required that it become part of the common sense of war, in the nature of things 'inevitable'.

Grave births; rubble memories. In 1964 the citizens of Darmstadt produced their own account of the raid, *Die Brandnacht: Dokumente von der Zerstörung Darmstadts am 11. September 1944.* What strikes the reader about this is the vast predominance of images of Darmstadt after the bombing in which the rubble has been cleared away. All is disturbingly tidy, as in the photograph of the Luisenplatz that opens this chapter. Time thickens, takes on flesh, precisely there, where the rubble borders the street, for this surely is what I earlier called a time-place – a chronotope, this strange margin where the essential oneness of time and space is apparent.

This is akin to the threshold of the house, which Bakhtin identified as one of the key chronotopes of literature.[39] Past and present unite along these margins, the dead city asserting its second coming; it is at once dust and rubble, yet stands to attention in the same straight lines in which the old towns and cities stood. Order is made out of disorder – rubble and decay on the one side, the astonishing cleanliness and seeming order on the other, a tribute itself to the industry of the survivors and to beginning again. Many photos of London – and the one of Portsmouth, above – have the same stories to tell. A bombed-out St Charles Square, site of what would later be my Catholic Kremlin, is among these images, the destruction standing in mute attention beside the commerce of daily life.

In the bombed cities themselves, the threshold had before the end taken on a terrible immediacy. This was the threshold between the house and the grave, for the house might also become the grave. The cellars of the German houses, like the shelters of the English ones, were refuge and grave alike. Anthropologists use the term 'liminality' – the quality of ambiguity or disorientation that occurs in the ritual process when persons, and through them communities, are poised between the old state and the new, standing at a threshold. These transitional, disordered moments seem to be central to all cultures, and perhaps their deep historical embeddedness explains something of how the timeplaces of the threshold lodged themselves in the memory of the survivors.

In the German and British cities, there was much agony concerning the transition between these two states, safety and death, as it was important to cross the threshold and leave the bunker, the cellar or the shelter at the right time, and this depended on what had happened above. One might face the slow death of asphyxiation in the cellar and shelter, or consumption by the fire outside. In Germany, as the houses were destroyed the bunker became an abode. Once the bunkers were filled, the cellars came next, and the cellar was the experience of the vast majority of those seeking shelter. The threshold between the cellar and the fire outside had another terrible immediacy, too – one concerning the enormities of Nazism, willingly embraced by many of those who sheltered from the bombs. In the bunkers and cellars alike, what Jews were left were excluded, as were prisoners of war and foreign workers, whether or not the latter were forced labourers.

In the Darmstadt photographs, the houses are there but not there. The old road pattern of the city is blazoned forth as never before, yet the road seems to serve what is almost an empty city – one defined by the rubble mounds that are the ghosts of the old houses, themselves emptied graves, or sometimes ones still with the bodies in them, the pulverized human remains eventually carried away with the rubble. The rubble was stored exactly upon the places where once the city existed, reproducing the street patterns of the dead cities. The city too, then, is there but not there, vigorously asserted in its original shape, yet empty, at once mysterious and baleful, the site of murder perpetrated and suffered, yet expectant, seemingly waiting – a past that is waiting to become the future through the work of memory.

So often in these photographs the sun is shining, and destruction seems almost beautiful, the ruined cities losing their horror.

It is then possible to move on, away from the past. This is the technological sublime at work again: the photographs of the German cities convey that a just punishment has been carried out. However, these images became part of the imaginary war for Germans, too. Rubble photography became a genre. Nonetheless, the lovely ruins are still graves, the houses graves, and the past will not go away. Most often in these photographs there are no people.[39] In the account of the Brandnacht (the firestorm night) of 11 September 1944, alongside the 'eye-witness accounts' and the various *Statistik* and *Dokumente*, the destruction of the city is represented to the city in a series of around 150 photographs. All are of the rubble. With the exception of a handful of what seem to be US soldiers and a few survivors, not a single living person is apparent in the vast majority of the pictures. The dead town, perfectly ordered, dominates everywhere.[40]

The past as destruction came to be built into the material fabric of German cities after the war. After these pictures were taken, the rubble itself was deposited in great mounds upon which the new German towns themselves came to be built. People lived upon the past, constantly working down into its foundations to found their new life. Rubble mountains, so-called *Trummerbergen*, are evident in many great German cities. They have even acquired colloquial names. *Trummerfrauen*, rubble women, laboured upon these sites after the war. Wikipedia supplies the height and volume of each of these mountains. The *Birkenhof* in Stuttgart acquired forty metres of elevation after the war. It was reported by survivors that at the summit there were many recognizable facades.

Trümmerliteratur is a genre of immediate post-war German literature, of which Heinrich Boll was an exponent. It is mostly about the returning soldiers, and not the civilians and firestorm victims. In Britain, the bombsite rubble of London served an equally utilitarian, but now also fatal purpose: in hundreds of thousands of tons, it was transported by thousands of trains to make the runways of Bomber Command airfields in East Anglia. Birmingham's rubble was used to make runways for the US Air Force bases in Kent and Essex. In rubble the history of the war is written.

7

The Work of the Dead

We are strangers in the world, we come from the realm of the
dead.

Joseph Roth, 1927

In 1882 the Frenchman, Ernest Renan, posed himself the question: 'What is a nation?' Since that time, his answer has become canonical among students of nationalism:

Forgetting, I would even go so far as to say historical error, is a crucial factor in the creation of a nation, which is why progress in historical studies often constitutes a danger for [the principle of] nationality. Indeed, historical enquiry brings to light deeds of violence which took place at the origin of all political formations, even of those whose consequences have been altogether beneficial. Unity is always effected by means of brutality; the union of northern France with the Midi was the result of massacres and terror lasting for the best part of a century.

Of the French king who eventuated this unity of France, he continued: 'The nation which he had formed has cursed him, and, nowadays, it is only men of culture who know something of his former value and of his achievements.'[1] The deed and the man are alike forgotten.

Renan, a passionate Breton as well as Frenchman, goes on to tells us that a nation is what, in what to us is old-fashioned language, he calls 'a soul':

Two things, which in truth are but one, constitute this soul or spiritual principle. One lies in the past, one in the present. One is the possession in common of a rich legacy of memories; the other is present-day consent, the desire to live together, the will to perpetuate the value of the heritage that one has received in an undivided form.[2]

Of this past, he observes that it is inseparable from suffering, and he continues:

One loves in proportion to the sacrifices to which one has consented, and in proportion to the ills that one has suffered. *One loves the house that one has built and that one has handed down* [my emphasis]. The Spartan song – 'We are what you were; we will be what you are' is, in its simplicity, the abridged hymn of every patrie.' Suffering in common unifies more than joy does. Where national memories are concerned, griefs are of more value than triumphs, for they impose duties, and require a common effort.

Despite the antiquated language, Renan still speaks to us today, showing us if not quite who we are now, then certainly how we got here, for this older ideal has a long history, and is still with us. Just as remembering one thing means forgetting another, so unity is always effected by means of brutality: the founding violence of nations that is the baptismal forgetting, that of the mass destruction of humans. In part, therefore, forgetting is inevitable. Social as well as personal life depend on some measure of forgetting. We should go mad if we could not forget.

Furthermore, there is a sometimes necessary shared forgetting, required if the claims of retribution are not to run on endlessly.[3] But it is also the case that 'forgetting' is often a matter of never even knowing these forgotten things, especially their horror, because the forgetting has been done for us by others, for their own ends but in our name, so that we are nonetheless complicit in it. We also sometimes say that things happened 'a long time ago', so that they become consigned to what we call 'history'. Thus, paradoxically, history-writing can be a means of forgetting, too.

But what is important to remember? If there is a *habitus* of the nation – a set of inherited and embodied assumptions by which we mostly unknowingly live our lives – then suffering, and collective suffering at that, is what makes us. The suffering of women and men who now are old, of a generation and less before me, still has a powerful hold on the imaginary life of the British. We see this at the annual commemorations of war, and in the perennial cycle of anniversaries for battles, treaties and historical calamities. These elders are ancient and watery-eyed, seemingly from a world before our own. In one sense they are a lost world, standing there, or sitting in wheelchairs, in their blazers and regimental ties, their berets carefully placed, their medals on show.

Britain was built on such lost worlds, for these men have for long been conscripted for a second time – conscripted in the cause of the state, though they are themselves mostly willing conscripts in the amnesiac story of the nation that is told through them. They attest to the durability of the myths of a world that can be regained through Brexit. Not only them, but the next generation, my own – the generations profoundly shaped by war, and in consequence shaping Britain in the image of war. And onwards, all the way to the wars in Iraq and Afghanistan.

It has been said that to be human is to dwell, and moreover to dwell with the dead, as they do with us. To be part of a nation is to dwell, too, in the house of the nation as a home, and with the nation's dead. As Renan says, it is suffering and grief that unite us most in love for the past generations, for the ancestors, and for home. Can it be, as Renan suggests, that the nation is rather more literally than we suppose a house, one in which we may or may not find or make a home?

The dead, the grave, secured the ruined cities for the future. How could the *Trummerbergen* and the lesser rubble of British cities be walked over, ridden over, in peace after the end of the war? For this the dead must be dead, allowed to die so that the living might live. For the dead to be properly dead, there must be evidence of death – a body, a grave in which a body lies, a name, so that there may be a place where what was once a presence finds a mark, and where 'evidence' can be located. Even if remains may not be found or are without a name, a place is sought, a place where even ashes can have a memory and some sort of 'house', even though they are already dispersed in the elements. These are the ashes made in the ovens of the camps, but also in the firestorm's consuming consequences. We see this pitiable desire to put the dead in place in the awful evidence of unrecognizable remains dragged to burial sites by the survivors of mass bombing in Germany.

This being at home is necessary so that the past is allowed to be the past, in order that the living may live and the world be remade, and that the living may not be haunted. Thus, only the properly dead secure the future. But what is it to be properly dead, so that the cities and nations may commence their second coming after war, and order replace disorder? How can the threshold between past and future be passed, enabling release from uncertainty and disorientation? The answers are to be found in the memory work of the nation-state: the politics of memory.

The types of forgetting and remembering here are what Connerton calls 'humiliated silence' and what I call 'triumphant sound', apparent in German and British post-war responses to the war. There was the humiliated silence that flowed from the futility of the suffering undergone by the defeated in post-war Germany, when all the sacrifices had been in vain. However, if humiliation bred silence, it also fostered a remembering of its own kind, as we shall see. All was not quiet. On the British side, there was the triumphant noise of the victor, of the justified.

The remembering of the conqueror was, in fact, a very British kind of noise; the British have always been the conquerors, not the conquered. The post-war period in Britain was a time when the country thought of itself as an unvanquished power.

Thomas Laqueur has written of the epochal shift after about 1800 from the local churchyard to the cemetery – an institution that now served not God and the locality, but the nation, 'society' as it came to be called, and the individual. With this went the rise of the naming of the dead, and also an interest in the individual death – the actual moment of dying and the narrative of the human being's progress to and from this moment.[4] To have a name was now to be part of a political order; not to have one, like the slave population of the United States, was to be outside this order. The dead had to be in place; they had to be safely dead, and the name helped enable this closure.[5] Laqueur estimates, however, that between 90 and 95 per cent of the entire war dead throughout history are unnamed.[6]

The difference between the First and Second World Wars was that the enormous slaughter of the Second World War was so often beyond naming. Unlike the First World War, it was disproportionately a war upon civilians, whose naming was a task that lay outside the bureaucracy of either the army or the state. The difference between the two wars represented a transition from naming to merely numbering, though even numbering the dead in the Second World War remains a source of deep contention. Naming the dead helps to enable them to be safely dead in a double sense: to be safe for the grieving, so that they may know peace; but also in the sense that the institutions of this naming, primarily the state, come to own the names. It is the unnamed who are not safely dead, and who, in the years after 1945, came to haunt Europe.

In the first war, the drive to commemoration through the name was overwhelming, when the naming of the British dead acquired cult significance. The British unnamed military dead amounted to 200,000, and the named dead to 340,000. The former could not be left out, for, as Renan says, the nation's 'griefs are of more value than triumphs'. The Tomb of the Unknown Warrior in Westminster Abbey was dedicated on the same day as the Cenotaph in Whitehall, in November 1920.[7] Here the public led the way in calling for the memorial, but then the state quickly appropriated the mass emotions that were released.

In the Second World War, who might have named, or even numbered, the dead Russian civilians? Was the dead peasant family I puzzled over as a child in *The War in Pictures* ever identified or counted? Over a third of the military dead of the Soviet Union are still unnamed: 4 million souls. The Nazi killing machine was famously efficient in the naming of its victims, though there is still great ignorance about the vast numbers of German military dead who perished on the Eastern Front. Friedrich tells us also of the nameless dead in the bombing of Germany – in the cellars of the Café Hauptpost in Darmstadt, for instance, where coke had been smouldering previously because of the intense heat, so that people were boiled alive in water or charred beyond recognition.[8]

Hitler forbade mass graves, and the unnamed were burnt in enormous funeral pyres (techniques and technicians fashioned in the disposal of human remains at Treblinka were on hand in Dresden).[9] The photographs of these funeral pyres in Dresden are horrific in a particular way: these are the bodies, the still clearly discernible and clothed limbs and faces, of recently living men, women and children, now only beginning their coalescence in the putrefaction of death. We are so used to seeing what the dead of the camps looked like after liberation, to seeing mass death in this way, that the similarity to these German dead is disturbing and provokes thought. At the same time, Susan Sontag reminds us that pictures of the camp living, naked and semi-clothed as they were, at the point of but not yet beyond starvation, are in fact unrepresentative, because this was not the everyday life of the camps.[10]

Remembering the bombed cities, W. G. Sebald, in his *On the Natural History of Destruction*, writes of what he calls the 'profound disturbance to the inner life of the nation' in Germany, and of the repression of memory. He talks of 'the well-kept secret of the corpses built into the foundation of our state, a secret that bound all Germans together in the post-war years, and indeed still binds them more closely than any positive goal'[11] – the corpses of Germany's bombed cities, the dead cities as they have been called.[12] As will be seen, this was a silence about guilt, the Germans after the war presenting themselves as victims. But in other ways, as historians have now revealed, there was anything but silence about what had happened to them. Sebald and Friedrich write as if they were breaching the veil of silence for the first time. They were not.

And the British state? Are there not corpses built into its foundations, too – a state reborn through war, erected upon the corpses of the German cities? This was a war where the British dead were all in the right places, safely dead, the German ones forgotten. David Edgerton opens his book *The British War Machine* with the words: 'Britain won the Second World War. Yet that victory is hardly commemorated.' By contrast, the early war years, a period of defeat, have become the subject of 'an almost obsessive fascination'. Dunkirk, the Battle of Britain, the Blitz, Britain 'alone', Vera Lynn singing 'We'll Meet Again' – all of these are at 'the centre of national narratives of war in which a new inwardly focused nation was born'.[13] Of course, the Normandy landings, El Alamein, Burma and the other campaigns are remembered, but not with anything like the obsessive and enduring intensity as the early war years.

It is into this nation that I was born, and in it that I was raised, the 'British nation', as Edgerton calls it in his fine new history of twentieth-century Britain.[14] The simplicity of just being of 'Irish descent' when young was matched by the simplicity of also being part of one Britain, easefully elided with England: the Britain of the war, of the welfare state, of social democracy in the ascendant – the last two as mythic as the first. And part simply of the legerdemain of history, of growing up thinking how things were, and how they were said to be, was how they had always been.

As a consequence of the invention of World War Two, described by Edgerton, 'Britain's technical genius, exceptional mobilization and emergent welfare state could be celebrated" ('The People's War' in short). Empire and Commonwealth were mostly written out of the history of the war, also the support of numerous allies, including the United States. And it is only in the last decade that the British Empire dead have been remembered. About 2.5 million Indian soldiers fought in the war, and many from the rest of the Empire, though casualty rates were nowhere near as high as in Europe. But the Bengal famine of 1943 was greatly aggravated by wartime conditions. And then there are all the other imperial dead, barely remembered – for instance the awful civilian slaughter in French Indo-China, in the Dutch East Indies, and of course in China.

It was in 1945 and not 1940 that the idea of Britain 'alone' became central to the emerging political alliance of the national and the popular, on both the right and the left. Contrary to the notion of Britain alone, Britain at war was, as Edgerton writes, 'a first-class power, confident, with good reason, in its capacity to wage a devastating war of machines. This was still a great power, which thought of war not in martial but in material terms, as befitted an industrial giant, one which remained at the heart of the world's trade.'

In 1940, 'Chamberlain left office and left Britain with the world's largest navy, the greatest aircraft production of any country, and a small but uniquely mechanised army'. Hence, Britain could avoid putting the majority of its servicemen and women in harm's way.[15] And so, for all the suffering, Britain got off lightly in comparison with much of the rest of the world. It fought a war of technology and machines, not a war of mass slaughter as in the killing fields further east. In this sense, my reading as a child was accurate; in *The War in Pictures*, war was techno-war. The richest nations in the world, the United States and Britain, got the best of it, and some of the poorest – the USSR and China – bore a terrible cost. 'The British war was fought with radio waves, aeroplanes, tanks and ships, and a vast destruction by fire and steel of Britain's enemies. It was not a people's war, in short, but a technocratic, technological war.' The real peoples' wars were fought in Europe and Asia.

What of 'the people' themselves? In the myth of 'the Blitz', the class differences that marked the experience of the bombing war are often forgotten: the working class had no cars, no phones, usually no friends outside the cities. They had little ability to replace lost belongings, or to navigate the complex system of post-raid administration. The class tensions that surrounded children and parents when they were evacuated out of the British cities are better known than these ones. Until the bombing of the West End of London, the East London poor were near mutiny. All this is much better known now than it once was, but known only fairly recently, and it is the seventy years of forgetting that needs remembering.

On the German side, historians born long after the war have shown that in post-war Germany people did not simply forget the war and just get on with making the future – although this was the view of many at the time, Hannah Arendt among them. There is now a new social history of the civilian bombing, which is more attuned to the actual experience of everyday life in Germany.[16] In recent German historiography there is also an understanding that things were more complicated than this brute forgetting, and that suffering and loss themselves do not stand still but are constantly shaped by history, especially by political change.[17] For instance, like Germany itself, public memory was divided between the Communist East and the 'free' West.

In West Germany, there were fairly clearly defined phases that the shaping of public memory of the bombing went through, and to some extent these were similar to the equivalent process in Britain. In the first twenty years after the war's end, the role of Christianity was very marked, the primary aim of all the churches being to put the two nations together again, East and West. The simple fact of the indiscriminate nature of the civilian destruction, in which all suffered irrespective of creed and politics, if not always of class, meant a certain degree of reintegration already existed below the surface. This was perhaps given foundation most of all through a shared sense of local identity. For the civilian dead of the bombed cities, there was a concrete space and visible location for remembering, even if it was a ruin, a place where people could gather and remember, in Berlin, Darmstadt or Pforzheim, as in the East End of London.

Civilian death lent itself to Christianization in a special way. Unlike military death, it was not 'normal'. On the one hand, in military death there is a clearly delineated bureaucratic framework in which death occurs. Soldier death can be presented as a 'natural' disaster, unlike mass civilian death. The space of the unnatural was rapidly filled by the supernatural. On the other side of the North Sea, the invocation of godly terror and apocalypse served to obscure the question of German guilt and complicity. This invocation of pure 'evil' was a kind of ecclesiastical parallel to the total war argument: if the war was a product of evil as a daemonic force on all sides, then all sides could be held to be equally responsible, just as all things could happen in total war.[18] The Christian vocabulary of death, resurrection and salvation was shared between Britain and Germany, as is evident, for example, in the Christian movement to reconcile Dresden with Coventry – a reconciliation in which the appalling extent of the bombing of Germany, and the vast imbalance of deaths, could more easily be lost to view.

On the German side, from the 1960s a more secular phase of public remembering was evident. Museums and local history initiatives developed in tandem with the idea of *Heimat*.[19] The

Darmstadt history book of 1964, mentioned in the previous chapter, is one example of this. However, the collective experience of a homogeneous community victimized by forces beyond its control remained dominant, and it was not until the 1980s and '90s that the oscillation between victim and perpetrator fully emerged, then coming to haunt German minds. From the 1980s, professional historians began to integrate the air war with local experiences of the war as a whole, and therefore with the Nazi regime. They resisted the urge to universalize the war.

A third phase emerged from the 1990s, in which Friedrich and Sebald played a key role. Friedrich's *Die Brand* sold over half a million copies in Germany, and created a sensation. The bombing now occupied centre stage in the work of the dead. The official politics of bombing remembrance were seen by many, correctly, as inadequate – as speaking thoughtlessly about things people had no experience of. After this, the notion of the air war on civilians as a 'crime' was spoken openly.[20] In a strange way, there was also something akin to the reworking of the old Christian strand of memory work, with the emphasis now on lamentation and 'pure' mourning, so that guilt sometimes retreated once again. Nonetheless, the courage of Friedrich and the great qualities of his book are remarkable.

The human face of German suffering is revealed in a remarkable book of photographs of war children, *Kriegskinder*, by Frederike Helwig, published in Germany in 2017.[21] There is a photograph of a man in his eighties called Werner Weber. His look is contained but direct, somewhat distant but not at all hostile. He sits at a table, on which his hands rest, between them what looks like a fine china teacup and saucer – a sign of a more gracious time. I am in my seventies, and so naturally feel a kinship with his generation, for they hold the lived memory of the raids. The same is so on the British side, although one hears little mention of this in Britain, nor of the mental suffering here caused by the sights such as Herr Weber saw there.

In Germany, there is more public discussion and concern for this 'forgotten generation'. The *Kriegskinder* often claim that they have led a normal life despite what they saw in the war. Normal is as normal does, and one gets on with life as best one can – so who can gainsay their opinion on this? The word 'trauma' is too easily thrown around, especially about whole generations, even nations. But that child suffered horrendously then and there, in that time and place, and that suffering is enough, that infliction upon the innocent. This is what Werner Weber saw as a child:

> One day a hanged man is lying in front of our house in Berlin. A German. He had tried to hide from the war in a ruined building and they hung him from the crossbar of the lamp post. When he was dead they cut him loose. He lies there for days with his mouth open and we children throw pebble stones into it. Eventually they take him away and bury him on the side of the road. Because no dead bodies can lie in the city streets trucks arrive, dig him and others up and throw them onto the trucks. We children watch. Then we have to go and have lunch. It's maize porridge for lunch, but I can only think of the corpses with their tattered clothes and bones sticking out and I feel sick.[22]

With Herr Weber and his like, the sense of different and yet parallel lives is awoken strongly in me, the kinship of generation, but underneath this also the kinship of a burden carried from the war. In March 2017 I talked with Jörg Arnold, one of the brilliant new generation of German historians of the bombing. He was born in 1973. I am of an age to be his father, who was born a year after me, in 1946. Jörg's father was raised on a farm in the tiny peasant village of Ringau in the Netra valley, which is on an important road connection between Leipzig and Frankfurt. Its former prosperity declined after the war, as it was too close to the East German border for its own good. The local town is Enschwege.

Jörg himself was raised by his parents and grandparents, and this gave him a strong sense of generational differences. He tells me that his work on the bombing war was at many levels an engagement with the life of his grandmother. I am struck by his comment as to how, until relatively recently, the future in Germany was a sort of shadow on the present. This arises from the sense that the past is a burden. Germans of particular generations, his parents and grandparents, only have an 'after-life', by which I take him to mean that the war was such an enormous reality that what came after was but an appendage to real experience. Yet, for his own generation, Jörg says it still feels the future as some kind of shadow, but that it will be the last generation to feel so.

This shadow, like so many, was cast by silence. The war was never, or hardly ever, talked about by Jörg's grandparents and parents. Guilt and complicity were hidden, and Jörg talks about his father's and other local people's capacity to square awareness of their neighbours' and their own kin's support for Nazism with their personal knowledge of these people as in some sense 'decent'. This silence was of course also a consequence of living in a culture – and the same was so in Britain – in which talking through one's life was not an option. Even if people had wanted to, they did not know how. His village and town were not bombed, but nearby Kassel was, and his terrified relatives escaped to the farm for refuge. The losses and suffering were direct as well as indirect. Tiny Ringau's local war memorial has forty or so people listed as killed in the Second World War. Jörg's grandmother lost a well-loved brother, who left for the Russian front and was never heard of again. This woman took a substitute brother in the unlikeliest of forms, for she cared both for the person and the memory of a British pilot whose aircraft had been shot down nearby.

Yet she was an avid National Socialist – not so much antisemitic, I am told, as a 'peasant Nazi'. This was a strong strain in Nazism, one based on the idealization of a peasant world that was in reality at the time undergoing great change. His grandmother felt that the Party would bring back the pride she once felt. So did many of the young men marked in the Ringau memorial, most of whom, after 1942, were lost 'in the east'. There are countless such stories to tell of the end of peasant Europe in the twentieth century.

There are stories to tell even of Jewish peasants, for there were such despite the popular cultural notion of the wandering Jew and the rooted peasant. In Enschwege, as all over Europe, the Jewish population had been rooted for generations in Germany. The Jewish population of the town reached a peak of 549 in 1885, in what was then a very prosperous town. A substantial synagogue was built in 1838, and reduced to a ruin on Kristallnacht in November 1938. The Jewish population was luckier here than most other Jewish ones in Germany and further east: 421 emigrated in 1933, many of them for the United States. In 1941 and 1942, the last hundred or so Jewish residents were deported to the death camps. Entschwege has three names of historical note, making up an astonishing historical conjunction: Rolf Hochuth, the controversial playwright, and friend of David Irving; Alizia Olmert, writer and wife of the former Israeli prime minister Ehud Olmert; and Edouard Weiter, the last regular camp commandant of Dachau.

After the war, many Germans came to Ireland in search of a peasant Shangri-la, balm for the wounds of a shattered Germany, and for some it became a substitute for a peasant world they had lost, or felt they had lost. In Ireland, especially in the west of Ireland, that oft-imagined Newfoundland of healing and renewal, they seem to have found what they were looking for. Most notable among them was Heinrich Böll, whose *Irish Journal* was first published in Germany in 1957. Reading it again, how absurd it is – Germanic Oirishry. As an adolescent going back to the West in the 1960s, German-bought houses, down by the lake below us, were dotted here and there, models of tidiness. Not all were holiday homes – some stayed. They were good neighbours but kept to themselves. One neighboured Paddy Kenny's house, returning for funerals now and then.

Unsurprisingly, the post-war work of the dead in Britain was a different kind of labour. Britain had won, and in contrast to humiliation there was justification. These feelings of justification are merited, of course, and it was a good war if not the Good War, given the nature of the conflict and whom it was with. But this is separate from the public culture of the war in general and the bombing war in particular, for these tell a story of a different kind of justification. In contrast to the German side, the militarization of memory was central. The realities of the air war on Germany itself, if not expunged, have been tidied away in the boxes labelled 'Military necessity', 'Us or them', 'They deserved it'; 'We gave them back what they gave us'; 'It helped win the war'; 'Total war' – and so on. When the bombing war on Germany is mentioned, it is most often a matter of the familiar, dehumanizing technology story, plus the heroism of the pilots and crews.

In British bookshops, the 'military history' section is often among the largest. British football supporters continued to sing 'Two World Wars and one World Cup' at the 2010 World Cup, just as they had at the 2006 tournament in Germany itself. This alternated with 'Ten German Bombers', sung also by Northern Irish football fans and those of the sectarian Glasgow Rangers. All this might not matter if football was not so much part of the 'national psyche'. Paul Gilroy has identified the connection between sport and nationalism as a symptom of what he calls 'postcolonial melancholia' – a form of mourning for a lost empire.[23] Be this as it may, the armed forces play up unceasingly to all this, for Britain since the war has become an extremely martial country, deluded by the image of plucky victory long ago, and by its continuing pretensions to Great Power status.

Britain has been at war or engaged military conflict in one place or another continuously in every year since 1914. This includes Operation Banner in Northern Ireland between 1969 and 2007, the longest twentieth-century deployment of the British army outside the world wars, and the one involving greater loss of service life than any other since 1945. There has only been one year (1968) since the Second World War when a British service person has not been killed on active service.

The late Michael Moran claims in his recent book that in perhaps no European country bar Russia is militarism so powerfully ingrained as in Britain.[24] When still part of the European Union, Britain was the only member to recruit below the age of eighteen. Almost a quarter of all recruits in 2015–16 were children: boy soldiers. It is also the only European country that allows the military to enter schools for the purpose of recruiting schoolchildren. In 2012 the government initiated a range of schemes designed to promote a 'military ethos' in schools. Military spending and military production are uniquely high for a state the size of the United Kingdom, and the economy heavily dependent on this spending.

The webpages of the RAF Benevolent Fund, charged with curating the memory of Bomber Command, replays the command mottos, 'Strike hard, strike sure' and 'The bomb will always get through'. The site also choruses the 'Dam Busters' theme. My generation was raised on this saga ad nauseum, told among many other places in the film of 1955. The custodians of Bomber Command history tell us of the civilian bombing: 'The truth is, it was a time of total war, and ideas about the boundaries of conflict were very different then than we have today. Only those who have lived through similar times could understand or pass judgment.'[25] The old lie of historical necessity again, negated by the fact that people of the time could and did think very differently.

Those who did live through those times were perfectly able to see what the 'necessity of history' could do to you if you did not watch out. There were those who stood up, the well-known and the more obscure, though the government of the day effectively managed what disquiet there was, and many who stood up sat down again.[26] In Britain at the end of the war, the arrival of the photographs of Armageddon, now seen at ground level and not simply from above, only intensified the idea of just retribution. Christianity became wedded to the revelation of the sheer power of devastation that the photos showed. Bomber Command, as an expression of the unity of military and civilian endeavour, was integrated into the idea of the People's War, though it remained secondary to the exaltation of the Battle of Britain and the timeless sacrifice of the ordinary fighter pilot. September 1945 saw the first celebration of Battle of Britain Day, the Christian symbolism of sacrifice and resurrection lending itself to this more readily than to Bomber Command.

'The Few', unlike in the early days of war, were in the post-war period given a social-democratic gloss. Those who made the aircraft were included in public ceremonies, and people like my mother became briefly state heroines. The Royal Air Force Chapel in Westminster Abbey joined the Tomb of the Unknown Soldier in the public iconography of remembering. At the ceremony to open the chapel in 1947 there was no specific mention of Germany, but only of 'evil' and 'the beast' the nation had been facing. In the 1960s, the Battle of Britain was still seen in terms of the economic struggles of the present being an extension of the People's War.

In 1961 the four-volume *History of the Strategic Air Offensive against Germany* was published, and created a considerable public stir. Firstly, its judgment on the management of the air war was damning.[27] Did this mean that the 55,000 British aircrew killed had died in vain? The question does not seem to have detained public opinion for long, and, as the historian of both bombings, British and German, Dietmar Süss writes: 'In spite of criticism, however, there was hardly anyone who doubted that the bombing of Germany had been necessary and at least an indirect success.' There was no lasting shock, and 'in the end, the consensus of society about the reason for and purpose of the war was too strong'. After Webster and Frankland's four volumes, 'the government of the day could draw a dividing line, consigning area bombing to "history".'[28] Amnesia's prize, atrocity's dustbin.

Two decades after I had seen *War in the Air* on television and beheld the images in *The War in Pictures*, in 1973–74, British television screened an epic series on the then three-decades-distant war. At the time, *The World at War* was lavishly praised, widely watched, and deeply influential. One of the twenty-nine almost hour-long episodes, called 'Whirlwind', concerned the bombing war. Nothing much had changed in the decades since the earlier representations of the bombing. The episode was a familiar account of strategies, campaigns, logistics, missions and responses on the other side, with a few personal accounts thrown in. About twenty seconds were given over to the experiences of those being annihilated under the bombs. Grim as those images and voices were, it was all over in a flash.

The bombing was also covered in a later episode, called 'Nemesis', on the end of the Third Reich. The programme led off, for only three minutes of its fifty-five, with the bombing of Germany, predictably with the Dresden raids. Horrific, but again brief, the commentary sardonically mentioned that in 'the technical language of the experts this was a case of severe over-bombing'. This glancing irony was as morally deep as the account of the air war went, and the minutes were at once consumed in the account of nemesis – nemesis itself a fitting 'monument to total war', as it was put. The technological sublime of air war was dominant in both programmes. Contemporary comments by air crew included: 'Gerry had it this time, it certainly was a wizard prang', and 'Let's get The Kraut in his bed if not in his factory', and if 'Granny Schicklgruber next door' cops it, then so what?

Churchill's role in the politics of memory was contemptible. As Süss writes, 'When the historians writing the official history of Bomber Command put questions to him about Dresden he gave the curt reply that he could not remember. He thought the Americans had done it.'[29] Famously, his end-of war speech made no reference to Bomber Command. The dirty secret that all the slaughter need not have happened had to be kept. Belated public recognition of Bomber Command came in 2012 in the form of the Bomber Command Memorial in Green Park, dedicated by the Queen. Aluminium from a crashed Halifax bomber was used in the construction of the memorial. Perhaps it was one of the Halifaxes my mother helped build.[30] 'Amnesiac classical', as one critic of the Memorial put it at the time, 'an inadvertent echo of the fixed thinking that directed the flattening of German cities'.[31]

Six years later, 2018, marked the centenary of the RAF. The BBC broadcast hours of programmes on the centenary, including much coverage of Bomber Command and the bombing war.[32] The broadcasts were breathless in their adoration of the men, but even more of the machines of war, especially the 'iconic' Lancaster.[33] In the same year, the BBC released Berlin Blitz for VR headsets. In this, to old commentary from a raid on Berlin in 1943, viewers seventy-five years later can enjoy an 'immersive' experience that takes them right back to what in the original commentary is called 'the biggest fireworks show in the world'.[34] The moral repulsiveness of all this is as usual unremarked in British public life – an absence in line with most public opinion in Britain.

The quiet dignity with which Darmstadt remembers its night of fire each year contrasts with this British Bomberfest. At five minutes to midnight, when the raids began, the bells of the city ring out, and the mass graves of the Waldfriedhof are visited. The tiny atom of the Altstadt that remains – the ruins of an old chapel – have been preserved to honour the victims of both National Socialism and the Brandnacht. Three large placards showing images of the destruction, with explanatory texts, are kept permanently in highly frequented public places. In September 2018 there was a special event on the Brandnacht for school children, held at the Central Station.[35]

Not all British memorialization of the Second World War is as big and bombastic as the Green Park Memorial, of course. In keeping with other aspects of the national self-image, it can be low-key and reserved. This is evident in the vast number of war memorials in almost all British communities of any size. On these, names proliferate that are intensely local, native to that place, telling a story of an older and more rooted England than that of the present. Commemorations of the 1918 Armistice are genuinely community affairs, yet the military note is strong even here. The armed services veterans' organization, the Royal British Legion, is the dominating influence. Ceremonies remember what are called 'the fallen' – not the shattered bodies of the real dead, least of all people like the 10 million forgotten, mutilated survivors who, as we have seen, 'haunted the streets of Europe' in the 1920s, the dismembered rather than the remembered. If the settlement is big enough, the local army cadets will often lead the procession. The 'Last Post' is heard. There is a march. The local clergy lead events. A very British kind of militarism is on display – moderate, in concord with the pendulum of the National Middle Way – and the nation deludes itself that this is not militarism at all.

At a national level, the British Legion organizes the annual Festival of Remembrance in the Royal Albert Hall, complete with military bands and standards, and what is called a 'drum-head service', a religious service held as if it were happening in a field of combat. The grotesque appropriation of real suffering again goes unremarked. The monarchy is in attendance, as are the leading politicians of the day. They reassemble at the Cenotaph Memorial Service on 'Remembrance Sunday'. This 'invented tradition' has become deeply rooted, and has so well done its work that veneration of the national dead becomes our second nature.

As the late Michael Moran remarks, 'The cult of military remembrance is powerful because it arises from features long engrained in the British state and in British society. It defines the British in terms of military providence – the notion that the country is endowed by historical fate to pursue military adventure.'[36] Moran writes further: 'The annual national ritual of Remembrance Sunday has become both more significant and more invested with transcendental meaning in recent years. Following victory in the Falklands it was revived by the state, and was transformed much more explicitly into a civic ritual blended with religious overtones'. Military remembrance, of which Remembrance Sunday is the central part, is 'the most successful civic ritual created by the British state in the last century'.[37] The British become more militaristic, not less, as time goes by. The 'remembrance' of anniversaries is relentless, arbitrary and superficial. Anniversaries make us forget more than remember.

The civilian bombed of Britain, never mind Germany, barely rate a mention in all that goes on. There are few memorials to the dead and injured of the air war in British cities. London does not have a single collective, national public memorial to the civilians who suffered in the London Blitz. What it does have is the Civilian War Dead Roll of Honour, tucked away in Westminster Abbey. The concentration of memorials in the abbey means that memory is sanctified in the image of the state, the abbey itself being essentially the state Valhalla. It also means that national memory is located in a London that many people visit only very infrequently, if ever. As it now costs £20 to enter the abbey, the state seems to be blindly pricing itself out of existence.

A small collection of wall plaques testify to the civilian dead in the city at large, though even here the 'home' defence forces are honoured rather than the civilians. The only memorial that even pretends to a strong public statement about the London civilian population at war is that to the civilians of the East End in Wapping – and that had to wait more than sixty years to appear. There is also a small memorial to peace in Bethnal Green, recently defaced. Individual disasters rate a little better.[38] Most memorials that do exist are the result of private effort. This includes the Animals in War Memorial in Park Lane (2004), funded by the super-wealthy. It is considerably more impressive than any memorial to civilian humans. British sentimentality about animals being what it is, the disparity is not surprising.

Meanwhile, the various branches of the Imperial War Museum get about 2.5 million visitors a year. Of these, about 1,000,000 visit the money-spinners – all charging for entry – of RAF Duxford; the underground War Rooms in London (£19 a throw), which is a shrine of the Churchill cult; and HMS Belfast, on the Thames by Tower Bridge. What do people want at such places? They seem to get what they want. At places like Duxford one has 'fun': necro-euphoria. War becomes pleasure there and in the other parts of the leisure industry; the dead have to perform all sorts of tricks and contortions for the living in order to please them.

The permanent exhibitions at Duxford have the character one might expect from their titles: 'The Battle of Britain', 'Air and Sea', 'The 1940 Operations Room', 'Historic Duxford'.[39] The last of those includes the following on its webpage:

> Get to know Duxford's people; fighter 'ace' Douglas Bader, First World War clerk Muriel Derby and the coalminer's son who became one of Duxford's most celebrated fighter pilots ... Explore the sights, sounds and smells of Duxford ... Immerse all your senses with our creative hands-on experiences. Try on a replica uniform, fill a pilot's brain with flying knowledge, and get up close to the personal items of the people who lived and worked at Duxford ... the Bader aviator scarf. This 100% silk scarf is inspired by the polka dot scarf often worn by the famous Battle of Britain pilot, Sir Douglas Bader ... Shop now.

Or: 'Take the helm of HMS Belfast', and 'journey through this floating city' (a city made in another city, Belfast, by die-hard

Alamy

Kenneth More as Douglas Bader, *Reach for the Skies*, dir. Lewis Gilbert, 1956.

Loyalist labour, and launched by Neville Chamberlain on my saint's day in 1938).

I was brought up on figures like Douglas Bader. The film of the wartime experience of the legless pilot was released in 1956, and I saw it soon after, aged twelve. The image of Kenneth More seemed everywhere at the time – More, the epitome of the hero in British war films, which then relentlessly followed one another as a staple of cinema entertainment. The film was also highly popular in Europe in its day, More playing the role of the essential Briton both at home and in a devastated Europe. This gave way in the 1960s as the whole thing began to seem absurd – Britain a land, as we joked, of cravated fools and blazered buffoons, pipes clamped between their teeth, like More. Nonetheless, the foundations of the idea of war that More represented had been firmly laid by then, and our sense of the unreality of British pretensions proved too weak to counter the grip of a reality all the firmer because of its absurdity.

This is all now part of the 'heritage industry', the politics of which is to have no politics at all. The aim is to present an anodyne past free of pain and conflict. This is because the purpose of heritage – a political purpose, of course – is to bring people together. At Duxford and places like it, one has an 'experience'. Indeed, one is 'immersed' in experiences, as if baptized in the holy water of war. One feels good with the dead, and *through* the dead, so that they become only a means to an end. One gives up one's life, one's experience, to the museum's projects, in an obscene and uncanny echo of the original lives given up. I was there, I empathize, I 'see through the eyes' of the British people and the people of the Empire, as the IWM online has it. The parallels with reality TV are everywhere apparent: this is reality war, in which the world is presented to us through what are held to be our own eyes, so that we can come to have it as our own, part of the 'ordinary' life of 'ordinary' people just like us. The Second World War galleries at the IWM are in preparation as I write, opening in 2021, a mere seventy-six years after the war's end.

The museum's own research into their visitors' knowledge of the war shows that visitors only 'half knew' or recognized names and places, and 'often lack the confidence to talk about the Second World War'. Poignantly, they recognized a personal connection to the war, but 'felt guilty that they did not know more about it'. Many said it now seems distant and incomprehensible. The commonest sources of knowledge were film and television, 'which has led to stereotypical understandings' of the war. At the same time, and most poignantly of all, visitors felt somehow that the war was the most important event to shape the world in the past hundred years.[40]

The National Arboretum in Staffordshire was created in 1997 as a 'Centre of National Remembrance'. There are around 350 individual memorials, the vast majority of which are military. It is funded by the National Lottery and sponsored by the British Legion and the Ministry of Defence – another national Valhalla that, strangely enough, relatively few seem aware of or have visited, impossible to get to by public transport as it is, appended to a tiny and ancient village. It has around 300,000 visitors a year, nonetheless. However, this public face seems less its purpose than is publicly announced, as there is a kind of privacy to the place – the privacy of the institutions of war as they nurse memory by means of these memorials. These, institutions and memorials alike, are overwhelmingly military. Civilians hardly get a look in, unless they have some quasi-military purpose (firefighters, ambulance men and women, and so on); and, of course, the civilians bombed on both sides barely rate a mention.

Among the monuments are those of the Ulster security forces, including the notorious Ulster Defence Regiment, and the even more notorious 'B Special' Constabulary. There is an 'Ulster Ash Grove' for them, but nothing for the civilian dead in that war. It all seems more *their* place, these particular institutions, than a national monument – and, because of this, in many ways it seems to have more integrity than many of the big national ones. However, at last in Britain one finds mention of the bombed civilians of both sides – though in only one memorial among the hundreds here, in the shape of the British–German Friendship Garden. It is small and modest, which has its virtues when set beside the pomposity of the Bomber Command monument. Its modesty is in proportion to its obscurity.

The historians have now put the bombing and the war at large into what is called 'historical perspective', and this is a priceless gain; but something lost still lingers after this. In Germany the local rootedness of managing loss defied, and still defies, all attempts to put the bombing into 'perspective'. Memories were acted out in the spaces that had been directly affected, and this sense of place gave them their peculiar, enduring quality.

Nothing for the survivors seems commensurate with the loss itself. The more we know of the history, of how memory operates, the more the dead and wounded seem to recede. Worse, the more public memorialization we have, the more they disappear altogether – and with them goes apprehension of the sheer otherness of war, of the depths of suffering. Suffering is occluded by the very rituals that are supposed to put us in touch with it. This is why Friedrich's impassioned work on the bombing is so important.

In her book *Regarding the Pain of Others*, Susan Sontag comments on those who have known war first-hand: 'Why should they seek our gaze? What would they have to say to us? "We" – this "we" is everyone who has never experienced anything like what they went through – don't understand. We don't get it. We truly can't imagine what it was like. We can't imagine how dreadful, how terrifying war is; and how normal it becomes ... Can't understand, can't imagine.'[41] In particular, photographs betray us, for when we gaze on the suffering of war, 'the imaginary proximity to the suffering inflicted on others that is granted by images suggests a link between the faraway sufferers ... and the privileged viewer that is simply untrue ... Our sympathy proclaims our innocence as well as our impotence'.[42] We just don't get it, and we never will understand the pain of others in war. "Can't understand, can't imagine." That's what every soldier, and every journalist and aid worker and independent observer who has put in time under fire and had the luck to elude the death that struck down others nearby stubbornly feels. And they are right.'

Of photography, Sontag writes: 'photographs ... everyone recognises are a constituent part of what a society chooses to think about. It calls these ideas "memories", and that is, over the long run, a fiction. Strictly speaking, there is no such thing as collective memory ... What is called collective memory is not a remembering but a stipulating: that this is important, and this is the story about how it happened, with the pictures that lock the story in our minds.'[43] The rituals in which we make the dead work for us are indeed for us, not for them; for our consciences and comfort, not for their suffering.

Joseph Roth, a Galician Polish Jew, was one of the greatest chroniclers of the effects of war in the twentieth century, in his case the war of 1914–18. He had fought in that war and witnessed the death struggle of the Austro-Hungarian Empire, of which he was so passionately and ambiguously a part. In his *Flight without End*, first published in 1927, the protagonist, Tunda, is a soldier returning home from the vast remoteness of Siberia. He speaks for all the casualties of war – those who set out from home, and those who stayed but suffered no less:

The blue light shone on the grave of the Unknown Soldier. The wreaths withered … Tunda had already passed by this memorial a number of times. There were always tourists standing around, hat in hand, and nothing upset him more than their marks of respect. It was like globe-trotters, who happened also to be devout, visiting a famous church during the service, and kneeling, guidebook in hand, before the altar, out of habit and in order not to incur self-reproach. Their devotion is a blasphemy and a ransom for their conscience. The blue flame burned under the Arc de Triomphe not to honour the dead soldier, but to reassure those who survived. Nothing was more gruesome than the unsuspecting devotion of a surviving father at the tomb of his son, whom he had sacrificed without knowing it. Tunda sometimes felt as if he himself lay there in the ground, as if we all lay there, all those of us who set out from home and were killed and buried or who came back but never again came home – for it is a matter of indifference whether we are buried or alive and well. We are strangers in the world, we come from the realm of the dead.[44]

If we just don't get it, the pain of others in war, and we never will, should we just shut up? Silence is better than the mechanical devotion to the dead that Roth despises: 'Nothing was more gruesome than the unsuspecting devotion of a surviving father at the tomb of his son, whom he had sacrificed without knowing it'; the horror and sadness of this sentence reverberates down the years.

W. G. Sebald, inhabiting the poetics of memory, knew the importance of silence, not this continuous and deafening noise of commemoration. He writes that silence may be the true 'natural history' of destruction, and of the paralysis, the 'impaired' speech, of the survivors of the bombing. This is the impaired speech of those eyewitnesses who are today so valued for the 'empathy' we can have for them.[45] The victim has a right to silence as well as to memory – and sometimes silence is better.

In the face of the horrors of the war, Sebald teaches us that another kind of silence may just give us the possibility to speak – a silence that is the proper ground of speech. The work of Samuel Beckett points us in the same direction, and Beckett was someone who also experienced war directly. So too does that of the great German-language poet, Paul Celan, born Paul Antschel to a Jewish family then in Romania, now in the Ukraine, in a city then called Czernowitz in German.[46] He was a prisoner in the German camps. Paradoxically, like Hannah Arendt, he felt that language was the only thing that remained secure after Auschwitz, and the German language at that, his *Muttersprache*, which his mother taught him as a child in Romania. But for this to be the case, he says in his Bremen Prize speech, language 'has to go through its own lack of answers, its terrifying silence, through the darkness of murderous speech'.[47]

What is possible in a world stripped of meaning by the Holocaust and the air war, both of which were a surrender to vengeance? What eventuates in Sebald's work is a kind of loneliness, and with it depression, and this is embodied in the haunted figures that are Sebald's concern – people in exile, people seemingly forever on the move. This loneliness is constituted by the memory of the meaning that once was, but has now been destroyed. One is cut off from the past, bereft. Rather like the Germans themselves, in another kind of flight without end, Sebald's characters are also restless, forever moving on, travelling, searching in the thickets of silence for a language that will do something to make us less cut off, less bereft, and more able to say something in witness.

Melancholia is the condition of his world: we are a species in despair, living, he says, unaware of the pain that surrounds us every day. He remarks on the silence of his own parents about the war, adding that they are people 'without a conscience'. He writes of a world draining away, and losing the capacity to have moral feelings. He also speaks of the loss of the places and objects that once had the power of memory. He imagines himself as the dog listening to the gramophone on the famous HMV record label, and thus someone who is now kept on sufferance and can only listen to His Master's Voice, like the dog.[48]

Beckett writes in *Molloy* that 'to restore silence is the role of objects'.[49] Sebald attempts to restore objects and places so that their silence will speak. For language to be made capable of speech again – Celan's *Muttersprache*, for example – it has to go through the terrible silence of murderous speech. And to do this it seems that, for these writers, the silence of objects must be listened to. In his *Le Monde du silence* (1948), Max Picard wrote that

> every object has a hidden fund of reality that comes from a deeper source than the word that designates the object. Man can meet this hidden fund of reality only with silence. The first time he sees an object, man is silent of his own accord. With his silence, man comes into relationship with the reality in the object which is there before ever language gives it a name. Silence is his tribute of honour to the object.[50]

Seamus Deane, among other things a poet of the Troubles, writes this on Sebald:

> The muteness of objects becomes in this world a matter of fascination, for their muteness is like ours. In part we make ourselves, and in part we are made mute to survive the trauma of destruction. We are unable to grieve, we can't even count the dead properly. Sometimes it is only an object, perhaps, the familiar thing, that still bears the weight of these feelings that have otherwise left us, the meaning that has left us. It may be an heirloom, in a literal but also a metaphorical sense. The past is embedded and embodied in objects, which has to be prised out of them, out of their muteness. Their opaque nature says, at one level, that there is no meaning, but at another that there may be.[51]

Sebald's writing is about objects and about 'facts', the objects distilling the facts into writing that provides a form of witness. In an interview, he speaks of 'the shining vitrines of fact', and of how these might be enough. He also speaks of being essentially interested in social and cultural history.[52] The artistic image stands in the way when blankness or silence may be closer to the truth. In the interview he follows this comment with reference to a particular 'fact', where he had written in *On the Natural History of Destruction* of a grief-crazed mother fleeing the destruction of the bombing, carrying what remained of the body of her child in a suitcase. The suitcase is an object that, in restoring silence, makes his speech possible. He also writes about boots, which do the same thing, drawing on Victor Gollancz's surveys and photographs of immediate post-war Germany, published in the English press in 1946.[53]

As so often in Sebald's work, it is the photograph of the object, itself an object, that punctuates the sad, winding flow of the narrative. In his lecture 'The Air War and Literature', it is photographs of the poor boots and shoes of German children. In the raids themselves, very young children, younger than five, did not have the words to express what had happened to them then; nor ten years later, when they were asked again.[54] One such child was Uwe Timm, a three-year-old, for whom 'the missing hand of a porcelain shepherdess continued to stand for all the family lost on 25 July 1943'.[55] Other children grieved over odd shoes lost, lost dolls. Mothers counted the pieces of china after a raid. Werner Werther remembered that they had maize porridge for lunch that day.

I think here, finally, of the remarkable poem of Ciaran Carson, *Dresden*, in which he, or the persona that writes the poem, considers the life and times of his protagonist Horse Boyle, who acquired that name 'because of his brother Mule'.[56] There is in the poem a constant counterpoint between the vastness of historical reality and the indirection, aimlessness and inconsequentiality with which we live and apprehend that vastness. The brokenness and power of memory are revealed, as Carson tracks the flow of what is most of the time silent, but always present. As the long, conversational, digressive poem meanders on through the life of Horse, time flows by, 'Or rather, she wouldn't ask; she would talk about the weather. It had rained / That day, but it was looking better. They had just put in the spuds.' Stories flow too: 'Take young Flynn, for instance, / Who was ordered to take this bus and smuggle some sticks of gelignite / Across the border, into Derry.' Places flow by: 'a place that was so mean and crabbed, / Horse would have it, men were known to eat their dinner from a drawer.' So too do people flow. And suddenly: 'Horse who – now I'm getting / Round to it – flew over Dresden in the war. He'd emigrated first, to / Manchester. Something to do with scrap – redundant mill machinery.'

On impulse, Horse joined the RAF. 'He became a rear gunner. / Of all the missions, Dresden broke his heart. It reminded him of china.' As for Uwe Timm and the mothers, it is the objects that speak, or rather, articulation of their silence is made possible, and speech prised out of the muteness of things:

As he remembered it, long afterwards, he could hear, or almost
hear
Between the rapid desultory thunderclaps, a thousand tinkling
echoes –
All across the map of Dresden, store-rooms full of china shiv-
ered, teetered
And collapsed, an avalanche of porcelain, slushing and cascad-
ing: cherubs,
Shepherdesses, figurines of Hope and Peace and Victory, delicate
bone fragments.
He recalled in particular a figure from his childhood, a milkmaid
Standing on the mantelpiece. Each night as they knelt down for
the rosary,
His eyes would wander up to where she seemed to beckon to
him, smiling,
Offering him, eternally, her pitcher of milk, her mouth of rose
and cream.[57]

One may draw strength from writing such as that of Sebald
and Carson, (and the forgotten Picard), comprising as it does
a poetics of silence and of memory. These men help us understand better the eloquence of things – in my case the things
that are real houses, roads and graves. I feel a kinship with
Sebald. He spoke of death being all around him as a child and
in youth. His work is rooted in the peasant Catholic culture
of the Allgau in southern Schwabia, in which he grew up. Of
the old Corsican peasant world he considers in *Campo Santo*,
he writes, as we have seen, that the dead are ever returning,
coming into the house at night. Sebald bore the weight of the
war with great courage, carrying the backpack of the German
past, as he put it. As he says, most do not even know there is a
burden to carry, for the past is always a burden.[58]

8

Other Wars: The Walls of Derry

Walk about Zion and go around her; Count her towers; Consider her ramparts; Go through her palaces, That you may tell it to the next generation.

Psalm 48:12–13

From one war to another, from one wall to another: after the exploded walls of the old war the walls of the Cold War: the Iron Curtain, and the Berlin Wall. In 1970 I sat in amazement in a state office on the other side of that wall, in the Deutsche Demokratische Republik (DDR). The photograph below of the Brandenburg Gate was taken about that time, from 'our' side of the Wall. My seat was, as far as I recollect, in a building to the right as one looks through the Gate, on the Unter den Linden – once the great central thoroughfare of an undivided city.

I had gone there in preparation for graduate work on German history that I did not in the end pursue. To my surprise, the letter of permission to visit had arrived shortly before. It was written on coarse paper, and typed with a machine clearly so old and used that many of the typed characters on the page appeared broken and incomplete. It has always served me as an image of 'the East' at that time, of how time seemed to have stood still on the other side of the Wall. The DDR had rebuilt the Unter den Linden in modernist style, but this served only to gloss over the dilapidation of the rest of the city. It seemed that the war had only just ended. The buildings were marked by the traces of bullets and bombs. There were still large tracts of empty, once-bombed land. The police-cum-military, guns

Looking east over the Berlin Wall, postcard, 1970.

bristling, rode around in motorcycles and sidecars, comical in their antique precariousness but still threatening, as was the whole city.

It was at that time that I first visited West Berlin, the ride in along the designated road from the West as revealing as the wall itself, as the road was nothing but one long wall on either side, across which it was totally forbidden to stray. The checkpoints were heavily militarized, the searches lengthy and thorough, the guards deeply hostile. It was on this visit that I first saw the *Woodstock* film, emblem of the new age on 'our' side of the Wall. This only heightened the sense of unreality as I looked out from the East side to the West. The western city was unreal in its own sense when you were in it, the force-fed western modernity of the Kurfürstendamm amidst the gloom of the rest of the city.

The GDR itself, on the other hand, was to me a wonder when I first came across it that year, the prosperity already evident, unlike in the London of the time. The giant Kaufhof supermarkets seemed to symbolize the economic miracle, but everyone seemed to dress alike, and the new buildings every-where were all alike, bland and anonymous, built at the same time, to what seemed to be the same design. And then, when you walked through the doors and behind the walls of what

restored older buildings there were, all was new. The dislocation at this threshold between different times and realities was
unnerving, as was sight of the older person sitting beside you
on a park bench in the new beige – always beige – overcoat.
What had they done, where had they been, a mere twenty-five
years before?

By 1970 other walls nearer to home were in the news. The
walls of Derry and the violence that had begun to build after
the civil rights movement had emerged in the late sixties,
emerged first in Derry itself. I had grown up with walls. The
walls that buried my father. The wall in the head that was an
effect of class in England. The Irish walls. The music I heard
as a child, the set dancing Irish music, echoes still, *The Walls
of Limerick* and *The Siege of Ennis*. These dances signified the
bloodbaths of the Irish seventeenth century. Derry is the only
remaining completely walled town in Ireland.

Irish strife has a long history: in the 1798 United Irishmen
Rising, my mother's hometown of New Ross was besieged,
this time by the rebels, its walls breached. Wexford was the
epicentre of 1798. In the aftermath of the worst battle of the
whole rising, at New Ross, hundreds of rebels were buried or
burned alive where they were sheltering, and the bodies of
many of the 3,000 dead were thrown into the River Barrow. In
retaliation, 100 were burned alive by the rebels at Scullabogue,
most but not all of them Protestants (the United Irishmen were
Protestant as well as Catholic in composition). As a child and
adolescent in Ireland, I learned the Wexford rebel songs and
thrilled to them, 'The Croppy Boy' among them ('Croppy'
was a name given the rebels because of their cropped hair, the
antithesis of the bewigged gentleman). In his poem 'Requiem
for the Croppies', Seamus Heaney writes of the barley seeds
in the pockets of the slain young Croppy boys sprouting anew
from the mass graves. New Ross had been laid siege to more
than a century earlier, in 1643, during the Cogadh na hAon
Bhliana Déag – the Eleven Years War or Confederate War.

Cromwell had retaken the town in 1649. There was a long history of wars.

Class may form one wall in the head. In the North of Ireland, this wall was composed of this, but of much else too – things more murderous than class, at least here. Wars are about territory, and so always about boundaries and borders. Borders are walls, often literally. The North was of course a territory made by 'the border', the great presence in Irish history, and in British history, too, if with urgency only since the start of the Troubles after 1968.

My wife's family are people of the border wall, of Louth, Cavan and east Donegal on one side, Down on the other – the county in which she was born (Malones and Dullaghans, names mattering along this border). Walls in the head may be breached, but a price had to be paid. One of Rosaleen's aunts made a 'mixed' marriage there, Catholic and Protestant, an uncle another such union. The price paid for safety was emigration – one couple to England, the other to the United States. For those who stayed at home married, silence was also the price. Another uncle negotiated the murderous political geography of Belfast's internal walls at the height of the violence in the North. Like so many before him, he joined the British Army in youth, and then returned from England to live in the Falls Road at the height of the Troubles, working – he was an intrepid man – as a local postman. Yet another uncle carried livestock back and forth over the border, and so knew the frontier intimately. A cousin drove the oft-disrupted Belfast-to-Dublin train across the border itself. And so it went on, goes on, with these big families.

A more distant relative, Bernard O'Connor, an innocent man, was brutalized at the notorious detention centre of Castlereagh, a bleak brick-walled building that was a barrack house of the Royal Ulster Constabulary. His case provoked a notable BBC television programme that exposed what was going on there – a breaking of silence about a place designed to break silence.[1] The programme in turn outraged the UK popular press and the national powers that be, denounced by both Roy Mason, the government minister, and his Tory shadow Airey Neave, who was later assassinated in Westminster by the Irish National Liberation Army. Bernard was eventually awarded 'exemplary damages' of £5,000 against the RUC. There seems to have been a non-exemplary going rate for damages for being roughed up by the RUC in the unlikely event that it came to court – a modest £1,000.[2]

Walls, designed as they are to separate, are also about silence, silencing the presence of both those without and those within. Silence follows silence in my story: the silences of war. Noise follows noise as well – that of bombs, bomb following bomb, on Darmstadt, on Paddington, in the North of Ireland, and the bombs that detonated in Britain during the so-called Troubles. There are many kinds of silence, and from the great grow the lesser, so that silence is like a tree. The boughs grow from the trunk, then the branches, and from the branches in the spring the buds that renew the tree of silence. This tree flourished in Northern Ireland. This is the country where the act of 'telling' has more than one meaning, so that to tell is also *not* to break silence but to maintain it. For in this divided society it was and still is necessary to know who is who, and to be able to *tell* from which side one comes, so that telling is as often as not a way of keeping mute, and so maintaining the silence that enables the status quo to prevail. This way, a manageable life may be maintained. The more difference is negotiated, the more it is reinforced.[3]

In the bad times, silence might be a question of life and death – as Seamus Heaney famously put it, a matter of 'open minds, as open as a trap'. His words are echoed in the famous injunction of the place: 'Whatever you say, say nothing.' 'Smoke-signals are loud-mouthed compared with us', Heaney writes.[4] The North still lives in the shadow of all this. Residence, the minutiae of dialect, name, school, how one pronounced the alphabet, if one could recite the 'Hail Mary' – a hundred and one ways I am not privy to – all these told, and tell.[5] 'O land of password, handgrip, wink and nod.'

Aside from through my wife's family, the conflict came into my life most urgently in the form of the IRA bombing campaign in London. Of the nearly 500 bomb attacks in England, most were in London. Britain effectively meant England in IRA thinking, and Scotland and Wales were not targeted, the former because it was thought a Celtic nation. The Glasgow pub bombings of 1979 were carried out by the Ulster Volunteer Force (UVF) against Catholics. During the thirty-year campaign, fifty people were killed and many more injured in London. This was my town they were attacking, but my loyalties were divided. Certain bombs are remembered: the Notting Hill Gate bomb in Kensington Church Street (1975), near the bus stop I sometimes waited at, outside the K shoe shop where I looked at shoes I wanted but could not afford. This bomb killed the person defusing it, Roger Goad, a forty-year-old father of two.

In 1983, there was the Woolwich King's Arms bomb, too, near where I had worked, and the Regent's Park bomb, which I heard in the distance as I sat beside my dying mother in St Mary's Hospital. On that day in 1982, eleven soldiers were killed in Regent's Park and Hyde Park, the parks of my adolescence and childhood play. On the same day that the innocent Guildford Four were convicted of the Birmingham pub bombs, the Provisionals attacked the home of Hugh Fraser, the Conservative MP in Campden Hill, just over the other side of the tracks of my west London. Later on, there was the Manchester bomb of 1996. My daughter was in the city that day – mobile phones a thing of the future, and the public phones overrun. The bomb was the largest detonated in Britain since the Second World War. It weighed 3,300 lbs and devastated large parts of the city centre.

Bombs and funerals: in the Kilburn church in which I had been a pageboy and became a married man, a Requiem Mass was held on 7 June 1974 for the soul of Michael Gaughan. His funeral procession led from the Crown pub in outer London's Cricklewood to Kilburn's Sacred Heart Church. My father drank in this pub in earlier years, my uncle too. A crowd of over 3,000 people made up the funeral cortege by the time it got to the church. To the front of the procession, eight men marched in dark glasses and military-style uniform; a piper walking before them. They comprised an honour guard for Gaughan, who was a member of an IRA unit in London that attempted to rob a bank in Hornsey, for which he had received a seven-year sentence, part of which he served in the high-security gaol of Parkhurst on the Isle of Wight. After a sixty-four-day hunger strike, during which he was force-fed, he died in Parkhurst from pneumonia probably caused by the force-feeding tube having pierced his lung. He was twenty-four years old when he died. He came from the same county as my father, impoverished Mayo. Like my father, he had come to England in search of work.

For us London Irish in the 1970s, we daily faced the condescension of many of the British. The refrain 'Why don't they just get over it? Grow up!' was often heard, for the Irish inhabited a world held to be 'primitive' and 'medieval', in contrast to civilized Britain (or, more often, civilized England, in that so familiar elision of the two). Here in England, one was not 'obsessed' by history; our interlocuters seemingly unaware that Britain had inflicted much of this history – and that, unlike the history of the victor, it could not be shrugged off. Attempts to explain that the appalling violence of the IRA came out of a particular history were met by the charge that explanation was an excuse. Discussion was abruptly ended, tempers raised.

An old tune played yet again, and played too in the appalling stereotyping of the Irish by large parts of the British press.[6] As a result the press, and indeed many British people, saw the extra-legal violence of the security forces as legitimate. Force had to be met by force, and a pity for those who got in the way. 'Our Boys' were at risk, and it did not do to criticize their behaviour. But this was my country doing this to my other one. 'Our Boys' could never be my boys.

In London we were protected by our accents, but you needed to be careful with your name. For example, only a few streets from Ashmore Road, in the 'Avenues' whose little houses my mother yearned for, lived the Maguire family. The so-called 'Maguire Seven' were convicted in 1976 for the Guildford pub bombings of October 1974, supposedly guilty of handling explosives found at the scene. They were wrongly convicted, as were the 'Guildford Four' a year earlier. The verdicts were quashed and reversed in 1991. Three police officers were charged with conspiracy to pervert the course of justice, though found not guilty. Their shameful story is one of police corruption and incompetence, and of the complicity of a malevolent newspaper press. My namesake Patrick (Maguire), then a thirteen-year-old boy, was brutalized and imprisoned for six years, his life broken.[7]

I do not recollect these times with tranquillity, for Britain has in great part still not accepted that all of this happened *here*. The truth is that, just as the civilian bombing of Germany was rendered invisible, so in a sense was the conflict in the North. It was as if it all took place in another country – the invariable historical location, this other country, of the age-old Irish question. The Irish Free State in 1922, and its successor Éire in 1937, were the first new nations to emerge from the British Empire. They emerged out of the tragedy of partition, presaging another tragedy of partition ten years after that in India, the one as misguided and mishandled as the other. The greatest crisis in the post-war UK – at least until Brexit – was the civil war in Ireland. No other developed country in the capitalist world saw similar levels of domestic political violence after 1945, or was as a result so intensively policed or subjected to the abrogation of normal judicial procedure. Ireland was then, and has remained, central to British nationhood; but you would not know this from public life in England, where ideas of national sovereignty are dependent on the fiction of a united kingdom, the constitutional virtue of which has for decades been under threat from the EU – virtue now at last rewarded by departure.

For instance, in Robert Tombs's recent bestselling and Brexit-sympathizing doorstopper, *The English and Their History*, the English are said to have no national character because liberty engenders diversity, not uniformity, so that the English are defined by 'inclusion'. That the inclusion that really counted for these liberty-loving English was that of others in their Empire seems to have escaped the author; inclusion, that is, until political expediency called for the washing of hands. 'The Troubles' does not fit in this story: in Tombs's 1,012 pages, three paragraphs are given over to the subject. There was an independent parliament of Northern Ireland until 1972–73, so that Britain could have clean hands and be a united kingdom at the same time. In this way the myth of Unionist blameless-ness could be preserved, and so too the relationship with the British state.

The sheer power of the Northern Ireland state machinery before it was challenged in the late 1960s is striking; like the scale of its suffering, this is in need of recollection. The police, the judiciary, the entire governmental and administrative struc-ture in fact, were thoroughly politicized, thoroughly Unionized. The British government indulged the Unionists in their power, well aware of the injustices involved. Northern Ireland was hardly top of the Labour Party agenda, either. This was a war.

As in Germany, statistics have their story to tell, and thus we need the Irish numbers, too. There were 10,000 bombings, in some accounts more. In 1972 alone there were some 10,000 shooting incidents. Thousands of houses were destroyed. In a population of 1.5 million, 3,725 people were killed, around 43,000 were injured, and an astonishing 500,000 people have been identified by the Commission for Victims and Survivors as victims of the conflict.[8] Rubble memories again; the lost house and the lost home within it.

The 'geography of violent death' reveals how this catastrophe was concentrated in particular areas of the North, and in particular locations within those areas. Nearly half of the killing in the North occurred in Belfast, and there – and in some other locations with a high 'body count' – particular enclaves were more lethal than others. Three-quarters of the Belfast deaths occurred in the north and west of the city.[9] Yet, if violence was concentrated, the shock waves of the killings and injuries were felt all over this intimate province. Most of those killed were Catholic civilians. The killings were concentrated in the areas of highest social deprivation (where there were few cars to escape in, few phones to call for help, few jobs to make life bearable).[10]

A civil war? The poet Michael Longley calls it a civil war, remarking that 'civil war is a kind of oxymoron, since it combines an idea of community and an idea of its fracture'. It throws up, he says, the question: 'What is meant by home?' In his poem 'All of These People', he itemizes victims of the bombing, including 'Our assassinated Catholic greengrocer who died / At Christmas in the arms of our Methodist minister.' The poem goes on: 'All of these people, alive or dead, are civilised / Who can bring peace to people who are not civilised?'[11]

It has been estimated that, if the equivalent ratio of victims to population had obtained in Britain as in Northern Ireland in the same period, some 100,000 people would have died, and the number of fatalities in the United States would have been over 500,000 – about ten times the number of Americans killed in the Vietnam War.[12] If we extrapolate the number of those injured and dead in the province to the British population as a whole in 2001, we get a figure of around half a million casualties. There were perhaps some 30,000 people who were members of paramilitary organizations at different times, most of them Ulster Defence Association members.

The British Army's 'Operation Banner' lasted from 1969 to 2007. It has been estimated that over a quarter of a million soldiers served – a figure not including those in the UDR and its successor. In Derry, it is claimed that not far off a thousand people were imprisoned for IRA activities between 1971 and 1986.[13] There were, in total, what the official army account terms over 10,000 'terrorist arrests'. This was war. In Britain itself, by as early as the mid 1980s, around 55,000 people had been interviewed under the Prevention of Terrorism Act, and between 1974 and 1990 about 7,000 people were detained. In Britain, 115 people died and 2,134 were injured. The 'peace-keepers' themselves – the quarter-of-a-million British soldiers who served in Northern Ireland – are themselves a testament to this production of invisibility; they are a ghostly presence in the land, a remarkable social phenomenon scarcely remarked on now, their experiences leavening British society in countless ways that are not understood. They are less ghostly, however, when absolution is demanded for them now by the army and the Conservative press, in the name of history – all of it being history now, all so long ago.

Derry, this place of the last wall and the first upsurge of the trouble to come, seemed like the city in which to try to understand a little better what went on. Walls separate, defend and proclaim, and thus seem to speak with some eloquence about this province of division. Besides, the city has a pull for me because it is linked strongly to one of London's innumerable pasts: 'If walls could speak / then London's name should sound / who built this church and city from the ground', reads an old inscription at St Columb's Cathedral in the town. The other name of this city is Londonderry, 'London' itself a kind of wall.

In the eighteenth century, Presbyterians outnumbered Episcopalians here in all heavily Protestant districts in the city's hinterland, so that the usual colonial binaries broke down in this place. The Dissenters loathed the Churchmen, making for the development of radical Protestant patriotism and republicanism.[14] Differences of class largely underwrote these religious differences, organizing the society into elite Episcopalians and more plebeian Presbyterianism.[15] But the settler–native distinction was reconstructed from the early nineteenth century, with the failure of political Enlightenment and the later advent of the Home Rule question. Nonetheless, the past was not black and white. 'Catholic' and 'Protestant' are themselves imagined categories to describe 'identity', and something of the differences within each of them comes out in what follows. But it is the making of the two 'camps' that concerns me here – its realities and realization in the walls themselves.

Like many before me, I am impressed on arrival to Derry by two things: the beauty of the city's natural setting, and the overwhelming sense of political power that the walled city represents.[16] The city overlooks the river Foyle, which opens to the north into Lough Foyle, and then the Atlantic. To the west is the beautiful promontory of Inishowen, and then Lough Swilly, an even greater natural harbour than Lough Foyle. The jagged coast of Donegal stretches to the far west. The coast to the east is huge, uncluttered, a delight. The city has today far outgrown its walls, if not its past.

Not only the last remaining walled town in Ireland, it is reportedly also the last one built in Europe. This is how the great philosopher George Berkeley, Dean of Derry from 1724 to 1732, described the walled city:

> The city of Derry is the most compact, regular, well built town that I have seen in the King's Dominions, the town house (no mean structure) stands in the midst of a square piazza from which there are four principal streets leading to as many gates. It is a walled town, and has walks all round on the walls planted with trees as in Padua.[17]

This Padua on the Foyle was nonetheless a war machine, a gigantic device for exercising physical and symbolic domination. In

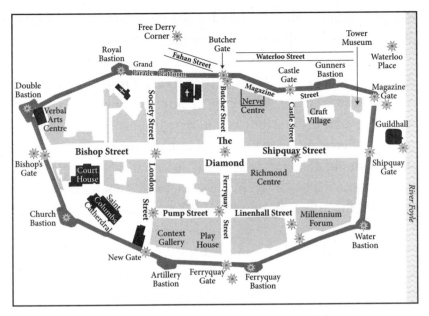

The walled city of Derry, west at top of plan.

the Troubles, the British Army erected enormous surveillance towers on the heights of the walled city, looking down on the Catholic Bogside and Creggan below.

Reproduced here is a map of the modern walls of Derry, and the surveillance of the Catholics below that would have been going on over the years would have been mostly from this side, to the west. The bastions on the walled town along this side are marked left to right: Magazine, Gunners, Royal, Double, with the gates Castle and Butcher. On the right side of the plan is Shipquay Gate (opening north), and on the left Butcher's Gate (looking south) – the business sides of the walls, as it were. The space enclosed by the walls is fairly small, far from Paduan size – the circumference only 1.6 km. Though the streets are few, some are long, the houses and other buildings close together. The plan is a slightly anachronistic one for my purposes, for in the top-right corner is something marked 'craft village', part of the attempted post-war regeneration of a once devastated city. The map is itself a tourist product – a fact that is relevant to the history, the anachronism useful now. I hope this plan will situate the place for the reader, as I wish to write about some of the points on these walls.

The religious and political geography of the place was once simple: the Foyle lies to the right, and so to the north on the map, though the river quickly bends to the east and so runs along the bottom of the map, and it is schematically marked. Ferry quay and Waterside bastions will be noted at the bottom of the map (the city is oriented to the north-east). Until Catholics began to move over to the east side after the end of the conflict, the east side, 'Waterside', was Protestant-Unionist. The west side, 'Cityside', was and is Catholic and Nationalist. The epicentre of Protestant-Unionist 'heritage', St Columb's Cathedral, is marked in the bottom left-hand corner, the much-bombed Courthouse above it. One other of the three main 'Protestant' sites is marked, the Church of St Augustine, towards the top – but not what is near to it, the Apprentice Boys Memorial Hall. There are no 'Catholic' sites.

The Foyle itself was a wall of sorts. There is now a 'Peace Bridge' over it, but when you walk over it to the east you are very quickly in the parade ground of Ebrington Barracks, built first in 1841 and named after the lord lieutenant of Ireland, Hugh Fortescue, Viscount Ebrington. During the conflict, Ebrington was the headquarters of the 8th Infantry Brigade, which had fought in the two world wars. The barracks came under attack in the conflict. It is hard to walk away from history here, the sign of peace that is a bridge being also a reminder of war.

The walls of Derry, and the concentrated historicity of the stones of the city, proclaim: 'siege'.[18] The walls were made for the siege, and the siege of 1688–89 in turn made the walls of Derry the site of one of the two great myths of the Protestant north. The other is the Battle of the Boyne. The Apprentice Boys,10,000 of them worldwide now, adopted the siege, and the Orange Order won the battle. The buildings and monuments within the walls make together a symbolic weapon of

Protestant power that complements that of the material walls and fortifications. Like the walls, the major buildings within look down upon the lowlands, forming above the military wall another wall in profile against the sky. St Columb's Cathedral (1628), the first cathedral in Britain built after the Reformation, in a style known as 'Planter's Gothic', is by far the biggest religious building within the walled city. It possesses the skyline of the city as a whole. St Columb's is now dedicated to 'peace and ecumenism', as are the other places of religious worship I visit.

Just outside the southern entrance to the walls, and immediately over the wall from St Columb's, by the Bishop Gate and along to Newgate, lies the Protestant and loyalist district known as the Fountain, a lone bastion on this side of the river. The Union Jack and the Ulster flag fly high above the Fountain, and are visible from far away on the other side of the river. One enters the Fountain quickly from the walled city, from Bishop Gate to the south. The enclave immediately abuts the city walls, while with time the Bogside on the west has withdrawn from them to the low land beyond, below the wall, starting these days at Free Derry Corner. The Fountain remains contiguous with the walls, as if reluctant to let go of what still gives it strength. Pictured below is a gateway to the Fountain.

The entrance – 'Welcome to the Fountain'.

The entrance is dingy and forbidding, an iron box inside which is a barred gateway. A notice on the wall indicates that the gate to the Fountain is locked at 9 p.m., although there are two alternative 'exits' available after this time. Enclosed by high mesh fences, making up what is called a 'peaceline', the Fountain is now essentially a small housing estate. Notwithstanding the defences, it is attractive, the green spaces and houses well presented and in good condition. The district is at once an historical exhibit and a place of dwelling. The entrance tells us about its history, and about the museum and 'monuments' that are to be found within. The latter signify what these days is called 'heritage'; like everywhere else on the two islands, we are these days held to have heritages, not pasts.

No less than the walled city, the Fountain itself is a citadel, a high bastion of what is publicly proclaimed from within as West Bank Loyalism. The initials 'WBL' are to be found in several places, sometimes followed by the words 'We are still here.' In the conflict many Protestants left for the Waterside, so that the area has suffered dramatic population loss, becoming what some call 'the last Protestant enclave'. And so there is a feeling of being under siege in this city of sieges.

Here within the citadel, the image, in the form of the mural, has dominance, as it does in the province as a whole. In the Fountain there are many of these often highly elaborate wall paintings, dedicated to the past as they are, to not forgetting (the motto 'Lest we forget' is emblazoned on several walls). What must not be forgotten are chiefly the Siege of Derry in 1688–89 and the sacrifices of the 1914–18 war. The walls of the Cathedral Youth Centre are covered in these works. The more recent past must not be forgotten either, and, movingly, on one mural there are depictions of Derry before the Troubles – in the 1950s, I would guess. There was a time when things were better, perhaps even good.

It is the long past of the Fountain itself that is also commemorated, and one is aware that this territory, and the Bogside too, are not simply creatures of the Troubles, but that the discord of those years has deep foundations in communitarian pasts: the Fountain's Thiepval Gallery commemorates 100 years of the district's history. There are also images of the past of the enclave itself on that part of the great metal-and-wire fence around the Fountain known as the Peacewall, just outside Bishop Gate. The message of the images of pre-Troubles community life seems to be that we are all of us ordinary Derry people together, our 'heritage' of equal weight with the others.

The contradictions now come thick and fast: the 'Peacewall' is to keep people apart, and the images on it commemorate a heritage that is not 'shared', a Protestant inheritance. A 'Peacewall' is also part of a 'project', 'the Peacewalls Community Tourism Project', in which a fraught and still hugely unstable past is mobilized in the interests of tourism and employment and, some hope, as a means to inter-community amity. All this in a city that still does not know what to call itself. This is how the manager of the Project describes it:

> The rationale ... lay in the fact that both the Fountain and Lower Bishop Street, despite lying within the shadow of the city walls and five minutes' walk from the Bogside, have never enjoyed the same level of tourist footfall at either location due to a range of factors. These include lack of visitor signage, lack of information about the attractions on offer in both areas, lack of historical information and a lack of online presence promoting the two areas.[19]

And, of course, the lack of a cause like Bloody Sunday, too. After the riots of July 2018 and the shooting dead of Lyra McKee, the Unionists were concerned that the Peacewall should be raised to protect them.[20]

Words matter here as well as images – in particular, words that are close to images, short phrases (or initials) that encapsulate meanings directly and with drama; still urgent words that connect the past and tradition with the present, words that are like bullets. On the side of a wall near to the Cathedral Youth Centre there is a mural to 'Sargeant [*sic*] Lindsay Mooney', aged nineteen, a UDA member killed in 1973 when a bomb he was transporting to Donegal exploded prematurely. There is a ballad to Mooney's memory. The martyrs to the loyalist cause, as to the republican, must not be forgotten. There is also a song about the walls, 'Derry's Walls', sung to the tune of 'God Bless the Prince of Wales'.

> When blood it flows in crimson streams
> Through many a winter's night
> They knew the Lord was on their side
> To help them in their fight
> They Nobly stood upon the walls
> Determined for to die,
> To fight and gain the victory
> And raise the Crimson high.

Crimson is the historical colour of Protestant defiance here, and this is the crimson city, the city of blood. At the centre of the Mooney mural, amidst the crimson colours, are the words *Quis Separabit*, which translate as 'Who shall separate us?', the loyal band, the band of brothers. We are not to be separated one from another, but nor are we to be separated from Christ, for, the original continues, 'Who shall separate us from the love of Christ?' (Romans 8:35). 'From the love of Christ' no doubt, but also from the British Crown. The Crown surmounts the memorial to Lindsay Mooney.

Quis Separabit is the motto of the Ulster Defence Association, the loyalist paramilitary group to which Mooney belonged; the largest paramilitary group, which it is now astonishing to recall was legal from 1971 until 1992. He was also a member of the Ulster Freedom Fighters, the legal grouping's *nom de guerre*. *Quis Separabit* either is or was also the motto of the Royal

Memorial to Sgt Lindsay Mooney. The British crown surmounts the motto, and the colour crimson dominates the memorial.

Dragoon Guards, the Royal Ulster Rifles, the London Irish Rifles, the Irish Guards, the 5th Royal Irish Lancers, the North Irish Horse and the 4th/7th Royal Dragoon Guards. It was also that of the Connaught Rangers, 1881–1922, and prior to this that of the forerunner of the Rangers, the 88th Regiment of Foot, founded in 1793.

Quis Separabit was also the motto of the Ulster Defence Regiment, 1970–92. In the UDR the formal structures of the British Army merged into the shadowlands of the sectarian organizations of a para-state comprising the various loyalist groups – the Orange Order, the Apprentice Boys, and others. Almost exclusively Protestant, the UDR's members were involved in many sectarian killings. But this did not prevent the regiment in 2006 being retroactively awarded the Conspicuous Gallantry Cross. As for formal state structures themselves, the words were the motto of the Most Illustrious Order of Saint Patrick (1783–1922), a now defunct order of chivalry founded by George III. It served the former government of Northern Ireland. It also represented the institutions that helped form modern Unionism in the first place, such as the Ulster Defence Union, founded in 1893 to oppose the Home Rule movement. *Quis Separabit* connects and recalls all these times, time flowing back and forth through the words themselves, in the times and places of their enunciation, the past ever present in the two words, the Latin lending them an extra antiquity, and so an extra authority. To ensure that nothing will separate us, walls were built.

The city was an engine of war. The structure of the walls is enormously wide at some places, much less so at others. Appropriately enough, overlooking the Bogside on the west wall is to be found what is now a wide and splendid walkway, but was in the past a vast military rampart; from the Double Bastion to the Royal, the 'London Cannon' are to be found, these massive machines of death over a ton in weight each, requiring six men to operate them. The length of their recoil when fired was six metres, hence the rampart width. Roaring Meg is the most famous of these guns.

In an uncanny premonition of the bombs planted in the city during the Troubles, Walker's *True History of the Siege* records for 1689 'the Number of Bombs thrown into the City of London-Derry since the beginning of the Siege'. From 24 April to 28 July, 587 bombs were 'thrown in', 326 small and 261 big: 'The largest Bomb being brought to the Scale did weigh 272lbs.' On 23 July, '20 more before Dinner, and we could not compute them afterwards, they came so thick upon us'.[21] Perhaps 5,000 died on each side, the total number of deaths being about three times that of 'the Troubles' as a whole.

Moving along the top of the ramparts from Bishop Gate to Butcher Gate and Castle Gate on the west side, Catholic Derry is openly revealed below, as was the plan from the building of the walls between 1613 and 1619. This is what walled towns are for – to reveal what is outside and below. From this point, one has access to what is called a 'tourist panorama'; these days one is a tourist here, and the centuries of watching the outsider below are occluded. The elaborate signage identifies the chosen sights of the town, most notable of which is

'This is what walled towns are for.' A cannon above the Bogside.

the enormous Catholic cathedral church of St Eugene, which opened in 1873, a riposte to the walled city above on which sits St Columb's. Two-hundred yards or so below the wall is Free Derry Corner, and near it the kill zone of 'Bloody Sunday'. A steep grassed expanse now lies between the walled city and Free Derry Corner, aestheticizing the city and emptying it again of its historical reality. The Bogside once ran right up to the walls, and these were the poorest parts of that poor place, Fahan Street most notably.

This is how John Montague describes the city in the opening of his long poem 'A New Siege', dedicated to Bernadette Devlin. The new siege – 'Once again, it happens. / Under a barrage of stones / and flaring petrol bombs' – is set beside the old one, as times merge:

> Lines of history
> lines of power
> the long sweep
> of the Bogside
> under the walls
> up to the Creggan
> the black muzzle
> of roaring Meg
> staring dead on

> cramped houses
> the jackal shapes
> of James's army
> stiffen in siege.

Visible too from above are two of the great shirt factories that once sustained the town, giving employment to women, not men, so that the men emigrated. Poor then, poor now. Almost all the current UK government indices of social deprivation highlight the crisis in Northern Ireland. And within the province the further west one goes, the worse things are, until one reaches Derry. In 2011, of the seventy-five most deprived local areas of Northern Ireland, twenty were in Derry. It had the most deprived area in the entire province, and five of the ten most deprived ones in the North were in Derry City and Strabane.[22]

The panoramic western stretch of the walls from the Fountain to Castle Gate propels the walker once more into past conflicts, but now in a different key than previously – not heritage so much as history, or rather history in the service of heritage; better than the blandness of heritage alone, but history nonetheless with the argument left out, and certainly the pain. This is the history represented in the new signboards that appear periodically along the walls and present the city's history. These are withal informative and informed. The printed and online material on the walls is of a piece with the signboards. The walls are part of a so-called 'branding' project for 'Derry/Londonderry', and the author of the signboards is described online as a 'heritage activist'.

I once met at this place, by chance, a Derry council official, and with her a leading member of the Apprentice Boys of Derry, the latter fearsomely proportioned and seeming to know exactly what he wanted from the city authorities. They were there to discuss the stump of the memorial to the Revd. George Walker, co-governor and hero of the siege, the rest of which had been blown up by the IRA in 1973. We met beside the stump itself, on the Royal Bastion, not far from Butcher Gate. The problem then was the paintballs directed at the monument by the 'dissident' IRA.

Here the words on the new signboards do not bear the hardness of the bullet: instead they make up rational sentences aiming to interpret the past in a 'balanced' way – the English way, it might be said, as if what matters can be got at by always seeing both sides, by weighting them equally; and as if history was not a matter of moral judgment as well as rational explanation. Historians, of course, are drawn to rational explanation. The presence of the conflict is muted on the signboards, as is the physical presence of the British Army. Missing also are the bullet marks, the blood, the ruined bodies, the bombs and what they did – for the old city was ravaged by the bombing. These cannot be there, but some sense that they *were* there feels needed. I think again of the pitiably inverse quality of the ratio between the degree of commemoration and documentation of the civilian dead in the bombing of Germany and Britain and the ever-receding understanding of the real suffering involved. The search for 'balance' in the end leaves me blank. There are so many words here on display.

Everything but the real thing seems to be commemorated, and I recall the words of Susan Sontag on the experience of war: 'We don't get it … Can't understand, can't imagine.' Perhaps what is missing on these walls, I reflect later, concerns that sense I raised earlier of a silence that may be a precondition of speech about atrocity, an awareness of the privilege that must be accorded silence before speech is undertaken. Here in the North, breaking silence as a means of finding answers – a means of accessing 'truth' – has been found in 'storytelling'. 'Heritage' itself is a form of storytelling. This concern with narrative is about redemption and healing, and draws on religious and psychological sources.

However, as others have pointed out, the urge to tell one's story may lead to a bland consensus,[23] as if there were always one true truth, and 'truth' itself were not a troubled concept. Truth-telling is not necessarily reconciliation, it is also revelation; and what is revealed has consequences, bad as well as good. One person's closure may be another person's wound. In a highly politicized culture, many are anyway impervious to versions of truth that contradict theirs. However, while it is necessary to respect the silence of those who have suffered, the damage that the entrenched silences of years and centuries has engendered has to be reckoned with, too. How to make this reckoning, a terrible conundrum, is the question that the North faces as it seeks to arrive at 'truth' and 'reconciliation'.

The telling of stories and the breaking of silence, whatever the result, has produced to my mind extraordinary human documents, like Susan McKay's *Bear in Mind these Dead*, and the voices that come out of the air in the sound recordings of the WAVE 'Stories from silence' initiative – the voices, after so long, of parents and children on all sides directly affected, short interviews full of sorrow as the effects of murder spread inexorably from one generation to the next, just as in the other bombing war. Full of anger and horror, too, and shot through with details we observers do not appreciate until they suddenly reveal something of what it was like on that day, the weather, what was worn, what eaten ('we ate maize porridge'), and what it was like after, for instance, the difficulties of negotiating the lamentably inadequate compensation systems.[24]

But here on the walls and in the town, the answer seems to be that a reckoning *with* the past is to be carried forward by a reckoning through the *means* of the past, the means of heritage. The difficulties with this will be apparent: treating the past as a means for present purposes robs it of its difference from the present. The past is a foreign country. Heritage is not history, though it is confused with it; and this confusion, if not always its purpose, is often its result. History is, at any rate, another country from heritage, though not from the present for it is the present that informs what historians do and see,

so that the past is also *not* foreign, if foreign means severed from us now.

What is it that heritage needs to be? It is supposed to draw people together, which is good, but usually bland, as it cannot offend too much. Bland in this fierce place seems set not to work. Identifying something as heritage seems to set it apart from daily life, making it an object, in some sense an object of celebration and even of veneration. In setting some things apart, it separates them from others. Of course, heritage is also economic; tourism must pay for heritage. Above all, perhaps there is no such thing as heritage – only what is given that name, so that naming it is creating it, and creating it is having power over it, being able to govern it. And being able to govern the past means being able to govern the present – the bland leading the bland.

There is now a legally established Victims and Survivors Service, and a Commission, and a Commissioner for Victims and Survivors. Academics work closely with the state apparatus, including that of the EU. They are forced to use the language and thought-frames of economic managerialism, so that, in one example, a 'Dealing with the Past' project is one aspect of 'delivering outcomes' of a greater project (project upon project, like century piled on century). Other delivered outcomes carry the titles 'Implementing and Building Peace', 'Managing Transition', 'Peace Building Practice', and 'International Lesson Learning'.[25]

How might we prise open the meanings that are in objects? Out of the walls themselves, perhaps, listening to their utterance, so that the very thing I am walking on is the object that may allow speech, however inadequate. Objects do things as well as say things. The 'doing of Derry'? By this I mean the design and the making of it – not only the walls, of course, but the physical city it enclosed; and not just the design, but how this was lived out in practice year in, year out. If the physical walled city did not dictate its use in preordained ways to people, then its material forms bore down on them, affording them certain possibilities here, foreclosing others there. This living of the city, like most living, was a matter of habit.[26] It is through the physicality of things – the height and sight of walls, the stewardship of land (what land, what is grown on it), the layout of colonial villages, the making of communication systems, and much else – that historians and social scientists increasingly understand the constitution of human action, of power, and of the state.[27]

The mark of the new kind of state emerging in the seventeenth century was territory, only territory now actively etched into the natural world by engineering. Derry was no exception. The Honourable Irish Society was a consortium of the livery companies of the City of London set up in 1613 to colonize County Londonderry during the Plantation of Ulster. It was James I who pressured the guilds of the city to fund the resettlement of the area. The walls were constructed by the Society between 1613 and 1619. Remarkably, it is still the owner of these walls, from which it still draws revenues as it does from the nearby River Bann.

The rural area of the county of Londonderry was subdivided between the twelve London livery companies, the twelve 'proportions' so created being distributed among the companies by the drawing of lots – a deliberate echo of the biblical story in which the twelve tribes of Israel shared out the Promised Land. The livery companies brought system and design to the cultivation of their various 'proportions': the survey, the map, the plan – all laid down what became the planned or 'model' Plantation villages and towns of the area, with their gridded and cruciform layout, their walls (also in nearby Coleraine), their roads, houses, market houses, schools, churches, mills, cornstores, dispensaries; the list is long.[28]

Settlements were thus 'planted', and those who did the planting were called 'Planters' here and throughout the new empires that were then being born. To plant is to settle, to make a permanent home elsewhere, whether or not that elsewhere is somebody else's home. We also plant land: seed it, cultivate it, reap its rewards. We cultivate what we think is uncultivated – bogs and the bog Irish, in this case. The small towns of rural Ulster still have their English streets, their Irish streets and Scotch streets. The historian A. T. Q. Stewart argues that the topography of the North has created recurrent patterns of behaviour over long periods of time that have largely determined historical outcomes.[29]

The original Londonderry is held to bear a striking resemblance in layout to the late-sixteenth-century frontier-fortress city of Vitry-le-François, in eastern France, on the river Marne. This was built to the neoclassical, Renaissance plan of the French king, Francois III. Its neoclassicism was based on the idea of the Roman fort, the town quartered by two main intersecting streets, and thus easy to defend. The Roman grid layout of streets represented the idea of classical order and reason, as against the irrationality of what was outside, in this case the wild Irish.

In living the city daily, one might walk through the decorative Bishop Gate (1789), erected to commemorate the siege centenary. The words and images engraved upon a meaningful form – the Roman arch – these one might know; but perhaps mostly not. What counted perhaps more was what was learned by the body as one experienced the bulk, the solidity, of the walls, so that the senses were orientated by the architecture of power. Coming through the arch, one was literally *under* something above one, and forced to always go *that* way and no other. One might have come *up* to the city from below, so that one was in another way under the power of another who was always above one. Walls dominate imaginations, but also actions, from which imaginations are composed.

Within the walls, there is perhaps above all the powerful sense of something that is concentrated and dense. The city is small, so that this feeling of the contained-ness of the place is overwhelming. There is a conscious awareness of the density of historical reference within it; but, more than this, it is the experiential, habituated sense of being at once surrounded and yet protected and powerful which is striking. The walls have weight and are themselves 'planted', the city its own plantation. Reassurance for those within, domination for those without.

The politics of the senses were at work. Of sight: for the eye of the inhabitant observer is led down to the dispossessed and dispersed outside the walls, those that are 'other', those that are of the faith of unreason. The senses of both parties would have been shaped by the cultural connotations and the physical reality of height and lowness involved, including the inversions, when they happened, of Catholics promenading along the walls and Protestants looking up from the depths below. In the society as a whole, however, the Catholics tended to occupy the high ground and the Protestants the low: the poor uplands and the fertile lowlands. There the senses were reversed.

Olfactory politics, the politics of smell, also obtained, underlining the distinction between the regulated city above (how it smelt, what health hazards it presented) and the impoverished ghetto of the Bogside below, bereft of the Victorian gospel of sanitation and ventilation and so wrapped in diseased miasma. Those without and within heard the sounds of each other, too, could touch the reassuring firmness of the bastions themselves (bog and mud below, stone above), and taste the air surrounding them.

The physicality of the wall and that of the human body seem to interact, symbolically echoing and reinforcing one another; there is a profound correspondence between the structure of a society and the way it deploys and thinks about bodies.[30] There is the distinction between the pure and the polluted – the pure inside, the polluted outside, beyond the walls of the body and the city. The orifices of the city walls, the gates, are sacred, for they are the sites of regulation between the pure and the impure. Perhaps the whole culture is one of walls, and so it has been written of: a place of walls within walls, the designation of what is within and what is without permeating everything, even the core of the Orange Order.[31]

Fate is the child of habituation – the habituation the physical city ingrained in people. Eamonn McCann remarks of the Catholics he grew up with before the Troubles that they were not taught to hate Protestants, simply that 'it was best we kept away from them'. Protestant power was resented, but was a fact of life. It was fate, and so there was no outrage about unemployment or emigration. Industrialists were seen as benefactors, bringing jobs to the town and its fated Catholics.[32]

When, in 2018, I asked Seamus Deane, a native of the city, about this physical city, about looking up, this is what he told me:

> It was alien ground, for sure. Scarcely ever went on the walls except near St Columb's Hall, where there is a gap in the walls, which is also close to the Fountain. But it was, to me, foreign territory otherwise; but we used the Guildhall for Feiseanna, school choir competitions [primary school]. The worst slums in the Bogside were in Fahan Street, right below the walls, right up to Butcher's Gate; the smell was indeed awful at times. The poverty in the Bogside area was merciless, grinding, it smelt of shit and tea. But if one looked up it was always with resentment or dislike; no one was ever overawed by Unionists – an inconceivable idea – and their architecture was, like themselves, heavy, inert; more immobilized than immovable, their hatred of us leaden – the police carried it in their guns and truncheons and their heavy black boots. Protestants dressed with corpse-like respectability.

Shit and tea, the smell of Fahan Street below the walls, the smell of Southam Street in London's west in my nostrils still, poverty's reek. Our streets and senses in London were regulated, policed, governed from on high, as were our houses, their rents and tenancies, their habitability, whether they were 'condemned' or not (people lived for years thus condemned, given the housing shortage). There was the silent but eloquent regulation of class evident in property values, street maintenance and policing levels, courtesy in the first instance of the Royal Borough of Kensington and Chelsea, in Paddington the august administration of the Borough of Westminster.

Here in Derry, Protestant architecture was in Deane's perception immobilized rather than immovable, but still deeply *there*, still above, leaden, hatred in stone, in truncheons and tweeds, guns and striped ties. The walls, nonetheless, 'the walled rock', spoke the meaning of power's architecture. These words are from the first two of the three stanzas of Seamus Deane's poem 'Derry',

> The unemployment in our bones,
> Erupting on our hands in stones,
> The thought of violence a relief,
> The act of violence a grief;
> Our bitterness and love
> Hand in glove.
> At the very most the mind's eye
> Perceives the ghost
> Of the hands try
> To timidly knock
> On the walled rock.
> But nothing will come.
> And the hands become
> As they insist
> Mailed fists.[33]

In Derry, the walls and the buildings within are emblematic of the whole history of the North. The physical city and what it taught the body connects powerfully with the symbolism of a people within the walls as well as without, at once protected, embattled and surrounded – a people under the threat of being besieged.[34] A people indeed of the citadel, spiritual kin to John Calvin's Geneva citadel of the original faith. The people now of the DUP, a party born out of the threat of violence, a number of its leading figures (the spokesperson for its Brexit policy) with connections to the Protestant paramilitaries. The high places of the reformed religion, Mount Sinai, Mount Zion, Mount Horeb, were in the Protestant imaginary particularly sancti-fied – especially Zion, the emblem of Jerusalem, the City of David and of the chosen people. Zion is a citadel.

As Psalm 48 says, 'Walk about Zion and go around her; Count her towers; Consider her ramparts; Go through her palaces, That you may tell it to the next generation.'[35] And as Psalm 31 has it, 'Listen to me, and deliver me quickly. Become a rock of safety for me, a fortified citadel to deliver me.'[36] The commander and spiritual leader of the siege himself, the Rev. George Walker, spoke thus in a sermon to celebrate the 'raising of that desperate siege': 'We may through all the course of Holy Scripture, plainly behold that when the Almighty designed to work out a deliverance to His people, He made them sensible that it was not so much the Arms of flesh, as His Immediate Power that saved them.'[37]

The motto of the Presbyterian Church in Ireland is 'ardens sed virens', 'Burning but flourishing', after the burning bush on Mount Sinai. Aflame yet enduring, always suffering yet always triumphing, aflame in the fires of their enemies, but never consumed, saved by God's 'Immediate Power'. The citadel also speaks of a particular kind of Protestant silence, which is apparent where Protestants were *not* the dominant group, where they were a marginal and embattled part of the local population.[38] This silence is perhaps less well known than the loudness apparent when Protestant silence is broken, the sound of the drum and of the parade – what Seamus Heaney called 'the voodoo of the Orange Bands'.

Rural and Catholic south Armagh in the Troubles was one site of this marginality. There a disproportionate number of

Protestants were murdered, and people felt betrayed by their own politicians. Discussion of events and of the violence was often muted, among themselves as well as outside. Suffering in silence meant retaining strength and pride, having deep biblical resonances, like the citadel. One suffered for righteousness, so that silence became the only way of honouring the truth of what one had endured (Roman Catholics were too cute, too smart, too vocal, always wanting to tell their stories). Instead one drew upon the book of Isaiah (53:7): 'He was oppressed and affected, yet he did not open his mouth'; and Psalm (32:2): 'Listen to me, and deliver me quickly. Become a rock of safety for me, a fortified citadel to deliver me'.[39] One will, with silence, always be delivered from the siege. This silence is broken today as local Protestants join the many others who now seek deliverance by telling their stories as a means of getting justice.

Catholic silence in a vulnerable area, on the eastern coast this time, has another story to tell.[40] There is the obvious silence of necessity, of being surrounded, of the big Orange feast days; but there is also silence in the presence of a young woman's cousins in the South, who are always somehow 'more Catholic, more Irish, softer and more childish than us' – sometimes, indeed, they are even royalists. The Northerners are the poor relations in the South. The Irish in the North are Irish but not Irish, British but not British, and indigenous but often without the transgenerational connection to land and resources that Protestants have. They seem as if always looking for a home – the home that is the Irish nation – but in all manner of ways it eludes them. On the other side the home, the house of Ulster, seems always under attack, both from within and without, the Britishness of its inhabitants questioned – after all, they are not part of Britain, but of an unstable United Kingdom.

In Derry itself, there is a peculiar kind of isolation that the Catholics of the city often experience. In Derry people feel not 'in-between' but 'out-between', separate and apart from London, Belfast (especially) and Dublin, which have not listened to them, even though here they are not a minority.[41] I get a sense of the intimacy of what went on in the North when Eamonn Deane, brother of Seamus, tells me that he was taught by Seamus Heaney, and how Martin McGuinness lived not far away in the Bogside, and was taught at one time by Eamonn's brother Seamus.[42] After the Education Act of 1947, the children of the poor (the Deanes' father was a labourer, like mine), if they passed the examination at eleven years of age, had a chance of a good education – a good but a brutal one, for Eamonn tells me that Irishness was among the things beaten into them – the teachers, half of them priests, many of them southerners, concerned that their charges were not yet quite fully green.[43]

Around from Castle Gate to Shipquay Gate, there are within the walls the premises of the new city of heritage, tourism and culture – buildings that have been restored to a state not seen for many decades. Close to these, and announced by facsimile Irish Gaelic lettering, is the 'Craft Village'. It appeared to be almost empty as I passed on a summer's day. There is a sign offering free coffee as an inducement to come in. The Walled City Partnership describes it as 'the classic Craft Village. Dickensian in appearance and delightful in layout'. And grandest of all is the Guildhall outside the walls, which is where such tourists as there are wander. When I visited there was an exhibition called 'The Way They Were'. In this one might 'try on the clothes of a planter or an Irish person [*sic*] for size'.

Just as there is a Free Derry Museum (outside the walls), so too is there now a Siege Museum, the latter established in a new building beside the old headquarters of the Apprentice Boys (within the walls, near Butcher Gate). Both museums have an online presence, and parties of schoolchildren visit them both, one after the other, sharing 'heritages'. Both are funded by the EU's Peace I-IV initiative; but for these people, after Brexit, Europe is no more, and an uncertain future awaits.

PART III
NORTH

9

Industrial Jerusalem

... the cotton clouds, those white ones into which without a word the breath of legions of human beings had been absorbed.

W. G. Sebald

On his arrival in the city of Manchester in 1966, W. G. Sebald looked out to the west across a demolished Hulme, itself an industrial district that was a *locus classicus* of Engels's epic description of the world's first industrial working class.[1] In his novel *The Emigrants* (1996) he wrote: 'Views opened up across a wasteland towards the still immensely impressive agglomeration of gigantic Victorian office blocks and warehouses, about a kilometre distant, that had once been the hub of one of the nineteenth-century's miracle cities but, as I was soon to find out, was now almost hollow to the core.'[2] He wrote further, 'I never cease to be amazed by the completeness with which anthracite-coloured Manchester, the city from which industrialisation had spread across the entire world, displayed the clearly chronic process of its impoverishment and degradation to anyone who cared to see'.[3] He returned in 1989 and reported that nothing had changed. The buildings that were put up to stave off decline were now themselves in the grip of decay, and the so-called development zones already semi-abandoned.

Sebald came to Manchester and left; I came in 1979 and stayed. I worked in the same institution as him, doing similar work for almost three decades, sitting in the same university library, reading in its basement as he did, where he tells us he laboured over Paracelsus in the evenings (an activity surely conducive to melancholia?). I came to the city in a sense to leave it, for no one lived in the dead inner city then, and being from the inner heart of London I scorned the suburbs, so that a village some distance to the east on the Derbyshire border, at the entrance to the Peak District, became my home for what has become almost four decades.

In *The Emigrants*, a German Jewish emigrant called Max Ferber comprehends the greatness of the city through an account of the Manchester Ship Canal. Ferber tells Sebald of how the canal was dug from the Mersey Estuary by a vast host of Irish navvies, who shifted some 60 million cubic metres of earth in the period of construction, and built the gigantic locks that made it possible to raise or lower ocean-going steamers up to 150 metres long by five or six metres. Some 17,000 people laboured on its construction – 'navvies', from 'navigational engineers', an eighteenth-century term that bears witness to the importance of canals in the early stages of the Industrial Revolution.

That name was applied successively to the men who built the railways and the roads, eventually the motorways. Irishmen, too, many of these, like my father, and perhaps Carson's Horse Boyle, too – though he, having emigrated to Manchester for a while, had, we know for certain, 'Something to do with scrap – redundant mill machinery'. Many of the nineteenth-century Irish immigrants and those who came after them merged into the surrounding English soundlessly, like the ghostly ships that appeared on the Ship Canal on winter evenings to Sebald, vanishing into the white air around them, a sight he thought 'an incomprehensible spectacle'. The ships left, but not the people. In this city today, vast numbers bear an Irish name, and have an Irish ancestor, but have only the scantest knowledge, if any at all, of who has gone before them and the places their ancestors came from. Still, for others the generational merger was troubled and never complete, and the constant to-ing and fro-ing across the nearby sea presents a different picture to Irish-America – the hyphenation signifying the bonds of the Religion of America.

The Ship Canal ended in the largest inland port on earth, where 'the loading and unloading never stopped'. Manchester was then, Ferber says, the true industrial Jerusalem.[4] The canal carried its greatest volume of traffic around 1930; by the late 1950s, less than a generation later, it was abandoned. The Trafford Park estate, which grew up around the canal, was the world's first planned 'industrial estate', and for a long time the largest – at its peak in the war years employing over 75,000 people. Industrial Jerusalem industrialized destruction as well as creation, war as well as peace. Many of this vast number worked on the construction of engines for the four-engined Lancaster heavy bomber: the Ford Motor Company employed 17,316 workers in its purpose-built factory, producing under licence 34,000 Rolls-Royce aircraft engines by the war's end, most for the Lancaster, others for its developmental predecessor in slaughter, the Avro Manchester. Trafford Park itself followed the canal into disastrous decline in the 1970s and '80s.

The vast demolished areas that Sebald encountered when he arrived were 'like a glacis around the heart of the city'. There, it was only and always children that one encountered – 'restless shadowy figures', he calls them. In areas like Hulme, 'all that was left to recall the lives of thousands of people was the gridlike layout of the streets'. It is in a similarly silent memorial that he writes of 'the cotton clouds, those white ones into which / without a word the breath of legions of human beings had been absorbed'.[5]

I had first come to the city in 1971, two years after Sebald, as a young historical researcher, and I became a witness to the last days of the great industrial civilization. Like Sebald, I walked the dead heart where no one lived, and around it the 'glacis', the desolation in truth stretching further than this alone, out to the surrounding cotton towns of the east and north, themselves in decay. I had seen decay in London. I lived in the desolation of a razed Notting Dale in the late 1960s, but it did not compare to this vast clearance of souls, and of the houses in which they had once lived. All that was visible in the rotten mouth of the Manchester glacis were the public houses, left alone on the main roads out of the city like half-decayed stumps of teeth, places returned to from afar year after year by the expelled, the cleared out.

On the Ashton New Road in 1971, with the destruction of the Second World War still in my mind, I became aware that, however bright the future was painted for the young, my country had arrived at a new kind of destruction. I see now the kinship of these two great gatherings of rubble, the vast German *Trummerbergen* and these unnamed ones – smaller, more dispersed, the destruction erased for a moment by the stretches of remaining buildings. Time thickens, takes on flesh along these roads, as in the German cities, for again the rubble borders the street, but here it is in piles, chaotic, as if the line between past and future is itself ragged, outcomes oddly enough more uncertain. In rubble the history of peace as well as war is written.

The great clearances, Manchester, 1960s.

Mary Evans Picture Library/Shirley Baker

The photograph of Manchester is by Shirley Baker – a street photographer, like Roger Mayne, though much less known than him until recently, no doubt because she was a woman. In the background is a new tower building of the University of Manchester Hospital, and to the left of it the massive bulk of the Catholic Church of the Holy Name, built in 1871 to accommodate the armies of poor Irish immigrants still arriving. Sebald may have seen the city much as it looks here – he worked across the road from the Holy Name, as I did. The transformation even by the time I arrived in 1979 was enormous; today it is staggering. The university is a vast corporation, covering everything around.

The old houses that had been destroyed were reclaimable, many of them anyway, but they were nonetheless replaced by the new: boxes, towers, a botched modernism. Many disliked the new estates and found them unwelcoming; the housing blocks were set far beyond anything they knew, and were shoddy, decaying for lack of proper maintenance.[6] To others they were a blessed release.

The districts of Gorton and Openshaw lie to the east of the city centre, from which they are but two or three miles distant. Both were once at the centre of perhaps the most heavily concentrated industrial district in the world, at a time when Britain had the largest industrial proletariat on the globe. It was from areas such as these, from the seemingly endless rows of terraced houses that surrounded the great industrial works, that those rehoused in the post-war clearances came. Many stayed more or less put, however, rehoused as they were in the same places. The railways and the arterial roads to the eastern cotton towns cut through Gorton and Openshaw, including the Hyde Road, or A57 – the road I drive to the city from my home thirteen miles east. I have used this road for forty years now – either that or taken the train which travels much the same route.

Caught between the roads and railway lines were several major industrial enterprises of the age. There was the

Whitworth engineering factory, one of the greatest of the period, and beside it to the east the great railway yards of the Manchester, Sheffield and Lincolnshire Railway, which later became the Great Central Railway, terminating at London's Marylebone Station, close to where I was born. To the east of Whitworth was the Crossley Gas and Engine Works.

The industrially renowned and locally notorious Clayton Aniline Dye Company lay just north of these – notorious because of the high incidence of urinary tract tumours in such factories. Medical experts tell us: 'On hot days, when there is much evaporation of nitro-benzol, aniline etc., new workmen are often affected by such urgency of micturition that urine passes involuntarily into their clothes.'[7]

Many of these firms would go through changes of name and ownership (Clayton to CIBA-GIGY, for instance), but nonetheless lasted a century or more as continually operating entities in these locations. An industrial canal lies to the north of the railway and the Ashton and Hyde roads, canals reminding us of an industrial period before that of the engineering works in its prime, as engineering was from the late nineteenth century. Only a little to the north again were the giant engineering works of Mather and Platt. In 1943 L. S. Lowry, the genius of kitsch, painted factory workers arriving at the Mather & Platt Works in *Going to Work*. Lowry, a totem of the north, is himself another memorial to the industrial past, like the massive factories he painted. He retired to the Elms in Mottram-in-Longdendale – a house, one mile from mine, a house that he is said to have hated. This 'retirement' lasted thirty years.

Whitworth devised the standard screw-thread system, the first of its kind in the world, as well as the Whitworth rifle, which during the American Civil War was employed to kill officers of the opposing sides at a range of 800 yards – an enormous leap forward in the history of the weapon, effectively creating the first sniper rifle. Whitworth helped pioneer the machine tool, a device for handling or machining metal or other rigid materials, a development as important as any other of the great inventions of the industrial age. 'What Manchester thought today, the world thought tomorrow,' went the self-satisfied saying. The factory also produced armour plate, gun housings, cars and trucks, and eventually even aircraft. Crossley's became a leading vehicle and engine maker. Henry Ford visited the factory at the turn of the century: it is said that the invention of the assembly line owes much to Crossley's innovations. The list of great firms goes on and on. This industrial inheritance was squandered by Britain in the second half of the twentieth century, a tale witheringly told by James Hamilton-Paterson in *What We Have Lost: The Dismantling of Great Britain.*

The Great Central works are immediately north of Beyer and Peacock's once world-renowned locomotive factory. The locomotive works were always known locally as Gorton Foundry, just as the railway works are known still as Gorton Tank. At their peak, between the world wars, the two concerns employed about 5,000 people between them. The two big works are separated by the railway line I take to the city. Utterly oblivious to what lies on either side of them, thousands upon thousands of rail passengers have over recent decades looked out unknowingly at the desolation on either side of them – desolation relieved only by the majesty of what remains of Gorton Foundry, the vast, now empty and near-derelict, boiler and tender shop building. My own A57 lies only a little to the south of the foundry.

On the Ordnance Survey maps of the area everything is reduced to the line – the railway tracks, the streets, the houses seem to form ordered boxes and an ordered world. The world is not like this, not straight; but we would be hard put to understand it now, let alone control it, without these images. Reason and power are given form in these lines; these are originally military maps, after all. I have looked at such lines for a good part of my professional life as a historian, just as, when a child, I gazed at them, fascinated by all maps, colouring the sea borders in blue in my geography book. Those coastlines are not straight, of course, but are still full of the enchantment of the line – something at once abstract and concrete.

Paradoxically, the past, as if metamorphosing the straight line, seems now for me to live again in these maps. They take on magical qualities, the past suddenly appearing before the eyes in an act of legerdemain. It is as if the magic of the straight line gives the past a kind of solidity, a promise of endurance; what was hidden is now seen, seen from above, seen into, as if the view from above was our magic eye with which to see the mystery of what is within, of what once was. This is especially so on the larger-scale maps and plans, which are astonishing. The past thus seems to endure, but we know that solidity and illusion are one, and that the sense of something having endured lies as if in an embrace of the knowledge that everything has changed. The past speaks again as a kind of absence: we seem to see what was there only by its vanishing.

Around the big lines and blocks of the factories congregate the lesser ones of the houses. Just below the works of Beyer and Peacock, squashed between the arterial Ashton and Hyde roads (the latter now called the A57), going east out of the city, is a tiny universe of what were once familiar streets making up another tiny universe, just like my London one. The map lines delineate the extraordinary territorial rootedness that once marked this lost industrial world of the North. The past speaks again as an absence, this time through the street names as well as the lines: Isca Street, Townley Street, Cyclone Street, Siam Street, Bingley Street, Maripuris Street, all in a row, north to south. To the east, Wycliffe, Tyndal, Coverdale, Bunyan, Wesley, Whitfield; and a little further away, Cowper, Milton, Shakespeare, Johnson, on and on, seemingly endless, each a world. Many in these streets would have worked in the foundry and the Tank. All the place names, all the histories: as

Ciaran Carson writes of Belfast, 'At times it seems every inch of Belfast has been written on, erased and written on again … most of all, "Remember me, I was here."'[8]

The number of human beings who passed their lives working in these factories can only be guessed at – the number of families, too – for employment ran down through generations in the same place. But now, everything is forgotten. The walls of Gorton Foundry talk, and they write Britain's lost industrial past – for lost it is, not only in time and economics, but in memory, too. All this is what 'heritage' surely is, but the foundry and the Tank are known to few beyond the museum curator, the specialist historian, and the zealots of railway history for whom the engine means more than the people who made it – and of course the very old of the locality, and those of their children who listen.

Beyer and Peacock's was founded in 1854. Almost the whole world was locomotivized from this spot, Gorton Foundry. The company built a total of nearly 8,000 railway locomotives over its lifetime. Employment peaked when the enormous Beyer-Garratt large-gauge locomotives were being made. Eventually,

Mechanical Landscapes

The walls of Bayer and Peacock today. Small trees and plants now grow out of the walls.

almost 1,700 of these Garratts were run by eighty-six railway companies in forty-eight countries. Beyer Peacock & Co.'s *A quarterly review* for April 1929 tells us that, at the time, the company had locomotive representatives in countries from Argentina to Siam, and machine and tool representatives in India, the Malay States, Belgium, Siberia, Ireland, Northern Manchuria, among many others.[9]

The Gorton plant declined from 1958, and by 1966 all production had ceased, with devastating consequences for the community. The thirty acres of 'Gorton Tank', across the railway lines, were rendered a wasteland after an equally catastrophic failure in 1968. Even in the 1960s, the 1,700 or so who still worked in the Tank supported nine public houses in one nearby street.

In the Museum of Science and Industry in Manchester, the catalogue entry for Beyer and Peacock reads as follows: 'Objects 27,815; Documents 4,732; People 1,916'; and for the Great Central Railway: 'Objects 18,515; Documents 2,907; People 1,048'. I explore the headings under 'People', and the references are to business transactions, to the higher reaches of the organizations, those in white collars upstairs in offices, and not to the blue-collar generations who laboured below. The archive is phenomenal, but it is a business and technical one; the man who made it, and who also made the museum itself, a remarkable accomplishment, is a historian of technology of the old school, one interested in how things, and not men, work. For me, in part a social historian of objects, it would take a long time to make these objects speak, sing, write themselves, and I do not have time now as I grow old.

Nonetheless, a few voices remain. I forage for these, literal voices now, in the large sound archives of Manchester Central Library and the Manchester Museum of Science and Industry. Among all their holdings, I found only a few voices out of the tens of thousands who worked at Beyer and Peacock's (the rate of return is even less with the other enterprises around).[10]

The interviews were mostly recorded in 2007. The respondents were born between 1928 and 1938. They would have worked there from the 1940s to the 1960s. A number of the respondents had been apprenticed – so-called journeymen. But the labour pool of skilled men in the city was large, and 'skill' is a relative term when applied to practice in a number of the shops within the factory. Organization and precariousness went hand in hand.

These men had pride in the machines they worked and knew them intimately, as the firm sometimes made its own machines, a number of which were said to be in use for 100 years, since 'things worked for ever'. Parts might need replacing, but it was people then, not machines, who had built-in obsolescence. These workers had been mostly skilled men, almost universally union members, and they had some control over their lives this way; but at the same time a number of them had become stuck for years, because promotion possibilities were limited. One man remarks almost casually that, for eleven years, 'I went slotting' – in fact a relatively routine job making coupling rods, semi-skilled at best.

It should be remembered that these were the days of union power, union numbers swelling in the inter-war years and then massively boosted in the Second World War, especially those of the giant Amalgamated Engineering Union, which at one time boasted almost half a million members. But it was not always thus, and the employers' faith in the twin gods of Political Economy and Divine Providence was firm. One man in the works talks of how, if your union subs were not paid up, you were sent home that afternoon, remarkable as this now seems. The green union card gave you entry into a particular works, and the black card was the key that opened all the city's engineering works.

Men sheltered in the community of the individual shop, although these shops might themselves be large, sheltered against what they perceived to be the vastness of the enterprise, the size of which in several cases they exaggerate, counting 5,000 workers whereas half that number were employed. Their lives were hard; they had to put up with noise – the scream of the turning machine, turning five-inch-diameter steel, or the relentless thumping of the steam hammers. James Hicklin only remembered three men in all his time at the works who made it to the retirement age of sixty-five. He was deeply rueful at the adage that hard work never killed anyone. They had been destined for this life, one man describing how in his youth school trips were organized to all the leading manufacturers in the city.

Women were the custodians of order, teaching the boys who would grow up to be men. Dorothy Lord, born 1933, worked in the office of Beyer and Peacock's until 1963, having joined in 1947. She remembered how everybody in the works was 'stunned' when it closed in 1966, and how the local shop-keepers were decimated, the pubs especially. Like so many, her father and grandfather worked in the foundry. She worked in the office as a clerk, and was impressed by the order she saw all around her, in the offices and in the various shops that made up the Foundry. She was insistent on her respectability: her home was spotless, she said, with the piano on display. She talks of the churches and chapels as great meeting places, and says she attended worship from time to time.

She values obedience and order above all. They were a result of a harsh upbringing, she says, as her father died young and they were poor – a big family in the two-up two-down houses of Gorton and Openshaw. School, too, was a matter of discipline and order: learning to speak when spoken to in tightly serried rows where total silence obtained. Home life was spartan and disciplined, and she was a great respecter of law and order, she says. Her husband Fred was an engineering turner, born locally in Openshaw. He remembered long walks each day to find work when things were bad – as far as Bolton, ten miles and more away. Order and disorder went hand in hand too. So did independence and dependence; as in Derry, there was often the feeling, despite the union organization, that industrialists were benefactors, bringing jobs to the neighbourhood.

The history of these people is partly mine. My father-in-law, Hugh Malone, born in Louth village in 1920, was a blacksmith. After working first in his own County Down forge, tending to the needs of countrymen, he emigrated to England in the late 1940s and worked for decades as an industrial blacksmith in Eastleigh Railway Carriage Works, just outside Southampton. In Ireland the life was hard, with only the Protestant farmers paying him in cash, the Catholic ones in chickens. Two sons of four served apprenticeships in Eastleigh.

Spaces of shelter are small as well as large, boxes within boxes. My wife keeps a box of what is left of her father's work life, mostly unopened so that his smell may not be dissipated. It is the smell of the person and of the works combined. The box

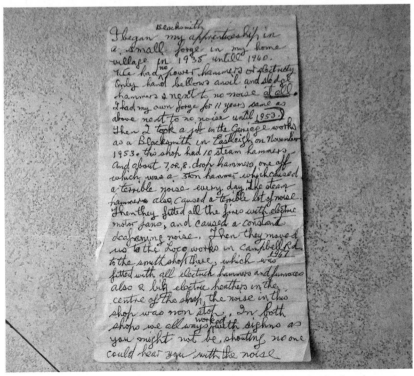

A document. Work note of Hugh Malone, Eastleigh Carriage Works, Southampton.

is small, the objects left few – Hugh's British Rail notebook as a checker of parts made in the shop for 1976–77; his union card for 1985–86. There is a larger book of drawings of parts he had made and took pride in – especially the tools which, proud of the place he had left behind, he always stamped with a tiny shamrock. Like many of the men of Beyer and Peacock's and Gorton Tank beside it, Hugh's lungs were ruined, and he died too young, of emphysema, a disease of the lungs.

Reproduced above is an image of one of the contents of my wife's box. It details noise, not fumes, and is about the lack of power-hammers in Hugh's shop – the ten steam hammers and the eight drop hammers in his works causing 'a terrible noise' every day. Alongside this is 'a constant deafening noise' from the electric motor fans. He is moved to the Loco shop and it is worse, so that everyone had to communicate in signs, year in, year out. The letter was written to his employer in application for compensation for his work-created deafness. It opens by mentioning how he was apprenticed in a forge in his home village in Ireland, and how there was 'next to no noise'. Reproduced below is a picture Hugh managed to take of himself working at the Eastleigh Works (how few images there are in the archives of people actually working since the Industrial Revolution!).

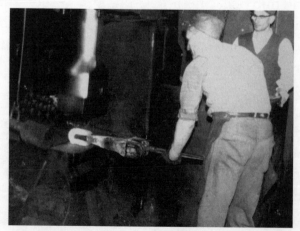

Hugh Malone, Eastleigh Carriage Works, Southampton.

The place from which I make my journeys into the city past Gorton Tank and Gorton Foundry is called Broadbottom – a name comically northern to southern ears, and to mine when I arrived after tasting the awfulness of inner-city estate living in London in the sixties and seventies. Broadbottom is a place full of Sidebottoms, Shufflebottoms and Heginbottom's, names that are to be found on the village war memorial. The place has a street called Summerbottom. A 'bottom' is a valley floor. These local families had lived in the village for several genera- tions, people who had laboured in the local cotton mills, at one time almost 2,500 of them alone in one vast mill in the village centre, a reality now almost impossible to comprehend.

In 1979, when I first arrived, understanding this old reality was a little easier than now, for a few mills still struggled on and there were many who knew mill days first-hand. I had come to the North having written a history of the cotton factory districts in the nineteenth century, but I found that I had come to live among people still not culturally distant from their own past. Before the final and then still pending triumph of the supermarket and the motor car, this place of about 2,500 souls in 1979 had five pubs (including the Conservative Club, an ecumenical drinking den), several shops, and a post office. Only forty years before, in 1939, a list of business premises enumerates thirty-six enterprises, mostly food shops, including four 'chip shops'; several butchers, including a 'tripe shop'; the shop of a hawker of lamp oil; an enormous co-op, in which one might get a suit made to measure; and a bank – as well as the five pubs of 1979 (there is but one in 2020).

There was in 1979 a rawness about the place; as cotton had declined, so had the village. It was itself a little indus- trial Jerusalem fallen upon hard times, though subsequently it has prospered, unlike the 'metropolitan borough' it is part of, Tameside. I belonged to the first generation of 'middle-class' incomers, people who mostly worked in the city, many the chil- dren of working-class parents escaping the restrictions of those parents' lives. Some were pushed out, in the great clearances of inner-city demolition, from east Manchester, or places like the wasteland of Hulme, on the west side – getting out, like me, through the escape hatch of education.

What was once named the Manchester, Sheffield and Lincoln-shire Railway (formed 1847), runs through the village, 400 yards from my door. Five miles from the home where I now write this, the line goes over the Woodhead Pass, which leads across the Pennines to Sheffield from Manchester. There, earlier Irish arrivals than Hugh Malone had helped to build the Woodhead Tunnel through the hills – railway men of another sort, navvies again.[11] Built by the labour of some 1,500 men, at peak times it was for a short while the longest rail tunnel in the world. In fact there are three tunnels, the first completed, after eight years of digging, in 1845, the second in 1853, and the third in 1953. There is a small chapel near the top of the pass, St James's. This is a wild place, but in daytime full of the sound of motor traffic as it goes by unheeding below, the occupants unaware that just above them lie buried many of the navvies who died building the first two tunnels. Around two-dozen died during construction of the tunnels, and two-dozen more from a cholera outbreak that struck the work camp in 1849. Many of the workers were Irish, just like the builders of the ship canal later. In Woodhead the navvies, like my father, lived more or less on as well as by the job, and so were buried here, where they fell.

The field behind the church is bare. It is said Irish Catholic workers, and some of the family members who often accom-panied the navvies, are buried there. It has the uneven, broken ground one might expect from a huddle of unmarked graves, like the unbaptized children's graveyards in Ireland. Catholics were not allowed to be buried in Anglican churchyards, and so they lie here, in 'unconsecrated ground'.[12] But there are only locally named headstones here, and it is likely that as many of the unmarked dead are English as Irish, the two now as one in death.

By the mid 1850s the twin tunnels were facilitating the passage of an astonishing 250 trains a day each way below these graveyards. The line is disused now, but nearby, below ground, are the great reservoirs that still serve the city, and below these another vast engineering miracle of industrial Jerusalem matching that above: the great network of giant tunnels that takes water to the city. Many died in their making, too. The Invisible Revolution – the bodies and the tunnels in the ground.

The road is the same as the railway, another line on the map. It is with amazement that I now compute that I have driven the A57, the Hyde Road, in and out of the city perhaps 4,000 times each way. As a child my habituation to the city was through walking, as an adult through the car. The difference is epochal: the street, Southam Street or Ashmore Road, is where all one's senses were alert, where one constantly 'took in' what was around in such a way that it has never quite left. Roads are now so often not for walking but for driving, and for *keeping*, cars, so that one no longer sees the street in its intended form. For me, therefore, London when I visit is always occluded, the real city not there. Millions now grow up never seeing this real city. I remember more of the 2,000 walks of Southam Street than of the 8,000 drives on the A57. It is on this driven road, the banal A57, that I have dreamed much of my life – the driving daydream, the semi-automatic mind at work in the automated reverie. In the car one is enclosed, 'safe'. Alone, if not lonely.

But is this not really a 'non-place' the likes of which the French anthropologist Marc Augé writes about – one of the places of transience now so common, like motorways, corporate hotel rooms, and airports, through which, in these times, we seem always on the move?[13] Such places are also the sites of what Ágnes Heller calls 'the absolute present' – a present in which many now live, so that it is in a time and not a place where people feel 'at home'.[14] This time is shared by all the non-places we are in, so that we are divorced from both real pasts and real places. The 'non-place' may be opposed to the 'anthropological place', where we interact with people and things, as in my walk to school.

The railway journey led to a new envisioning of the world, something that has been called 'panoramic perception'.[15] The world seemed framed through the window as a constantly changing 'picture', something nineteenth-century travellers marvelled at but which we now take for granted. From the car, the world outside is different, at least in city driving – fleeting and fugitive. One's eyes move up and down the road constantly, but are also drawn from side to side, and one is aware and unaware simultaneously, so that one seems to take in the surrounding world in a disjointed and interrupted way, time itself being disjointed and interrupted. The flow of time between past, present and future is constantly broken up and reconnected in strange ways. This is 'drive time', at once a tyranny and a time of reverie. It becomes possible to appreciate the vast number of times, present and past, that one is passing through, but only fleetingly, dimly, because you are past before you can be present, whereas in walking things are slower and more enduring.

Inner-city east Manchester has remained a desolate place since the clearances, and the purpose of this road is essentially to get me as fast as possible between two places – home for 'tea', as northerners of all stripes say. In this road, as well as in its rail lines and canals, the history of industrial Jerusalem is written – the old history and the new: the 'regeneration' of this area has been called the greatest post-industrial reconstruction seen in Europe.[16] Like the Manchester bourgeoisie that Engels described in his 1844 book, people travel in and out of the city oblivious to what is on either side of them, as if in a tunnel. Nothing changes as regards not looking: 'The town itself is peculiarly built, so that a person may live in it for years, and go in and out daily without coming into contact with a working-people's quarter or even with workers'.[17]

The A57 begins to talk, more and more volubly. The road,

like Carson's river Farset that runs through Belfast, 'remembers spindles, arms, the songs of mill girls. It remembers nothing: no one steps in the same river twice.' The road speaks about the people who made industrial Jerusalem. Gorton Foundry's originator, Richard Peacock (1820–89), designed every inch of the first factory himself. He is buried in the yard of the church that he built on the road, Brookfield Unitarian Church. Its large steeple is visible all around. Peacock lies with other family members in the Peacock Mausoleum, the graveyard and the tomb now vandalized. The large Sunday School to one side is now a residential home. The church steeple contains a peal of eight bells, all named after members of the Peacock family. I have never heard these bells rung. The Unitarians were the most progressive of all religious denominations in his day, especially in this city, though Peacock was a Home Ruler.

The road talks loudly – but no one listens, and the cars go by. Charles Frederick Bayer, the other founder of the firm, was a Jew, the son of a poor handloom weaver from Plauen in Saxony. Plauen was also a considerable textile centre, and later, in the twentieth century, the first town outside Bavaria to host a chapter of the Nazi party. When he moved to Manchester, Beyer became a dutiful Anglican, another patron of local churches. In Sebald's *The Emigrants*, Ferber considers nineteenth-century Manchester to have had the greatest German Jewish influence of any European city outside the Jewish homelands. He says of the city that he has come home, the city reminding him of everything he was trying to forget; home amidst the black facades 'to serve under the chimney'.[18] He seldom leaves; does not want to, does not like moving. Lodz – the Polish Manchester, as it was called – looms over the close of Ferber's story, the path leading back, and so too coming from, this other city, the fates of its then vast industry and vast Jewish ghetto and that of Manchester entwined.

Men like Beyer and Peacock were part of a small group who can be said almost literally to have made the Industrial

Revolution. They pioneered the machines that made it possible, so that world history now winds itself in and around the line of the road. Thomas Telford, Richard Roberts, Thomas Maudesley, Beyer and Peacock – these men, in London and Manchester, my two cities, lived, worked, visited together, along this road. So did Friedrich Engels and Karl Marx. The now-anonymous A57 was then the pivot of the whole world to be. The 1861 census states that Beyer lived at 9 Hyde Road, age forty-seven, an 'engineer employing 800 men', born in Saxony. In the house beside him lived Charles Sacré, a Frenchman aged twenty-nine, his chief engineer. Sacré shot himself after the Penistone railway accident of 1865, in which nineteen died. By 1871 Beyer had moved to Stanley Grove, not far from here. The road runs alongside Belle Vue Gardens, then already on the way to becoming the supreme pleasure ground of the northern English working classes. It fronts onto the Hyde Road, and is now a no-man's-land of aborted hopes for rejuvenation.

At its height, Belle Vue covered almost 200 acres and had 2 million visitors a year. The Rolling Stones, Jimi Hendrix and the Beatles played there. Beyer's neighbour, at 5 Stanley Grove, then nineteen years old, was Arthur Schuster, from Frankfurt, later the first Beyer Professor of Applied Mathematics at the University of Manchester. Beyer was, and remains, the most important of all that institution's patrons. Another neighbour was Salomon L. Behrens, aged eighty-three, a Jew, the founder of S. Behrens & Co. bankers, which was heavily involved in the textile industry in both Manchester and Saxony. Behrens introduced Beyer to Richard Roberts in 1834.

Friedrich Engels, cotton factory owner and revolutionist, lived parts of his peripatetic Manchester career close by, rather secretly it would seem, trying to avoid the attention of the Prussian police and what he called 'the philistines'. He also lived on the site of my own university, reached along this road as Gorton gives way to Ardwick, and then south to Chorlton-on-Medlock, where I and Sebald laboured. Mary Burns and her sister Lydia (known as Lizzy) were the daughters of Michael Burns and Mary Conroy, Irish immigrants who lived first in the squalor of central Manchester. Engels lodged with them in different premises. Mary, who became his common-law wife, died in January 1863 at 252 Hyde Road, in Ardwick. Frederick and Lizzy left Manchester for London in September 1870. She is buried in Kensal Green in London, somewhere beside Kitty and Johnny, my parents. She and Friedrich had married just before her death.

Almost across the road from No. 252, the Hyde Road is crossed by a railway bridge that has conveyed generations to and from the city to London. On 18 September 1867, just out of Ardwick, a police van was ambushed under this bridge. It was on its way to the giant and forbidding Belle Vue Gaol, now itself completely obliterated by time. Inside the van were Fenian prisoners. A group of thirty to forty Fenians attacked the horse-drawn van. In the attempt to blow off the lock, Police Sergeant Charles Brett, travelling inside with the keys, was shot and killed. The two prisoners inside escaped: they were Colonel Thomas J. Kelly and Captain Timothy Deasy. They had attained their ranks in the Union Army during the American Civil War, when they had fought against the Southern states whence came the cotton that made Manchester the industrial Jerusalem. However, another five men were arrested and tried for the attack. Three were hanged, death then being the only penalty for murder – a crime then construed more broadly than it is today.

William Philip Allen, Michael Larkin and Michael O'Brien, all members of the Irish Republican Brotherhood, were hanged on 23 November 1867 outside Salford Gaol. In one of the last public executions in Britain, they met their end on a wooden edifice constructed on the prison walls, their agonies on view before a crowd of 10,000, almost all English; the Irish had stayed away. Over 2,500 police were deployed in and around the prison.

The public executioner, William Calcraft – whose body count was said to be in excess of 450 – reportedly nervous of executing Fenians, bungled the job, just as his successor in the post, William Marwood, would do with Myles Joyce only fifteen years later. Calcraft had to rush below the gibbet and pull the legs of the prisoners, in effect strangling them by main force – although strangled is what they would have been anyway in the old 'short drop' method of death. Marwood, a technician in his task, developed the 'long drop' technique of hanging, which was supposed to break the prisoner's neck instantly, resulting in death by asphyxiation while they were unconscious. As we know from the case of poor Myles, this new technology had its glitches.

The day after the executions, Engels wrote to Marx: 'So yesterday morning the Tories, by the hand of Mr Calcraft, accomplished the final act of separation between England and Ireland. The only thing that the Fenians still lacked were martyrs.' Their deaths, he continued, 'will now be sung to every Irish babe in the cradle in Ireland, England and America'. And so here the road sings: 'God save Ireland', the de facto national anthem of Ireland for the next half-century. One of the verses is as follows:

Climbed they up the rugged stair, rang their voices out in prayer,
Then with England's fatal cord around them cast,
Close beside the gallows tree kissed like brothers lovingly,
True to home and faith and freedom to the last.

The song was set to 'Tramp, Tramp, Tramp, the Boys are Marching' – a song intended to give courage to Union soldiers captured and imprisoned in the Land of Cotton.[19]

I had travelled thousands of times, in my ignorance, under as well as along the reinforced concrete bridge that has now replaced the old railway arch – the bridge carrying the West Coast Main Line, the busiest long-distance main line in Britain.

There is a plaque there now, added recently, but the driver is hard put to see it, small and tucked away by the side of the bridge as it is, and not many walk this road made for cars.

The road talks on, but then the voices begin to stutter, and then speech starts to die as the end of industrial Jerusalem comes. The fall of industrial Jerusalem has been long-drawn-out, but from the 1960s through the 1970s the descent reached such a speed that the end came at last, the road becoming ever more mute. We have a privileged way of witnessing this final fall. Between 1950 and 1972, the Manchester Amateur Photographic Society, aware of what was coming, carried out an almost complete street-by-street survey of the city, showing its streets before, during and after the great clearances. There are, astonishingly, something like 800 images of the Hyde Road and adjacent streets alone (all the city is covered, in thousands upon thousands of images, available publicly online). These photographs are unusual – a document in the strict sense, the etymology of the word telling us of its Latin root, *documentum*, 'lesson, proof'. A 'proof' of what is now lost to vision, and,

The fall begins, getting ready for it, back street, unnamed, Gorton, 1965.

Manchester City Archives, DPA

Falling, breath expiring, falling, 1972.

Manchester City Archives, DPA

with the death of the occupants, lost to re-vision in memory: however, it signifies something that decidedly once was there and lends the force of this facticity to the cry of 'I was here.'

The first image of the unnamed backstreet conveys the pathos of old shop products, Dura-glit, Senior Service Tipped, Jubbly (nice frozen), Nulon; the pathos of the shop window, nothing in it much – the few cars, the dirty gutters: the gutter and rubble, the marginal gutter, the liminal space of transition. If the gutters are uncleaned, times will be bad. In the second image from 1965, the seedy premises of Slack and Cox, the Eue de Salz company, the makers of Vitonica: their bottles are collectors' items now. There is one in London's Science Museum. But the glory days of Vitonica are gone forever.

10

After the Fall

Place management is the process of making places better ...
the underlying common factor is usually a desire to maximise
the effectiveness of a location for its users, whether they are
residents, shoppers, tourists, investors, property developers or
business owners.

'Place Management', *Wikipedia*

Gorton, notorious as one of Britain's forgotten places, offers
an image of the very essence of what is called 'post-industrial
blight', in an unconscious echo of *Am an Drochshaoil*, 'the
time of the bad life', the Great Famine. Those fleeing from the
Great Famine in fact travelled its road, my A57, and lived on or
beside it, and some of their descendants still do. Like my father,
these people journeyed from blight to blight. The popular UK
television series *Shameless*, which depicts the life of the unrespectable, benighted, 'rough' inner-city English working class
was mainly filmed in West Gorton. The characters have Irish
names, but the names are all that remains of the Irishness.
The parade of shops used for filming was built on the site of
St Mark's Church, in Clowes Street, off the Hyde Road. This
church was the birthplace of Manchester City Football Club.
The first rector of the church was Arthur Connell – an avid, not
to say deranged, Orangeman.

In the Britain of 1951, in a total in-work population of some
22 million people, manufacturing was by far the biggest category, with almost 9 million people – not too far from half the
population. Mining, manufacturing and building accounted

between them for 11.1 million workers. Public service and professional occupations accounted for 3.3 million. On a generous estimate, of the total occupied population, only around 8 million people could not be considered 'working class', in the sense of not having a manual occupation. Thus, the manual working class constituted around 70 per cent of working people.[1]

Nationally the 'golden age' of manufacturing continued into the 1970s; but absolute numbers peaked in the 1960s, with the first portents of decline in the car industry and shipbuilding. Manchester itself, the place where it began, declined first and fast. From the 1960s, especially in the east, the fall was dizzying. The political story of 'national decline' is a complicated one, and decline was to some degree inevitable after other countries caught up after the war, and then surpassed Britain. A service economy painfully and only partially replaced a manufacturing one. In terms of national output and the proportion of the total labour force that manufacturing made up, the change was staggering. (National output is the total value of all goods and services produced in an economy.) In terms of labour alone, there was a fall from 35.1 per cent of employment in 1964 to 16.3 per cent in 1993, and then 9.5 per cent in 2007.[2]

Between 1954 and 1974, 90,000 houses were demolished in Manchester City and 71,000 new ones built – council boxes and towers. This was the city proper; the numbers are vastly higher when Greater Manchester is taken into account. The population of the city itself is only around half a million, and the giant, contiguous conurbation around it now 2.75 million. Manchester City Council is separate from the Salford Council's jurisdiction, and is part of Greater Manchester, but Salford is really the other part of the city's heart, just across a river that is little more than a brook. Its population is a quarter of a million. Between 1955 and 1965, more dwellings were demolished in Salford per capita than in any other city in Britain.[3] By the end of the 1970s, almost 50 per cent of Salford's homes had been

built since 1944. On the city's south side, the Hulme–Moss
Side area was one of the biggest rehousing schemes in Europe.

When Manchester's commercial centre was badly hit, many
firms relocated elsewhere.[4] The shoddy modernism of the
1970s city centre was the answer to 'Regeneration'. The vast
city-centre Arndale Shopping Centre was the symbol of this –
one of the largest in Europe. This was the Manchester Sebald
saw on his return at the end of that decade.[5]

The fall of Jerusalem was from the old life – that world
of order and control, disorder and chaos, independence and
dependence that is glimpsed in the Beyer and Peacock interviews. An ordered life was what came with the order of
industry, with fitting life around industry's routines, for industry was the source of life. The ordered life meant keeping one's
head above water given industry's ups and downs: it meant, in
fact, being industrious, like the bee that is the city's symbol. A
worker bee, however, lives only to work, dies young as a result,
and is infertile. For beneath the gaining of order, of self-control,
lay the ever-present danger of disorder and the reality of powerlessness and dependence, from which some sense of control
over life had to be wrested.

Respectability is the name so often given to that fragile possibility of control, and its price was often terrible. Of course,
respectability might not be attained at all, or might be rejected
in the first place, and the counterpart of the respectable was
the 'rough' working class, consigned there by recalcitrance, circumstance or social obloquy. One was the mirror of the other,
and together they made up a class system within the working
class that was just as strong as the wider class system itself.

Some key works by insiders to this culture – a culture similar
across all of Britain – profoundly illuminate it.[6] These include
the works of Robert Roberts, on the Salford he grew up in
above his parents' corner shop in the first quarter of the twentieth century; those of Richard Hoggart, born thirteen years
after Roberts in 1918, and raised in Leeds's Hunslet district,

which was similar to Gorton; and of Jeremy Seabrook, born into deprivation in shoe-making Northampton a generation later than the others, in 1939. These works have always spoken strongly to me. Roberts was an acute, unillusioned observer whose acuity was sharpened by the minimal distance he had from things, living above the corner shop. In 1957, Hoggart was already lamenting the loss of the world he had been raised in before the onslaught of what he called mass culture; he was a man who raised up to dignity the laws and codes of the culture he analyzed. Seabrook, meanwhile, caught the bleakness of lives given over to survival more than the others.

What I take from these three figures is a sense of a life obsessed with the sanctity of boundaries, and thus the preservation of order in the uncertain world of industrial capitalism. In Roberts there is the awareness of the class struggle as what he called 'a perpetual series of engagements in the battle of life itself', rather than the Marxian class struggle. In all three, there is nonetheless a recognition that a clear sense of 'Them' and 'Us' obtained; though alongside the solidarity of 'Us' ran profound social conservatism, even fatalism, as well as a sometimes crippling sense of self-limitation. You had to put up with things, life was hard, but you just got on with it, didn't rock the boat. The 'wall in the head' was high in this life – the one you had not the education, the courage, or the resources to look over, let alone surmount.[7]

Respectability was at once a ladder, a hierarchy, and a code – a code enshrining order and marking boundaries evident in the details of everyday life: you put your best foot forward in the house, for example, with its lace-curtained windows, its pristine and mostly unused front room, its unplayed piano, and its unused best china. There were codes for who should use the back door, who the front. There were the unceasing repetitions and rituals that made life manageable – those of the week, the day and the year; rituals, for example, like those being performed by the women in the following image, in an

Cleaning the front step, Openshaw, Manchester, 1950s.

Openshaw street in the 1950s, out in a row scrubbing the front step and then the pavement outside on 'washing day', after first cleaning the house.

There were codes for who you could interact with, and how, and who not: the rough, one's betters. Marginal and therefore threatening times and spaces were carefully patrolled – those to do with 'outsiders' as well as one's own rough. To do with the Irish as outsiders, and then the West Indians and Asians. In this culture of the boundary, drink, gambling and sex were potential sources of disorder and excess, and thus they needed to be highly regulated; there was a correct time for the spree or splurge. The homosexual presented particular problems – someone on the margin, not quite one thing or the other. Language echoed and reinforced the social milieu. The language of 'Us' was concrete, the language of 'Them' abstract: the one immediate, the other appraising, so that 'middle-class' speech conferred security upon the self. It distanced and classified, while the other code was immediate and personal.

On the one hand, there was the escalator life, on the other the carousel, as Raymond Williams put it. The wall in the head was built high, by both them *and* us. The rough were on their own carousel, refusing the disciplines of boundary and control:

their homes, the look of their children, how much the husband brought in and by what means – all spoke of the disorder. These are the people of Southam Street, of the poorest parts of Manchester, the people of *Shameless*, and of the unlicensed spree, the splurge at the wrong time.

Though this industrial world was markedly different to London, places like Gorton in 1950 nonetheless had much in common with the city I grew up in, and were if anything more prosperous. If the city is a body, the heart in the middle, then the arterial roads like the A57 and my Harrow Road are fed by the arterioles that issue out from the warren of streets on either side, which are themselves fed by the capillaries of every path and ginnel, all walked, all known, all written upon. Gone with the old streets is a way of life the streets themselves enabled – for instance, the significance of corners and intersections between streets for social and economic commerce, for seeing and being seen; the view across and along the street; the almost invariable siting of pubs and shops on corners. The utmost importance of the street pattern is evident, the underlying street structure the key to a sense of continuity; when this goes, memory is deeply afflicted – obliterated almost.

Glimpses of the lost world are to be found in local newspapers – the *Gorton Advertiser*, for instance, which by 1956 had already been going over 100 years. The intense localism is evident from even a glance. The whole community was concentrated in the newspaper's pages. The front page was full of personal ads, public announcements, deaths, church notices, situations vacant. On later pages, 'Heard in Audenshaw' and 'Gossip Grave and Gay', by 'Wayfarer of Gorton'. Victorian moralism was alive and well; and there was a 'Gems of Thought' column in the paper, passing on wisdom from those such as Seneca and Matthew Arnold – words to the wise.

Almost all the adverts were for local shops, many on the Hyde Road. This was a world of local clubs and associations, and these were covered in great detail. The British Legion was there, as well as Gorton Townswomen's Guild, workingmen's social clubs of all sorts, political clubs, works clubs and sports clubs. There was even an Ashton Methodist Football League (in which Anglican church teams played). The great summer communal-religious Whit Walks were still going strong, as were the century-old Sunday schools – powerful, but now largely assertions of local belonging. Going out rather than staying in still dominated.

As had been the case for a century, all of this life was psychogeographically centred on workplaces small and great. And people were buried around the factories, too – in Ardwick Cemetery, in Rusholme Road Cemetery, and others (in Kensal Green, factories abutted the Catholic cemetery). Ardwick Cemetery operated until 1950, by which time some 80,000 people had been buried within its grounds. The remains of the great scientist John Dalton and the Chartist leader Ernest Jones lie there; also those of Robert Thornton, who won the Victoria Cross at Delhi in 1857. But the graves are disregarded now, and the traffic roars past.

In 2006 Manchester City Council inaugurated a multimillion-pound redevelopment plan for the Gorton District Shopping Centre. The old market and retail areas were demolished, and a new market hall and Tesco Extra hypermarket added, followed by a Subway, a Coral betting shop, an Age UK, and eventually a KFC. In Britain this litany of premises is familiar. The last remnants of place were erased, and this became Anyplace, England.

In the map below the A57 is marked towards the bottom of the map, and runs south-west out of the city to Hattersley, Broadbottom and Tameside, ten or so miles east. The area mapped is around six miles from east to west. Gorton is at the bottom of the map, unmarked here, but West Gorton is marked. Bradford is more or less interchangeable with Beswick, as marked below (though not quite to the inhabitants of these once ultra-local communities). Just north of the black dot on the A57 towards the lower right-hand corner of the map lies

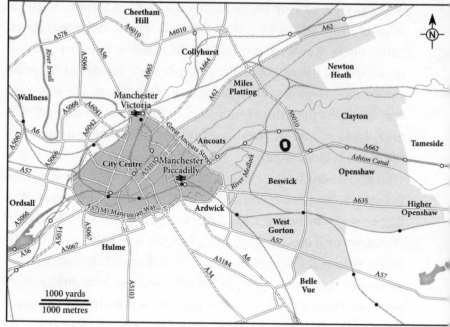

Inner-city areas, east Manchester.

the Gorton Tesco. Gorton Foundry and Tank were in their day just south of the Higher Openshaw sign.

On the other, southern, side of the Hyde Road (A57) stands Tesco's enfeebled competition – shops that frequently change owners and functions: GB Mobile, Pennies to Pounds, Manchester City Furniture Co. ('Private Landlords Welcome', house clearances a specialty), G & S Cash and Carry, Friss Hair extensions, Bootleggers, Gorton Payless – the latter its real, unconsciously cruel name. But there are also the All Nations Barbers, the tiny Bensonni Classic 'Italian tailors'; Rise and Shine Christian Ministries, now boarded up; Manchester Next Level Lounge; African and European Foods; and the Wembley Restaurant. For Gorton now has many immigrants, especially African ones, and this is their place. Anyplace, England becomes a real place again. Behind these shops are the old terraces that still exist from the century before last – mostly poor-quality rented accommodation, now catering to immigrants. It is from people in these streets that the poorer high road premises make their money – those in private-sector housing that they must occupy as they try to force themselves up the housing ladder.

On the northern, Tesco side of the Hyde Road, in a great arc stretching to the north of the city, lies the new world of 'regenerated Manchester'. The immigrants remain on the fringes of this land of opportunity, unless they have been here for some time. In this land of regeneration, things are at last, if slowly, improving; but this is only after almost half a century of degeneration – and it is the wasted years I think of. The population in this great arc is mixed, but mainly white; as one goes out of the city east, to my borough of Tameside and the old cotton towns of Ashton, Hyde and Stalybridge, it becomes whiter still – the white working class, as it is now called in public commentary. Tameside voted roughly 60–40 for Brexit, Manchester City itself the reverse of that. The latter result was driven mainly by the middle classes of the south, but also by non-whites; the city itself is a culturally mixed place, in large parts little different from London.

On the north side of the road is the 'Square', where a new covered market feebly echoes the great Victorian public markets that once prospered in these parts. It makes a poor competitor to the Tesco behemoth a few hundred yards away. The 'Square' itself is simply a large carpark. Many of the people on this side of the road look different to the younger, healthier-seeming migrants, who have their own shops over on the other side. In every face I see Blake's 'Marks of weakness, marks of woe'. People seem to walk with their heads down. I talked with the CEO of Tameside Council, a local man himself, the grandson of Oldham engineers and cotton workers – a man doing his best for the place, though also with a proprietorial air about him, a little as if he were lord of the manor. He also notices how people around the market in nearby Ashton walk with their heads down. He hopes someday to help them walk upright again. He tells me the average healthy life expectancy in the borough is in the late fifties – a shocking figure.

The Manchester Gymnasium Centre is along the road, evidence of previous regenerations gone bad. Barbed wire fencing runs along the top: if one parks, one is politely asked to leave, but it is unclear why, as the place is tightly shuttered – even fortified. Further along the road is the shabby 'new' library. There is barely a handful of books, or any other material, in what is called the local history section. History – more than this, the past itself – seems lost here.[8] There are remnants, but so feeble are they that they mock the past. Heritage? Not even that. The library stands on Garrett Way, the name a reminder of the great Garrett locomotive, though almost all who pass do so in ignorance of its derivation. They are reminded by a memorial in the form of a rail carriage wheel axle, but the words of explanation below it have long been erased by the weather, just as the past is here everywhere effaced. It is an image of the past as an absence, a hole in the present; but the object is stubborn, and the silence in it may one day be the basis of utterance in that place.

Heading out from the centre of Gorton and then striking north, the walker encounters a jumble of houses built at many different times, but mostly after the clearances. The houses, blocks and towers are in different stages of repair, past decades visible as strata of decay. The new homes – and there are increasing numbers of them – are sometimes good, clustered together in thoughtful ways, in a brave bid to make a sense of place where there is little. They are called villages in some places, as in the 'overspill' estate of Hattersley, a mile from where I live, which once vainly attempted to divide the large estate into 'villages'. It was to Hattersley that many of those cast out from Gorton and points north were sent in the sixties and seventies.

Moving northwards, into Openshaw and then Bradford, one is back to the vast empty lot, the walled enclosures of nothing, marking vanished factories, waste ground, and then ever more houses, streets – all mixed up, without coherence. The sense of time as well as that of place is lost, the very juxtaposition of the houses and their decades defying any logic, any sense of time as linear, of the past being connected to the present. There are, it seems, no shops, no pubs, no licensed meeting places. The streets always seem empty, as on Hattersley (one lives 'on' Hattersley, not in it, and one comes 'off' it, not from it; like so many similar estates, it exists as if suspended outside time and place, hovering somewhere above the ground on which the rest of the world walks).

The houses and flats are small, no bigger than the old houses left behind. Britain has amongst the smallest habitable spaces per person in Europe. Little cul-de-sacs proliferate – mini estates within estates, a world folded in on itself, bent on privacy. The estate of man is such here. Time thickens, takes on flesh here, too; but the sense of place seems less than in former times, the flesh thinner. A kind of emptiness is apparent, where once, for ill and for good, there was the huddle. The derelict and apparently abandoned premises of the Grade City Church look like some lost US storefront chapel. Where have the flock gone in their inconceivable rush to be somewhere else?

Going down Cornwall Street, a nearby offshoot of the main road, one encounters St James's Anglican Church, another beneficiary of the locomotive magnate Richard Peacock' s local paternalism. There are only two services a week here, and the place is locked up most of the time; but the new primary school is opposite the church, and when all else has fallen it is the churches that remain. This is especially true of Catholic churches, at least if there are plenty of immigrants around, and Manchester is still a very Irish and Catholic city. The Nonconformists, who historically did not control the schools, lost out to the other two denominations; but they hold on, religion still being a social leaven in godless Britain.

This is a rough corner of the world; the few public houses around are themselves derelict-looking, huddling along the road. And then another remnant of Peacock appears – the large, boarded-up Conservative Club. Along the way is a tangled, unkempt open space with a sign in front of it: 'The Peacock Centre', a rectangular space, filthy and full of rubbish, where the future never happened. Peacock Park stretches out behind and is decent enough, then on from the Gardeners Arms to the Steelyard Arms, on the corner of Preston Road. Here is where the two great works stood: the foundry and the Tank.

I circumambulate both, up first a silent Bessemer Street, then desolate Whitworth Street eastwards. The seemingly impenetrable wall continues, and suddenly there is the entrance to what is now the vast new Smithfield wholesale produce market, in the daytime completely quiet. This serves the city, just as in London the new Covent Garden has replaced the old – the old in the centre, the new outside it. These markets are a symbol of the great change that has taken place. The new markets are private spaces; the old ones were porous, open to the city.

Onwards to the south, then down Press Street into Cornwall Street again, and Railway Street; and now the great sheds of Beyer and Peacock become visible again, though still inaccessible, as they are now part of Manchester City Council's Hammerstone Road depot. The great sheds dwarf everything around, new and not so new, the so-called 'industrial units', which look like what they are: makeshift, provisional, like

The hidden sign, Gorton, October 2018.

the immediate area. And then there suddenly emerges from the ground a strange object, appearing like the head of some ancient, beached sea creature. It is the top of a large stone edifice representing the coat of arms of the city of Manchester, sunk into ground; and on it, barely visible, is the motto of the city: 'Concilio et Labore' – 'Wisdom and Labour'.

The stone is uncared for; pale green and yellow moss encrusts it in places, and it is strewn with the leavings of the nature that surrounds it. It tells of a real heritage, if that word has meaning anymore, because it is not heritage. It is haphazard, not considered worthy of that exalted status. The city's care for its real past is pretty hopeless, except where it is part of some sort of 'regeneration' project or, in the centre, an attraction for tourists. One must acknowledge the unknown city warrior who sank this stone in the ground. A tiny, lost plaque on a wall marks 'Little Ireland' in the inner city, the great Irish ghetto; Peterloo was until very recently similarly acknowledged, although there is now, on the 200th anniversary, at last a decent monument.

Ironically, the city ignores the very thing that made it great: industrial capitalism. There is very little public acknowledgement of the great factories that have now gone forever – only the skeletons of some of them now turned into expensive apartments in the city centre. There is an official history of the city, about how it is the home of what is radical and progressive in Britain; but what made the place a world city was capitalism red in tooth and claw. And what place can the city fathers find for this? What would a monument to industrial capitalism look like? Neither is there a statue to Engels, for that matter, except for a slab of political kitsch hauled from the Ukraine for the purposes of art, in a place visited only by people who get the joke.

There is, however, the People's History Museum, which has now rebranded itself the 'national museum of democracy'. Here the story is the familiar one of reform, the gaining of the vote, the worker unchained – a leftist version of the Whig version of history that is still a resilient presence in this country. The fatal nostalgia of the left: the past as political 'heritage', and just as bland as most other versions. You would not think, in this people's museum, that in this part of the world, and in Britain as a whole, generation after generation avidly voted Conservative, or that these people are part of the 'People' too. What the Marxist historian E. P. Thompson once cited as the 'flag-saluting, foreigner-hating, peer-respecting side of the plebeian mind' finds no place here.

And so this beached object of the lion's head in Gorton has to tell its tale alone, the past emerging out of the ground, the earth giving up the dead. In the coat of arms, the antelope is intertwined in a chain; the chain represents engineering, the antelope courage and harmony. In the middle is a great three-masted sailing ship, representing trade. Above it is the globe, and on the globe are carved the bees that have in recent times, and especially after the Manchester Arena bomb of 2017, become the city's symbol. But the chain seems to drag the antelope down, and the lion's face is that of one close to death, its grotesque, seemingly diseased mouth open. It appears blind, and the ample flow of the lion's mane presents a disturbing contrast to the animal's diseased face. The antelope appears like some kind of snake, the chain visible there by it. And the bees are indistinct, eroded by time, occluded, like the lives of the generations of workers that went before, a counter to the modern, sentimentalized bee. The object's silence tells a story both staggering and terrible.

Were the walker to go a little further north and east from Gorton, they would be in the district of Bradford, and the much-trumpeted Sports City, where Manchester City Football Club has its ground. Walking from the south into the area of the football stadium, a clutch of desperately poor housing is passed, then 'Mary D's Beamish Bar', looking more like a fortress than a pub (Beamish is an Irish stout). The stadium looms on the skyline, and here is the first shop in several miles:

'One Stop, Seven Days, 6 to 11'. The Stadium Chippy is on another corner, and there is a mounting sense of the limitations of regeneration – regeneration here courtesy of the rulers of Abu Dhabi, the whole thing piloted not as it once was by an elected city council but by the vanity and political needs of princes. The vast roads connecting the new sports facilities dwarf the tiny houses, which seem to hide from all this rather than embrace it. The roads go only to the different venues, or to a giant Asda supermarket. It is a space only for cars, and no one walks on the wide streets. All is guarded, fenced, private.

One crosses the strange, empty no-man's-land west of this and comes to Ancoats Vale and the filthy defile of the river Medlock. This is an edgeland,[9] a wasteland, similar to wastelands in all cities, on the edge of Britain, and of time itself too: no place, no time either. Occasionally one sees traveller people walking in the Vale, and poor Asian immigrants. Then, as one heads north, there are the endless scruffy streets through Miles Platting, long famed for its poverty. Suddenly, there is a dental practice, another broken tooth stuck in the mouth of nowhere, still working – though the iron shutters are nonetheless still down. And then, at last, one comes into the much more vibrant world of immigrant Cheetham Hill, once the city's Jewish homeland but now Asian.

Going further west from the City ground, one moves through edgeland and thence into the city centre itself. One does so under an extraordinary triumphal arch of twisted, pre-rusted metal girders, into the hip development of New Islington. There the forest of apartment blocks grows relentlessly, cranes everywhere – a spectacular sight these days, but especially these nights, when the cranes are dotted with red warning lights. The new city has been put there largely by money from Chinese sovereign funds. In one such block in New Islington, I entered, but there was no way out at the other side, the ramps and canal bridges leading in a circle back and out, cameras watching, some invisible algorithm or other sussing me out.

I take to the new city centre, especially knowing the old, and I am proud of it, especially when I show parochial Londoners around. The city has great heart and new hope. However, it is no city for old men, for it belongs now to the relatively prosperous young that crowd there. Of the very large number of those aged between twenty-five and thirty-four who live in the inner city, 35 per cent are born outside the UK. The city is said to be the fastest-growing in Europe in terms of its city-centre population. The extraordinary political economy of the relationship between the city centre and east Manchester has been analyzed by economists and sociologists at Manchester University, presciently challenging the much-lauded and much-boosted Manchester 'regeneration' model.[10]

The political story is a familiar one: the evisceration of city self-government by Thatcher's Tories in the 1980s and the pragmatism-cum-opportunism of a Labour Party–dominated city council that found it could get things done locally through a political accommodation with regional, national and international property developers. Getting things done meant, in effect, granting site-by-site planning permissions to construct what was most profitable, not most necessary.[11] Certainly this did not include social housing – though a little is now creeping back. It is the political story of all England, only this city was, as so often, ahead of the game.

The time of the bad life seems like an appropriate phrase for the failures of the past forty years. It is these that need remembering, even if there are signs of improvement in the city and Greater Manchester in recent times. Not that the present is enviable. In 2011, on a neighbourhood basis of around 1,500 inhabitants, 21 per cent of Greater Manchester's neighbourhoods were in the top 10 per cent most deprived in England, and Manchester City itself had a staggering 41 per cent. The outer northern boroughs of Oldham, Rochdale and Tameside (all in Greater Manchester) were in considerable trouble; as of 2016, they had been net losers of both private- and public-sector jobs for decades.

There is an acute shortage of social housing, with 120,000 names on the Greater Manchester housing waiting lists in 2017. The average mortgage in the city requires an annual salary of over £34,000, beyond the pocket of many families, who are then forced into the largely unregulated private sector. In east Manchester itself in 1999, 43 per cent of housing stock was council-owned, the privately rented sector accounting for 42 per cent. Over half of all households rented from social landlords, 37 per cent being council tenants. Since then, the council has handed over most of its stock to housing associations, which are providing a mix of housing for rent and sale at (mostly) affordable prices. In 1999, only 32 per cent of properties were owner-occupied, compared to 42 per cent in Manchester City and 69 per cent nationally.[12] Twenty years later, this had changed little. So this is England: a nation of would-be homeowners, would-be place-makers.

'One Manchester' is an important housing association in the city, and, as the name implies, it attempts to join up all the components of living in the city in one institution. Its staff are devoted people of the old council school of public service. They struggle against the economic and social constraints of the district, and of funding (their need to supply good rented accommodation is stymied at times by their obligation to sell houses). They also struggle against something else. The economic sociologist William Davies pithily defines neoliberalism as 'the disenchantment of politics by economics', by which he means that, in becoming subordinate to economics, politics loses its orientation around the civic, and so its moral sway, public life in the process becoming reduced to the economic evaluations and actions of a supposedly value-free market.[13]

In 2020, this may be changing; it is too early to say. But we still live each day in its wreckage, operating almost automatically in the techno-social grooves it has set down for our living over a period of more than thirty years – in education, in social welfare, in health. This is especially so in Britain, where our collective lives have become a matter of economic calculation more than in any other European country, as if love and care could be audited. Out of this a great contradiction emerges, one between those invited to 'win', invited to 'aspire' to win, and the truth that these aspirants are in reality's cold light set up to lose. The old rage for order meant knowing and keeping one's place, the new aspiring to get out of it, or at least being constantly told to aspire to get out of it, but in reality being always thwarted by lack of means. Neoliberalism devolves order upon a supposedly free self that does not possess the means of securing it.

Between those who win and those who lose, there is now, as Davies says, no sense of a shared reality. But there are winners and winners – the rich, who are Davies's winners, and those winners in what politicians now call 'the middle'. Between many of these and the poor there is little or no shared reality, though in practice these middle winners shade into the poor at many points, into what is now called the 'precariat', in effect poor winners; these days Britain is a precarious place, economically and politically. Shared reality, a shared social bond, a shared sense of nation – all these shade one into the other. Who is there to remake the bond, to remake a sense of a place belonged to?

One Manchester is there; Tesco and Asda are there. As the former's publicity proclaims, 'Our view is that housing associations are all about place-making'. In 2017, One Manchester launched its 'Social Investment Strategy', 'which involved ensuring that all areas we operate in can become Resilient Thriving Communities'. They are there to make 'happier people in our communities', to which end they publicly present what they call 'the key statistics from our Social Accounts' – accounts they record so as to be accountable to government. They must cut their cloth according to their accountabilities. And so Manchester is something of a centre for 'place management' – and the Institute of Place Management, no less, is based here.

This publicly maintains, the cliché unresisted, that the problem is not always solved by 'throwing money at it'. Their approach, they say, is 'something we call "social innovation"', and they believe 'in helping up, not handing out; inspiring and empowering individuals'.

Retail is most often the means to the end of place management. The science of Tescography emerges: the enterprise's making of place and community, its cultivation of aspiration through the government of the mouth, the tutelage of the stomach. Driving out along the A57 from Gorton, motorists leave one giant Tesco and arrive after twenty minutes at another Tesco, this one in Hattersley, part of regeneration, the valuable motorway-end site given to Tesco in return for a community 'Hub'. This 'Hub' is built beside it – built, as it happens, far to one side of the large estate, and out of reach of many.

On entering the supermarket there are the usual food banks, here for Hattersley itself. The food it sells is aimed at local tastes and pockets – food that makes you ill, that makes you obese; cheap booze. There are hardly any shops on the vast estate, so the clientele is captive. So are the workers in the shop, many from 'off' the estate. The hypocrisy is glaring. Noticeboards detail sponsored collections and engagements with local schools and community associations. There is a large board warning of loan sharks. The vastness of the place signals a complete lack of scalar sympathy with the surrounding area. All who enter and shop are once again in the arms of Big Data.

Hattersley has been the destination from Gorton for many. Myra Hindley grew up in Gorton, and both she and Brady lived there up to their arrest in October 1965. Their Hattersley house, once an unwelcome attraction for visitors, has been demolished. The curse continues. Dale Cregan shot two women police officers to death there in 2012. Less than a mile from this spot lived Harold Shipman, the greatest serial killer in British history.

Here people came from the west, from 'condemned' homes, from homes considered 'unfit'. The isolation drove some back, disturbed by the birdsong, while others rejoiced in the 'country'. In the early days, it was the women who did most of the place management, and then there were the bad years of the 1980s and 1990s – a generation lost, time just sweeping by unheeding, the estate drug-ridden, the poorly built houses deteriorating dreadfully. The schools were poor, the kids in the usual way educated to fail. As always, there is a Roman Catholic church, small here and built like a fortress.[14]

AW, who was born and brought up on the estate, is a Labour activist: he knows how the estate was seen until the very recent past – 'it's crap, but it's our crap; it's Hattersley isn't it?' He is a man in his thirties, and talks of the racism and homophobia of school days, how they linger in the older generation of even his own family, how the estate is all white, and how people hardly ever move off – they are 'stay-putters'. Family ties are very strong still, even though frequent divorce and separation complicate everything, and the children suffer.

Things are a little better now, but this is again a world folded in on itself. This is the new life of the house: cheap alcohol, home entertainment, the end of the pubs, but nonetheless houses, some of them, to be proud of and to spend money on, not houses to be got out of, as in so much of my west London. The old controls are gone, the new controls are now in hand – in the 'remote', and in that which makes a person remote. The streets are dominated by cars, and places within the estate are spread out, so people use cars more than ever. My wife grew up on an estate like this, in Southampton, near the docks, and I knew it well through its good days and its decline. All her nine brothers and sisters bar one got off the estate, though most of them not far.

The old mass, popular working-class order has gone. As the city merges into the old cotton towns, and as the A57 penetrates eastwards into Tameside borough, not only are family ties strong, but the people, who are overwhelmingly white, are also 'stay putters', with generations in the same places. The old order leaves generational traces, therefore; but the seemingly endless streets and terraced brick rows are a sort of illusion, too; though they echo the past, the lives experienced within the houses have changed. And the old cotton towns have suffered as much as the poor inner-city suburbs in recent decades.

Lynsey Hanley has become well known as an interpreter of contemporary 'working-class' life. She was born later than Roberts, Hoggart and Seabrook, in 1975, and in her memoir, *Respectable*, she writes of the life of the generation after mine. Her story is of the vast council housing estate where those in the great clearances so often ended up, in her case Chelmsey Wood on the edge of Birmingham – vast indeed, with 20,000 houses. She offers a penetrating and withering account of what respectability became, and still is. The old proletariat has been replaced by the new 'precariat'. It is as if, though the old supports of life have gone – steady employment in the known industrial locale and a recognition of one's status – the old symbolic structure and rhythm simply continue, only now endlessly repeating, ritual for ritual's sake: at best a source of obsessive consolation in a world that has completely changed, at worst self-destruction in the fury of *ressentiment*.

Hanley describes this obsessiveness and fury to chilling effect.[15] It is clear it has been an animating force behind support for Brexit, here and throughout the country. *Ressentiment*: suppressed feelings of hatred directed at those one holds to blame for one's condition. In fact, Hanley goes as far as to say that the essentials of life now are much the same as in 1950s Britain. It is with a kind of shock that I reflect upon the probability that she is right – that, while everything happens, nothing changes.

This resentment is directed without much discrimination, sometimes at the true source, more often at the imagined – the EU and the immigrant – the feelings these days no longer repressed. People wallow in such resentment, happily joining hands with those who put them in the shit they wallow in to begin with. As Joe Bageant puts it in *Deer Hunting with Jesus*, describing the 'redneck' America he knew first-hand, 'If you are doomed to eat shit, you may as well bring your own fork.'[16] Blame: blame for one's frustration; blaming acting as a kind of drug that cannot be easily satisfied once the hit is taken. Like all drugs, this resentment distorts reality. For the sense of weakness or inferiority from which it comes, the sense of having little or no control over one's life, is compounded with the ordinary frustrations of life to produce the toxins that have recently flown freely through British public life. Brexit was and remains a matter of control, of 'bringing back control' for its supporters – control over borders, over sovereignty, or at least their version of it; bringing back a time when control was once ours and can be so again, so that we will have again what the others now have, which is denied to us.

But inequality and powerlessness are relative, not absolute. It is also a matter of generations, so that people's attitudes are a function of where they started off, among their parents and their own people. Long-term economic growth has produced a measure of social mobility and affluence beside ever greater inequality, as better pay and conditions of employment, higher living standards and the consolations of consumption and 'life-style' have for many, over the long term, meant that people feel mobile and advantaged compared to their parents and their own early lives.[17] 'Individualized social inequality' is the name sociologists use for this. It works the other way too: the young have of course lost out, at least the better-off ones; and the large numbers of young people going to university for the first time are perhaps somewhere in the middle, feeling stalled, waiting in a kind of limbo, promises unfulfilled. Explaining Brexit in terms of poverty and powerlessness alone is wide of the mark for the country as a whole, therefore, when some feel their circumstances have improved – even though the middle is now too near the precariat for comfort in many cases, especially since 2008.

Yet in more affluent parts of the country, whether the affluence is real or imagined, a similar story of yearning and dispossession is apparent, too – a similar concern about 'control'. The nation itself has become the locus of an order believed to be lost – and, more than this, to have been taken away. 'Europe' represents the source of this dispossession. This sense of having lost something is redoubled for many older people. For them, a class-bewitched society was experienced not only or even mainly as social conflict and national disharmony, but as inclusion within familiar and comforting hierarchies. To know one's place was to have a place. To be keen to be out of it was to know both the place you had left and the one you might land in. This created the sense of a nation in which you knew where you stood, and which therefore meant something. When all this fell apart in the new demotic Britain that followed the disintegration of the old manual working class, the sense of loss was great – loss of the nation, loss of a hierarchic, ordered society, as the UK, but more especially England, seemed to be falling apart. People no longer felt at home.

11

Home

The Burnley Miners' Workingmens' Club is, and has long been, the world's largest consumer of the fine French liqueur Benedictine!

Tony Bell

What is it to dwell? By the mid fourteenth century, 'dwell' had the sense of 'making a home and abiding as a permanent resident'. The same name is used for the act as well as the means of being in the world, and this means also denotes a place: 'the dwelling'. Magnus Course, the anthropologist of the house, argues that the existential sense of place itself, of being 'here' in the world, is inseparable from the dwelling; as he puts it 'the wherewithal of place does not preexist the act of building but is created by humanity's mark'.[1]

Robert Pogue Harrison, the literary scholar, understands the dwelling as a constitutive part of the relationship between past and present generations, between the living and the dead. For the dead have a foundational role in human life. He describes how humans (derived from the Latin *humar*, to dig, bury), in inscribing their dwelling upon the earth itself, also inscribe this earth with their own mortality. As Harrison writes, the place of inhumation is the surest locus of place and the surest means to take possession of a place and secure it as one's own. He refers to the Sicilian baron in one of Pirandello's stories, who refused to let the peasants bury their dead on his land because he knew that if they did they would come to regard it as their own by natural right – to regard it as their house.[2]

All this is in turn related to what meanings we ascribe to 'home'. The sense we have of being at home in the world may inhere in other things than the actual dwelling alone, of course, just as being 'here' does not automatically confer the sense of being at home (after all, 'to dwell' comes from the Old English *dwellan* 'lead astray, hinder, delay', and, remarkably, is etymologically related to the Middle Dutch *dwellen*, 'stun, perplex'). Being at home may involve another person, an idea or belief, a race, and not just the sense of being in a place. Nonetheless, being at home seems deeply related to dwelling there, and dwelling itself to place. We know that, at the most basic level, dwelling involves the sensation of being enclosed and sheltered – perhaps in a room, a house, an apartment, or even just by something that at least covers a person, a doorway say, or even the plastic sheets and cardboard boxes of those people on our streets we now call homeless. Shelter is always had in a place. The Englishman's home is his castle.

As Ágnes Heller writes in her essay 'Where Are We at Home?': 'Privileging one, or certain, places against all others' is 'perhaps, the oldest tradition of the *homo sapiens* ... The privileged place could be the father's tent, the native village, the free city, the ethnic enclave, the nation state, the territory of the holy shrine and much else.'[3] However, as she recognizes, it is for us the nation-state that has a particular prominence. I recall the words of Ernest Renan: 'One loves in proportion to the sacrifices to which one has consented, and in proportion to the ills that one has suffered. One loves the house that one has built and that one has handed down. Handed down by the sacrifices of the national dead, past and present.'

In Britain today, most of all in England, that sense of being at home, 'here' in this place, is in question. Within the nations of Britain, England, in particular, seems to have been lost. Scotland and Wales do not seem to share this sense, except insofar as they feel British, while Northern Ireland is a different case again. Remembering that the nation is something *performed* in our daily experience, and so part of our daily life, it follows that many people must feel that they are themselves lost, that they have been uprooted from themselves, sundered. It is a big thing to lose one's nation. It is like losing one's house, one's habitation, one's home. I write this sentence in July 2020, amidst the dreadful onslaught of the Covid-19 pandemic. All the public talk now is of the nation as one, though events have revealed its divisions anew. Perhaps something better will come out of the pandemic than the nation that preceded it. Certainly the wounds need healing, but what unity there is now has been very short in the making, while the divisions have long been present.

What past of England and Britain might people seek to inhabit in the ex-industrial world of England's north? Not the post-industrial world, it should be said, as that is in Manchester. I searched for answers in the ex-cotton town of Burnley to the north of Manchester, one of a ring of such towns around the city – a town I had known well in earlier years. In such towns, replicated throughout Britain, people are in general less socially and culturally mixed and better off than in the cities. I knew the north Lancashire cotton-weaving towns a half-century ago, spending many months in them as a young research student writing their history, and since then have returned from time to time. Around 1900 Burnley was said to be the most important cotton-weaving centre in the world. By the early 1970s the town was beginning its 'modernization', and a good deal of the old town centre had already gone when I arrived, unlike in a number of the other towns, which held back for a little longer. I had not until recently visited them much in the last half-century. By all measures, these towns have been in a bad way for a long time. Great companies, once household names, have come and gone in Burnley; despite well-meaning 'regeneration', it is as if the town had never recovered from the fall of King Cotton. Yet it knew better days for a couple of decades or so, from the 1950s to the '70s when the big firms were there.

At the time of writing, about 10 per cent of Burnley's working-age population are on Incapacity Benefit. The livelihood of the town comprises a strange economy, in which some 20 per cent of its workforce cares for almost as big a proportion of the general population, since the number of those in the population that are unhealthy is huge. Poverty levels in Burnley are among the worst in the country, and child poverty is as usual worse than that of adults: in some parts of the town, over 50 per cent of children live in poverty. Nationally, something approaching a quarter of the population live in poverty, but just over a third of children do.[4] Vast swathes of Britain today are devastated. There seems little hope for the future when one considers these children; there is irreparable suffering here in the present as well as in the past, poor children the offspring of poor parents and poor grandparents.

Educational levels in Burnley are also among the worst in the country, especially for boys, and among these most of all for white working-class boys; but the figures for levels of literacy and numeracy nationally are shocking, too. Unlike in most other developed countries, older people in England have higher literacy and numeracy scores than young people. The average reading age of the national population as a whole is nine. At the same time the reading age of readers of the right-wing *Sun* newspaper is eight, while that of the quality press is fourteen.[5] In 2019, three-quarters of white working-class boys nationally failed to achieve the government's literacy benchmark at the age of sixteen. In the same year, according to the National Literacy Trust, a boy born in Stockton-on-Tees, in the ex-industrial north-east of England – a town with one of the worst literacy records in the country – has a life expectancy 26.1 years shorter than a boy born in north Oxford.

It seems to be a town in which there is a strong sense of something having been lost, and where the prospect of regaining it by standing alone and 'taking back control' has considerable traction. In the Brexit referendum, Burnley voted to leave by almost exactly 2:1 – the second-highest in ex-industrial Lancashire. Nearby Hyndburn and Rossendale, also part of the decayed cotton-weaving belt, voted to leave by roughly 60–40. In Blackburn, not far to the west, the split was 56–44; but there the vote was swayed by the very large Asian population.

Despite everything, Burnley itself is still a *place* to those who live there, albeit just about so. It seems at times as if only the now-successful football team are holding it together. It is a place, according to local feeling, that 'people never leave' – and, indeed, few do. It is in 'the arse-crack of Lancashire', the devastated top end of the Ribble Valley – a place surrounded by great natural beauty. Naomi Sweeney uses this anatomical metaphor when we speak. She is a teacher, as well as a child of teachers, and is, like many here, of Irish extraction – one generation from the North on one side. She was once a student of mine. She was born in the town and has spent her whole life there. She knows the place as intimately as anyone, and was once partnered with someone on the estates – someone who never got off. She says she has never really left Burnley.

We drive and walk together around the estates of the town: Barclay Hills, Stoops, Mill Hill, Wensleyfold, Shadsworth. One of these estates is the subject of a BBC TV programme, and so fabled in the land for its 'deprivation'. The kind of place where poverty porn is made. Of course, the tenants chafe at what they feel is condescending in these portrayals. Some of these estates date from the inter-war years, and have built up their own sense of place – but one perilously maintained and ruefully expressed. Naomi's grandmother was brought up on one of them. Stoops is particularly notorious, as the extreme right have traditionally been strong there, and it saw rioting in 1992 – part of a larger wave nationally, and strongly centred on the housing estates themselves.

Serious rioting also occurred in the town in 2001, as it did in other former mill towns, including Oldham and Bradford.[6] It occurred again in 2007. The *Daily Mirror*'s 'Hope not Hate

Bus' visited the Stoops and Hargher Clough estates in 2007, reporting that both were 99.1 per cent white, 'while the nearby Stoneyholme and Daneshouse estates have a large Asian population. The Stoops sports club brings the children from the neighbouring communities together for sport. For many of the white kids it is the first time they have had an Asian friend – and vice versa.'[7] A poll of 900 readers of the *Lancashire Telegraph* were asked, ten years after June 2001, whether race relations had improved. Only 10 per cent said yes.[8]

There are still rows upon rows of empty Victorian and Edwardian houses, and many of the old estates are almost in ruins. New and better estates and houses are on the way, if slowly; but it is the successive decades of neglect that are in my mind, as in Gorton and East Manchester – the failed generations, the failure of 'regeneration'. It is difficult to find the feeling of place here, as the estates themselves seem to have no centres, and the old town centre has given way to a formless blend of old and new – empty sites, carparks and semi-isolated blocks – an effect heightened by the grid layout of a town built *de novo* on cotton in the nineteenth century.

Charter Walk and its 'shopping centre' appear to mark the centre of modern Burnley. The Walk replaced the Victorian market hall, swept away in the 1960s and '70s like many other fine old buildings, including the imposing Weaver's Institute. Centenary Way and its flyover butted their way into the modernized town, as did the M65 later on. Trafalgar flats were built near the centre – the worst of modernism – and went into rapid decay soon after; then they were demolished. There is hardly a need to continue; the British reader will recognize this place, for such places are to be found north and south, east and west, though perhaps usually not so bad as here. Many readers will also be familiar with similar places in the United States and Europe.

In Charter Walk the signs proclaim: 'Top bargains, bottom prices, named brands'. The '99p' shop is huge. The YMCA once opened what they called the largest charity shop in Britain in this town. Just outside the Walk, in the deserted street, a man sits in front of the White Lion pub. He is dressed in the faux working-class clothes of a forgotten age, and plays Burnley 'folksongs' – or so his sign promises. On his hand there is a finger puppet as he plays, gesturing to no one but me as I go past.

Like me, older people here and throughout the country were brought up in a time when Britain promised them much – a bounty to be realized on the new estates and in the new town centres that were being built from the 1960s onwards, as here. They were betrayed, as were their children, and they are right to feel so. Betrayal comes out of the sense of a promise unfulfilled, and it engenders a sense of loss. That sense of loss in turn magnifies the brightness of those parts of the past felt to have been good, so that the sense of decline from some earlier, better state – a consciousness of falling – is sharply apparent in towns like this.

What people seem to perceive themselves as having fallen from in Burnley is associated less with the imperial past in general, or cotton in particular, than with the relatively brief days of better times from the 1950s to the 1970s. In those years the nation felt at home with itself – that Britain was Britain, even as it was being torn down and rebuilt. But this was also an overwhelmingly white past, though the legerdemain of empire made whiteness seem invisible. Only gradually did whiteness become visible, manifested as it was by the arrival of black and Asian immigrants – the former in significant numbers – in the cotton towns from around 1960. This white Britain very often did not like the Irish very much, either. This prelapsarian world was also a strikingly masculine one. This was the social-democratic age, as it is sometimes called, in Britain; but other parts of Europe were the same. This was the era of the Wirtschaftswunder in Germany, Les Trente Glorieuses in France, the exodus north from the Mezzogiorno in

Italy. If, in Britain, this meant never having had it so good, in the 1950s and '60s – for those of us around at the time – this was really not saying much; but it was saying something to our parents.

It was in fact during this third quarter of the twentieth century that various national myths played themselves out. Recent historical research re-examining the several social surveys of the time shows how, in post-war England, the memory of the thirties and the experience of the sacrifices endured in a victorious and glorified war made people believe progress was possible. The implementation of the welfare state and high employment levels had the same effect. People thought of themselves as if they were on a journey to better things. 'The people' were on the march. The economic dislocations of the 1970s and '80s, and the evident limitations of welfarism, meant that the dream was ended.[9] It was then that the failure became apparent of the great city-centre clearances – of Paddington, Salford and Gorton.

It was also at this time that what David Edgerton, in his important recent history of twentieth-century Britain, calls 'the central national myth' of the then-recent war was cultivated: the war of a unified nation and people.[10] The war has remained the central British myth ever since. Like much else in the same period, it was nationalized, so that the role of the empire was written out. The nation was Britain alone, in another instance of historical legerdemain. Nor did we appreciate the limitations of the other great national myth, the welfare state: that welfare was in fact thin and mean, restricted in the range of entitlements it offered and in the range of people whose loyalties it attached to the state.[11] When the system that had been established in the third quarter of the century came under attack in the fourth, it proved too weak to withstand the onslaught of market fundamentalism – just as the British nation was not strong enough to withstand the pressure for devolution, with the emergence of Scottish independence politics.

This is the view in hindsight, of course – though that is not to say we should not have known better, as some indeed did. And what of Burnley? Memory in towns like Burnley, as in many throughout the land, is very often archived within local newspapers, many of which have been publishing for well over a century, and most of which sit on vast amounts of photographic material. This material is recirculated online by amateur historians and by many small businesses, and is sold on in the form of heritage and nostalgia books and memorabilia (the self-described nostalgia trade is huge, and keenly aware of local tastes and desires because it is often locally or regionally based). This is not the only way in which the past is currently circulated, but it is revealing.

One such heritage firm is True North Books. It specializes in photographic accounts of what are called the 'golden years' – the term supplying the titles of a series of books on northern towns. The golden years encompass the third quarter of the last century; for Burnley and similar towns, these books thus tap into a lived past. The myths people live by are therefore not divorced from reality, not altogether irrational, as the post-war boom delivered a great deal. The books convey an unmistakable sense of a place and a nation lost, indeed of a certain bewilderment: *dwellen*, in its old meaning – to stun and perplex.

The cotton industry of the past is significant, of course; but the industry was in sharp decline by the golden years – a decline that had begun long before, after the First World War, and which deepened further during the Great Depression of the 1930s. For these towns – and the same is true in the Yorkshire textile districts and for the great manufacturing interests of Britain, once regarded as 'staple' industries – the history of decline stretches back across a century. Ironically, in these northern textile areas it was Asian immigrants who kept the textile industry going in its final days, in the fifties and sixties. The past of the cotton industry has receded, but is nonetheless presented locally as the most significant past. It is represented in the town by a heritage-conservation centre called the Weavers' Triangle, established in the 1970s like so many other parts of the heritage industry. The focus here is on regenerating the town; rather as at RAF Duxford, one may visit in order to embark on 'a trip back in time', an 'experience' – all in the present tense. You may visit a Victorian schoolroom and peer inside a weaver's dwelling, the interiors in a remarkable state of preservation, the smell of recent polishing in the air.

Golden Years of Burnley, and the many works like it, display years that, if not in reality golden, were in retrospect good ones.[12] These are the years when people my age and somewhat younger still had their youth – years also out of which loved ones are now recalled, those with whom the past is the link that matters most. In the *Golden Years* books, it is striking how few images there are of the new Burnley that emerged in the 1960s, when the old town centre was demolished and the new estates built – only two among hundreds of photographs in the Burnley book. Of course, these books aim at a particular age range, and in twenty or thirty years the golden age will have shifted – though it is hard to see what might be framed as 'golden' in any future account of the new estates and the new town centre.

What the photographs do not show – at least, not very often – is the smoke and pollution, including the clouds of cigarette and pipe smoke I grew up in; and there are no photographs of the early deaths, including deaths of children, the poor sanitation, the poor education, the poor and cold houses. What they do show, however, is images of a place, a town, since industrial Jerusalem was built around the notion of the identity and integrity of each particular city and town. The town was itself the great mark of place, the locus of dwelling – the house that made up home. The subjects in the book are predominantly occasions of collective urban action: Whit Walks, mayoral Sunday processions, carnivals, the visits of royalty, one picture of the East Lancashire Regiment as it marches through the town after receiving the Freedom of the Borough. Brass bands are abundant.

Life was lived in public then more than now. People assemble or process, the urban procession being a sure mark of the old urban culture of place. There are pictures of crowds at football matches, at town fairgrounds and theatres; and the collective enjoyment of the town parks is also depicted. The people are all white; the buildings various shades of grey shading to black. More than this, however, the aesthetic of the mill town is the aesthetic of stone, so that it is above all the sense of solidity that comes across after a century and more of industrial Jerusalem. The old town was built of local stone – stone sullied by smoke, but solid.

What is Burnley for more recent generations, who may not be the readers of these 'nostalgia' books? These are the words of Naomi Sweeney: 'As for what I love about the place, it is the house where I grew up, but I don't like that I'll never afford a house like that.' Price inflation is now rampant even in Burnley, where in the 1990s terraced houses sold for £5,000. It is the first house that draws Naomi back: 'I love the fact I know every inch of the place, and for the first ten years after moving away I went shopping there, as I knew where to get anything and everything. For example, a mincer with a turning handle.'

During the 1980s, when she grew up there, it was a place 'with enormous unemployment and real poverty amongst a generation of particularly young men who had the usual opportunities for economic betterment taken away. This left a bitter taste, in this area in particular. Deskilled dreamers on the dole, or working in a factory for very low wages trapped these people,' she tells me, and some remain stuck in a time warp, 'like the woman who pays too much for a new carpet every other year through the club, or the man who comes to the door for the loan shark payment each week'.

'What is singular about Burnley is the specifically local

knowledge and attitudes no one from anywhere else gets or understands ... the language and communication drips with underlying meaning.' In the not so distant past there was a conscious and publicly articulated pride in dialect, another echo of the nineteenth century, like the urban procession. Insiderdom and outsiderdom are still conveyed by urban dialects; to outsiders, what are small inflections mean a great deal to local people. 'There's a shorthand from where one grows up that others think alien when you move away.' The North East Lancashire Development Area has put money into the area, but local people 'dismiss it as "it's only Burnley" and will therefore "turn to shit"'.

Burnley-ites are defensive of their identity, to some extent aware of how they appear to others but also defiant, casting themselves apart as the 'other' that no one else knows or understands. The football chants speak here: 'We are the bastards in claret and blue.' The chief fan 'firm' once associated with the club called themselves the Suicide Squad. Firms are essentially young men's fighting fraternities. There is a history of the Squad told by one of their own.[13] The Squad is not representative of the fans in general, or of the town of course, but the name and the thing do stand for a kind of loyalty to the place, however desperate. England and Burnley go hand in hand in the account of the battle honours won by the Squad – a loyalty to nation and town that have a disturbing persistence over time. In late June 2020, an ex-member of the Squad hired an aircraft to fly over the Manchester City football ground as they played Burnley. The banner said: 'White Lives Matter – Burnley'.

The following are the opening words from the 'Story' of the Squad:

Nine years old and I was pissed ... That's the way it was where I come from. I was born in Burnley ... and shared a terrace house with my mum, dad and brother, Ade. Burnley Wood, the area where we lived, was a close-knit community – until the smackheads took over – full of rows and rows of terraces. Everybody knew each other.

The author was born in 1966, the year England won the World Cup, and for the author, as for the English football team, there was a long history of losing after that date. 'When you leave Burnley, you are judged,' Naomi tells me:

> There is something about the place that requires both humour and aggression to survive. This aggression is a mask, but it can and does spill into reality. Burnley fans are notoriously violent, but also laughed at for smashing up their own town when they lose a match ... Burnley people seem to be irritable and short on time, always rushing, making their interactions brief, loud and direct. Burnley people hate people from Blackburn more than they hate their Asian neighbours.

She cites an example of what she calls being stuck in the past, the Miners' Club: 'I had never seen so many mulleted double-denim men, old men in flat caps and dumpy elderly ladies bedecked in gold lamé with scraped-back hair in tight wet top-knots. The tragedy of a woman in her thirties with false teeth. The cackling of intergenerational shared humour.' [14]

The Miners' is one of the largest and oldest of the town's social clubs, a so-called 'workingmen's club', and when the term is used it is meant seriously; the tradition of the 'male-only room' is strong. So is that of the consumption of Benedictine liqueur, 'Benny', the club's history proudly announcing an annual consumption of 1,200 bottles – the largest in the world, it claims. The tradition is now over a hundred years old, the taste for Benny acquired by soldiers returning to the club after the First World War. Old attitudes die hard here, pleasure and pain mixed. In the club's history, one 'lady' is cited at length with unusual candour on her feelings about the men-only tradition:

It's living in Burnley I suppose. They can't help it, can they? Worked all their lives and nothing to show for it, have they? God! Wish I could get away from Burnley. You know, live somewhere nice. But I can't can I? It's like I'm trapped, you know? How can anyone get away from this rat-hole? Oh dear! I think too much, that's my problem.

She says this with a laugh; but it is 'a laugh without humour', the club historian reports.[15]

Were you to consult Google in search of contemporary visual images of Britain or England, and images from the nineteenth-century as well, you would not find places like Burnley. Indeed, among the many hundreds of images shown, there were in April 2020 only three (for the nineteenth century) that showed any industrial scene at all. One of the three is an L. S. Lowry painting. Hardly a scientific procedure, but instructive nonetheless; the industrial world that made modern Britain is but a fleeting presence in British literature and the arts. Exceptions will be found, but their number is infinitesimal compared with that which they fail to represent. This omission is incredible, literally – almost impossible to believe; but then this is what Britain has done to its past, one it does not wish to recognize, awful as it was, on the mainland and beyond it. Lowry is perhaps the most important exception, for his painting of industrial Britain – principally Manchester and Salford – were in the twentieth century the most enduring images of industry and its times.

As I turn into the A57, the Hyde road, on my way into the city of Manchester, I confront Mr Lowry seated on a bench a little set back from the roaring traffic that passes by unheeding. A couple of hundred yards back from the metal statue of the man at this crossroads is where the real man lived for the last thirty years of his life, 'The Elms' in Mottram-in-Longdendale. It was in this hated house that he did most of his work, and encountered the extraordinary fame that came to him late in his lifetime. He died three years before my arrival in the North. He is said to have liked the village well enough, but not to have been a great mixer – hardly surprising given the solitary nature of the man that is reflected in his work. It is unlikely that the real Lowry did much sitting on benches in the village.

There are several Lowrys: the brief political Lowry of the 1930s; the existential Lowry that followed – the solitary wandering in the deserts of modernity; and the 'English' Lowry, the Lowry that was perhaps the most influential. In this Lowry, his landscapes are seen as a sort of industrial pastoral – a version that, for a time, made it possible to embrace the North as part of one England.[16] There is now a fourth Lowry, that of the culture-led regeneration in the city in the form of the Lowry Centre, which itself is part of a massive redevelopment project in the area called Salford Quays. This was once the Manchester Ship Canal, part of the desolation Sebald looked upon, the cotton clouds of lost souls drifting above. The new BBC Media City is one of several prestigious institutions now situated here. The usual large apartment blocks are in evidence, but much of the rest of Salford Borough still lives in a condition of considerable want, which is putting it mildly, child poverty approaching 50 per cent in some parts. The Lowry Centre houses a large collection of his paintings.

In the 1950s and '60s, reproductions of Lowry's paintings were ubiquitous locally – a part, it is said, of the wallpaper of everyday life: on memorabilia, in calendars, on school walls. His ubiquity reflected his popularity precisely at the time when the world he painted was at its height, but already showing signs of its eventual and rapid destruction: the world of Beyer and Peacock, the world where the clearances of the old dwelling places of the city had not yet been accomplished, but were daily gaining ground – the 'golden years' of Burnley and places like it, in fact. His work was a salve for a sense of dislocation so widely experienced then, and a consolation for the consequences of this dislocation since. These images still matter to older generations, who may have beheld them in their youth. They still seem to matter to later generations; though for these people they are not connected to any real past, so that nostalgia easily tips over into sentimentality and eventually into the kitsch of Lowry's 'matchstick men'.

The scenes Lowry painted are mostly from the period between the 1920s and the 1950s – chiefly from a pre-war world, in fact, one of great deprivation and not of pastoral, but a world where the sense of being at home in a place was still intact. The sense is conveyed in *Golden Years of Burnley*, and extends to the years following the war and drawing upon it. This was a world whose ending had yet to be experienced – a world that, for those alive at that time, had persisted for generations, and so must have seemed capable of going on for ever. Lowry's paintings miss the vivacity of densely textured social life that existed in these towns – the life pictured in the *Gorton Advertiser* in the 1950s, for instance. He never shows the inside of workplaces or houses, and the real colours of life are not there; his palette is limited, repetitious, washed out.

Yet his paintings contain much that is true about industrial Jerusalem and its fall. They convey the reality of what I earlier called a culture of control – a culture shaped by the experience of dependence and necessity. They convey a powerful sense of place inseparable from this culture, without the vivacity but with the truth of subjection. He paints communal gatherings like those at football matches, on people's days off from work in parks – paintings such as his *Saturday Afternoon* and the *Sunday Morning* of 1949. He painted *A Procession* in 1929. Lowry was a voyeur, his paintings distanced and always looking on, and this enabled him to allow his public to be voyeurs of their own lives.

What is present in his work, and has been remarked on several times, is a numbness in him that conveyed the numbness people needed to survive in that world. All of his pictures are the same, the decades between them notwithstanding.

What they really convey is the darkness of industrial England and Britain. The workplaces, particularly mills, in his paintings completely dominate the compositions, as in the fearful *Coming from the Mill* of 1930. The workplaces overawe the tiny people scurrying in and out of them – harassed, trudging, bowed, leaning as if drawn in and sucked out of workplaces (and of parks and football grounds); people without identity. I am reminded of the bowed heads of Gorton and Ashton-under-Lyne in these present days. The non-work pictures are even more terrifying, for the workplace dominates and frames both the houses and the people in them, as in his *Saturday Afternoon* of the late 1940s. Attempts to escape result in the same domination as that which people wished to escape.

This old industrial world Lowry depicted has ended, and with it the manual working class of both north and south, just as the old peasant world I was privileged to know has ended. Thinking of the Britain and England I have dwelt in, I am in retrospect struck more by the similarities than the differences between north and south. They both experienced the same clearances, the same new modern world on offer, the same betrayals. Hyde Road in Gorton and Harrow Road in Paddington are in their essence not much changed. There have been endings, but at the same time I cannot shake off the sense of how relatively little has changed over my lifetime. Social inequality has persisted and increased, and the rewards of unparalleled economic growth have been squandered. How limited seems British intolerance of inequality still. Not far short of a century ago, R. H. Tawney wrote in his book *Equality*, in describing what he called the religion of inequality in 1920s Britain, 'One of the regrettable, if diverting, effects of extreme inequality is its tendency to weaken the capacity for impartial judgement. It pads the lives of its beneficiaries with a soft down of consideration, while relieving them of the vulgar necessity of justifying their pretensions, secure that, if they fall, they fall on cushions.'[17]

Attempts to escape result in the same domination people sought to put behind them, as in *Saturday Afternoon*. This could be a motto for Britain since the Second World War. If it is true that, in Britain now – more particularly in England – a sense of being at home in the nation(s) has come into question, then, in answer to the question, the past is invoked constantly. This invocation sometimes takes the form of what we call nostalgia – which is not necessarily escapism or irrationality. What *Golden Years of Burnley* and books like it reveal seems to be connected to real and not imaginary pasts, and so the nostalgia they reveal has a certain solidity to it.

The word nostalgia derives from the fusion of two Greek words: *nostos*, 'homecoming', from *neomai*, to return, get home; and *algos*, grief, pain or sickness induced by the desire for home. The German word is *Heimweh* – literally 'home-woe'. Nostalgia is particularly marked in the old, of course; but the sickness for home may be compounded with and so strengthened by other kinds of yearning. We may yearn for a past but not want to return to it ('things are better now'). Nostalgia has incredible power because it is so deeply rooted in our emotions. We should not disprize or underestimate it. It is these days taken more seriously than it once was.[18] Nostalgia has a long history. In the twenty-first century it has gone through a remarkable change, going from being a disease to a cure, and so psychologized as a nostrum for all manner of social ills (there is 'memory therapy', for instance).[19]

Contemporary desire for, recourse to, and simply interest in the past is so various as to defy generalization. But it seems clear that something has changed in recent decades with respect to time – certainly since Sebald wrote, in a time that itself now seems long ago, about the necessity of dwelling with the dead in a world in which they are increasingly crowded out by the vastly growing numbers of the living. When perceptions of time change, so do those of the past – especially the past as home. But it is difficult to understand this change, because so much has happened so quickly. Academics have maintained that nostalgia is a type of memory that is particularly dependent on a heightened sensitivity to the passing of time. This sensitivity certainly seems to mark the culture of the present – one of instantaneous communication, and of time as ever more pressing. In terms of perceptions and uses of the past, this feeds a culture of instant commemoration and anniversary, sometimes of things that happened recently but already seem long past, propelled as they are into the dustbin of 'history' by commemoration.

The Internet reflects and augments this tendency. Time is accelerated and compressed, so that things are 'done with' quickly, and one moves on to the next. The intensity of time is heightened, but this only increases the circularity of the effect; the next thing one moves on to only reintroduces one into the same intensity, ramped up in the interim. The Internet puts you 'there', as it has been put, privileging what is happening now, 'not opt in but always on', so that the value of depth is sacrificed to immediacy masquerading as evidence. I remarked in Chapter 1 that, just as the need to remember is eclipsed, so the possibility of remembering is enhanced. We are now capable of archiving almost everything, but the algorithmic and market principles of selection create an effect of randomness. A kind of mosaic memory results, the product of 'browsing', made up of information that is free-floating, bereft of context, and already selected for us. As the world is connected, understanding is disconnected. Of course, we are not pliant and passive users, and can fight back; but this often seems like an uphill task.

Space seems to retreat before time, in that the sense of place gives way to the timeless time of the present. The effect seems to be that people are desensitized to experiences of time as anything other than what is immediate and fast-moving. Past time thus becomes something akin to a void, something that people either have no time for or wish to flee to as a respite for the newness pressing in on them. Into this void comes nostalgia,

and what may be called pastness, so that nowness and pastness emerge together and run in parallel, complementing one
another.

Nostalgia feeds off pastness, and pastness thrives on the
feeding. Pastness is the notion that the past is stable, know-
able, and simply a continuation of the present backwards, and
the future a continuation of the present forwards. Something
seems to have happened to the past in the 1970s, just as something happened to time in recent decades. Up to the 1970s,
versions of the past drove visions of the future, energizing
them – which is not to say that this past was 'true', only that it
was felt to be directly and immediately relevant to the present.
When hoped-for progress receded, the past changed, too. It lost
its capacity to energize the present, since the present was on the
road to nowhere, and so seemed to have come from nowhere.
It became relocated in the realm of 'pastness' itself.

Heritage was one form of this phenomenon. 'The people'
underwent a similar change, and were now a focus of a more
present-minded individualism than before. Hope, if it existed,
became centred in present fulfilment, and in imaginary, more
individualistic futures. The once-progressive 'people' became
the object of appeals not to any real past, but to the fabricated
pasts of 'populist' politicians. And so, we are on the road to
Brexit, and indeed have arrived.

This broad picture accords with that of social historians'
accounts of what happened to the past, but is of course presented schematically here – for instance 'community' and
'individualism' are not only not mutually exclusive, but do
not map onto this picture of the change the past has undergone (golden ages of 'community', rampant individualism,
and so on). British nationalism itself began to break up in the
1970s, not least because of what happened in Ireland; or, at
least, the idea of a unitary Britain came into question. Out of
the 1970s emerged the myth of national decline and with this
there was a shift away from the idea of the people's war to a

Thatcherite identification of a patriotic war. The Churchill of late-imperial vintage came to the fore, a militaristic and racialized Britain became more manifest, and England took a more central place than in the past (it was the 'industrial spirit' of England that had declined, to echo the title of an influential book of the time).

The 1980s was the decade in which the new concern with 'national heritage' emerged, evoking the idea of one nation once again, but now a distinctly English one. 'English Heritage' was founded in 1983, with the motto: 'We bring history to life'. The National Heritage Acts were passed in 1980 and 1983, and the Heritage Educational Trust formed in 1982. This was followed by an astonishing proliferation of heritage sites – historical 'theme parks' as some of them came to be known. The economics of tourism became rampant in the new service economy of a deindustrializing Britain.

The past increasingly became simply the same old thing, and making history making more of the same thing. The past became the source of lessons – it was exemplary; but at the same time it was distant, apart and even exotic. The past we have inherited from those times has come to have its own pseudo-authenticity, which is mirrored by its political use as a marker of sincerity, integrity and commitment. The past also becomes the personal, and so pasts are selected through which an 'identity' is created, so that the past is a resource for self-fashioning, picked up and laid down at will. Pastness, which is the product of the absolute present, is the ground in which the myths of Brexit have blossomed.

In chapter 10, in reflecting on the old way of passage of the walked road and the new one of the driven automobile, I considered what anthropologists call 'non-places' – places of transience in cultures that seem always on the move. Ágnes Heller describes this new mode of existence as 'the absolute present', in which people feel at home not in a place, but in a time. She tells a story about this.[20] She writes of the owner of a small restaurant in the Campo de' Fiori in the Rome of some sixty years ago. This man does not know much of the world beyond the Campo, and his whole life has been spent there. This place is unreservedly 'home'. She contrasts him with a woman she met on an international jet flight three decades later, who could not understand the concept of 'home'. This woman tells her: 'Home is where my cat is.' The man is geographically monogamous; the woman travels light, and alone, without baggage, without a community, so that she is not in a culture of place but of time, 'the absolute present'. Everywhere she travels is the same, and she does the same thing in these similar places. It is as if, Heller writes, places move to her, not she to them.

People have always moved, of course, but they have carried their culture with them on their backs – the Jews and the Irish, for instance; but not her. She lives in the spaces of nowhere and everywhere, spaces that can be found in east Manchester as they can all over Britain. The limitations of a temporal life experience include, Heller writes, the lack of sensuality and emotionality; but these are found in other ways – in the self-cultivation of the body and the mind, for instance. (As someone growing up in the 1950s, it is, as much as anything else, basic things like food that present the face of change, in particular the now almost cultic significance attached to what is put in the mouth.) But the point of Heller's argument is not that we can go back to a world of space, but that we must live now in this new world of time. Nonetheless, we can choose to be at home in our spatial worlds, in places, as in religions or tribes; but what has changed is that we now have the *capacity* to choose, which is the result of life in the absolute present.

Heller's fable is schematic, but revealing. The people of Burnley do not dwell in the world of the woman with the cat. They are, like the man of the Campo de' Fiori, spatially monogamous; but, unlike him, they are married to a place where the sense of being at home in the home place is elusive. Racism is central to this; being in a place is being its rightful possessor, its authentic occupant. To have come from elsewhere was always to bear a stamp of inauthenticity in these very traditional towns, and this effect was magnified greatly in times of economic hardship – especially when the colour of elsewhere marked you out visibly.

Nonetheless, those living in Burnley, like all of us today, do live in this dimension of pastness: the absolute present. The absolute present, the eternal present – perhaps these terms are too dramatic, too absolute. Let us say, instead, the 'continuous present', acknowledging complexity and the reality that multiple times are always in play, because time is always experienced both privately and publicly. There are also the several tributaries that lead into the growing field of 'public history', including the family history.[21] This is history often written by amateur historians, the 'amateur' the one who does things through love. Nonetheless, the continuous present dominates. Heritage is its great expression, through which we are encouraged to dwell and find a home – along the walls of Derry, at RAF Duxford, on HMS Belfast, in the 1,001 little heritage museums that dot the country.

The political use of the past concerns our fate most immediately. There is the broadly political use of the past, as in the work of the dead in and through war, which we have seen; and there is the use of the past that is more party-political – though the two types intersect. In the former category, there operates across all parties, and no less in society at large, the pervasive idea of a liberal nation, an idea that more often than not gels with myths surrounding war. This is a version of 'national character' in which the nation is moderate, tolerant of all sides, sides which if they depart too much from the sacrosanct middle ground are labelled 'extreme'. It is a version of the long past of a Britain genetically liberal – a past frozen in time, seemingly able to accommodate all manner of hypocrisies and contradictions.

It is not fixed in permafrost however, as things can change dramatically, and nothing has dramatized the tumultuous return of the real past so much as the events that have come to a head in the summer of Black Lives Matter and Covid.

Liberal Britain has come to be defined in terms of the 'via media', against Continental extremes including those attributed to Catholicism. In intellectual terms, it includes the defence of stout English empiricism against Continental Theory; and it has for centuries happily coincided with visions of empire.[22] Liberal Britain, governed over long centuries according to the elements of liberal freedom – free markets, free people, free spaces – has nonetheless proved unable and unwilling to see that that freedom has as much to do with ruling people as with escaping arbitrary rule.[23] One historian of English identity, Arthur Aughey, writes of the idea of muddling through – of, as he puts it, 'muddling in the middle'.[24] As the Welshman Raymond Williams once wrote about the English, when in doubt they imagine a pendulum. Occupying the middle in this way is quite compatible with the all-pervasive idea of the 'island story' – the island alone amidst the seas, so that being in the middle is also being apart – even though England is not an island.

Already, Jeremy Paxman's bestsellers on the English of twenty years ago seem to describe another land.[25] But they are still bestsellers. To Paxman, the English live in a country that is 'firmly based in a tradition of personal liberty, that still believes in fair play, that is tolerant, easy-going and slow to anger'. And yet, the English 'remain convinced they're finished. That is their charm' – the same charm to be found in their 'glorious, fundamental cussedness'.[26] For Paxman, this is unchanged, as are the individualism and pragmatism. His 'new nationalism' is and will remain modest, individualistic, ironic. The embarrassing self-delusion and calculated parochialism of this horseshit is doubly apparent to those of us immigrants and immigrants' children born above the furrows of English culture.

Both the party-based and more broadly political registers

of the national past have had a profound effect on what it has meant to have a British or English identity over my lifetime, and on what it is to feel at home within it. In terms of the party political, historians have recently been revealing what has been going on.[27] While previous political uses of the past emphasized its capacity to make demands upon the present (Conservative duty and Labour obligation), this tendency has been sidelined in favour of a present-centred view of the past that can be rejected or embraced as is politically expedient. The past is used to set the present within a legitimating framework ('pastness', in fact) in which it appears constantly 'historic'. Parties and politicians are expected to remain true to their pasts, demonstrating continuity, integrity and authenticity; but they must also demonstrate that they are of their own time, and not lost in the past, so that they have time on their side. But political memory operates with a keen regard for the authority of professional history, as politicians are aware that they are part of history, and preferably making it – especially if they get in early enough with their diaries and memoirs.

Both main political parties are imbued by parliamentarianism, and thus by a particular belief in the liberal nation.[28] Labour has had a remarkable reluctance to change these institutions, being fixated on the distribution of wealth and not on the structures of power that keep it in place. There is now an account of the uses of the Labour past which employs the word nostalgia in its title – and in its subtitle refers to 'prisoners of the past'.[29]

On the political right, these structures of power are more intimately known and efficiently deployed, as is evident in the extraordinary continuity and political success of the Conservative Party since the war – a success that has had catastrophic consequences. The right has been even more enthralled by the idea of the nation than has the left. It is in the Brexit saga that we see most clearly the war myth being mobilized for political purposes. In this saga, it has been Britain 'standing alone', not its empire, that has mattered. The Eurosceptic right has been fuelled not by the idea of a return to empire, but by the idea that it did not really matter much in the first place. The effect of fixating on the nation 'standing alone' has been to reduce empire to a result of British power, rather than its cause. The empire was not something that Britain was, but something that Britain did, as has been said.[30] The empire has been written out of the story, just as it was from the Second World War.

It is myths of smallness, not of largeness, that have been in play ('gigantism' was, after all, Enoch Powell's term for imperial delusion), quixotically defining a 'Global Britain' as better off alone. The story is familiar, and infinitely wearying in its repetition, the protestations of historical exceptionalism and institutional distinctiveness projected back into history: the little islands of home under siege in Calcutta's Black Hole and at Mafeking; the defeat of the Spanish Armada by the tiny island; the heroism of Dunkirk and The Few. Smallness is the very essence of pastness, the flourishing of the absolute past. Smallness is related to sovereignty: go it alone on the right and the left, the Brexiteers on one hand, the equally deluded heirs of Benn's popular sovereignty on the other. Brexit, as we have seen, was a matter of control, of 'bringing back control', and there is nowhere better than an island on which to do so, and to be once again master of one's own house.

The materiality and symbolism of the island enact self-containment and invoke things that are integral – things like culture, traditions, states of mind, such as the straightforwardness deemed to be missing in more open, porous places, such as contiguous, and thus less fortunate, European lands. Islands enact the opposite, as well: movement and openness, outward and inbound; but it is precisely at the junction points of movement, borders, that the fears of islands are situated. What gives the island its force is the notion of home and of the house: that which gives shelter and security is at the centre of the idea of home.

My account of life in the continuous present is so far rather generalized and abstract. It might be better, in concluding, to focus on one place in particular: Stoke-on-Trent. The capital of Brexit, as it has been called, Stoke-on-Trent recorded the highest Leave vote of any large town or city in Britain. It is very similar to Burnley in its recent industrial history, though perhaps enduring a worse plight – poorer if anything. Its fall since the 1970s has been precipitous; iron and steel, coalmining, and above all the pottery industry all collapsed, though the latter, like cotton, had been on the way out over the long term anyway. This fall roughly coincided with entry into the European Union.[31] Stoke is called the Potteries; the name is used locally more often than Stoke-on-Trent. It is not a place most people go to, and it is like Burnley in this. It is perhaps only briefly glimpsed by rail travellers from London as they look up from their laptops and out at the city's remarkable neo-Tudor railway station during the train's brief stop. It is a place I knew between 1965 and 1969, when I attended the local university, Keele, itself sited on a hill away from the Potteries themselves, on the country side of the satellite town of Newcastle-under-Lyme. My knowledge was thus gained at a distance, though I have returned on and off since then. This is where I first saw the 'North'.

Stoke is still a distinctive place. It is made up of five individual towns, each still retaining its identity. Longton, in the south, was the greatest pottery centre. Stoke itself is neither North nor South, nor even quite the Midlands, separated as it is from the great conurbations of Manchester to the north and Birmingham to the south. Its patterns of speech are highly distinctive, and still persist. Men and women are called 'duck', as in other parts of the east Midlands, though it is not the quacking animal form that is invoked, but the Saxon word *ducas*, a mark of respect, similar to the Middle English *duc* or *duk*, which denotes a leader and a territory ruled over – a duchy. The same etymology is echoed in Dúiche Sheoighe, in fact – a vastly different place, but connected through the strange histo-ries that names give us.

There was until recently a popular cartoon called 'May un Mar Lady', written in the Potteries dialect, that ran for decades in the local newspaper, the *Sentinel*, which I once knew as the *Staffordshire Sentinel*. The *Sentinel*'s website now runs a 'Way We Were' column – what it calls its 'popular nostalgia' section. Clearly, there is more than one kind of nostalgia. It is said that older people use the dialect more than the young, and it is the same where I live further north; and 'dialect' is a relative term, since the richness of local speech has been progressively lost over the last century. Like the Irish language, 'dialect' is used increasingly as part of an effort to remember, rather than as something that emerges out of the exigencies of daily life.

The old cityscape, still evident into the 1960s, was an astonishing sight – a forest of tall chimneys interspersed with countless bottle-shaped pottery kilns – so-called potbanks; the industry had been one of hundreds of small manufacturers as well as the great ones, Wedgwood, Minton, Doulton and the others. The potbanks were crowded together with the houses, the two almost indistinguishable. There were once many ver-sions of the comic postcard of industrial towns depicted on both a clear day and a smoky day, but the Stoke version rang truest of all (identical blackness obtained on both days).

There is one place I remember above all from that time in Stoke – a place called Etruria. A remarkable place for its name and history, but a sight, then as now, of such utter desolation that only a Sebald could do justice to it. Wedgwood's Etruria Works had closed in 1950, after 180 years at the same site, moving south of the city and leaving hundreds of acres of abandoned land.[32] The great iron-and-steel works of Shelton Bar was nearby, and still going: photographs of the time show the great scourings of the land surrounding the works. Wedg-wood's fine eighteenth-century Etruria Hall stood intact in the desolation, cheek by jowl with the Bar and beside the Works.

Derelict potbanks, Stoke, 2019.

At its height, Shelton Bar (owned by Shelton Iron, Steel and Coal Company) occupied a 400-acre site and employed 10,000 workers. The company owned five coalmines, a complete railway system, and a by-products processing factory. Shelton Bar came under nationalized ownership in 1951, was denationalized by the Conservative government in 1953, and then renationalized in 1967, the main works closing in 1978. The BBC showed a film in 1973 called *The Fight for Shelton Bar*. What was left of Shelton Bar was closed by Corus, offshoot of the Indian steelmaker Tata, in June 2000. The half-mile-long steel-rolling mill building was torn down in early 2005.

I returned to Etruria in late 2019. Unsurprisingly, the place had been utterly transformed. Now a commercial and retail and leisure 'development', it was graced with a Toby Carvery, an Odeon multiplex cinema and a Homebase, the whole place now surrounded by long, flat warehouses and small light-industrial premises. Wide roads encircled the place – a place only cars could comfortably access, empty at night, creating an island. The one relief in the landscape was a pub called the Holy Inadequate. Here, you might say, was one home of the continuous present. But what was most remarkable to me about the place was the sight of the shiny new headquarters building of Bet365 – one of the biggest online gambling firms in the world, and the largest private employer in Stoke (even larger are the Council and the local hospitals). It struck me, on seeing Bet365 standing there, the workplace of around 2,500 people, that, just as so much of life in the continuous present seems to be about the pursuit of what is accessible but never achievable, I had in Bet365 the very image of this life.

Online betting enables betting not only for 365 days of the year, but for every minute and second of each day. One can be on almost anything and in multiple forms, not only sports, and there are an endless supply of sports to bet on anyway. As with the promptings of the Internet, time is compressed, and things are 'done with' quickly, so that everything happens in the present. Bet365 live-streams 70,000 events each year, it claims: 'Not opt in but always on'. What is accessible but never achievable, but more achievable than fixed-odds betting because the middle man is cut out and punter and Bet 365 divide the spoils within them, thus the incentive to achieve the unachievable is all the greater.

The journalist Martin Fletcher reports on the addictive intensity of the new betting, one now seamlessly giving way to another now. 'There are fewer and fewer opportunities to stand back and take a breather and consider whether you should be carrying on', says one respondent. A former employee told me Bet365 profiles its customers so it can target them accordingly. It has also developed one of the slickest websites and mobile phone apps: 'It's the best in the world. It's the most sophisticated.'[33] By 2017–18, Bet365 had 35 million customers, who wagered £52 billion annually. Its websites can be accessed in over twenty languages, and it is said to be the go-to brand for sports betting worldwide. It is reputed to have ways and means of tapping into the vast markets for gambling in China and India (gambling is illegal in China, but online gambling permitted in India). In the globalized in Etruria of 2019, Bet365 was the new British Empire.

It is important to realize that online betting is spread betting; the principles are exactly the same in financial as in leisure capitalism. According to onlinegamblingbible.com, one of many sources of wisdom in this occult world: 'Based on their estimation of the result of a sports event or the future prospects of an index or a share, a spread is quoted by the spread betting company. Based on your assessment, you can bet on rise or fall in the price or win or loss of a particular team' – or on the number of goals, or free kicks, or corners, or backheels, or players with black hair or bald making backheels, ad infinitum, so long as people are willing to bet. That is to say, you are betting for or against movements in pots of promises to pay or be paid – an already abstract market in money made even more so by dint of virtuality. You follow the pots of money as they grow or diminish – pots made in Stoke, Singapore, Milwaukee, Poznan.

Behind Bet365 is the phenomenon that is Denise Coates. She took the gambling side of the family business in hand in 2000. She is the highest-paid female business executive in Britain, and probably in the world, and one of the richest women in Britain. This is not difficult to bring off as, unlike many such companies, hers is family-owned, so that she pays herself. She is a favourite of the tabloids, though she and the company are very private, and in many ways very Stoke: a favourite because, between 2016 and 2019, she collected a total of £817 million in remuneration. The upmarket *Guardian* was on the case, too, estimating that over the same period she was paid an amount 18,500 times the income of the average woman worker in the city.[34]

She owns a Norman Foster–designed house said to have cost £90 million. In 2019, *Forbes* magazine estimated her net worth at $12.2 billion. Of the house, Piers Taylor, co-host of BBC TV's *The World's Most Extraordinary Homes*, told the *Daily Express* in 2018: 'Denise could have done a lot worse. Most new Cheshire millionaires build McMansions: a curious mash-up of a super-sized developer house that's mated with a Las Vegas casino ... It is one hell of a lot better than most of the houses that Cheshire footballers build.'[35]

Coates's father, Peter, made a fortune locally in catering and betting shops after leaving school at the age of fourteen. He has poured money into Stoke City Football Club, which he owns. Their stadium is the BET365 Stadium. In the 2019–20 English football season, half the Premier League clubs and seventeen out of twenty-four (second tier) Championship clubs were sponsored by online betting companies. Her grandfather Leonard was a miner from Goldenhill, in Stoke, had fourteen children, and was decorated for bravery in the First World War. They are great local benefactors, and in the city there is scarcely a word said against them. 'You could consider the Coates family to be the new Wedgwoods or Doultons of Stoke-on-Trent,' says Martin Tideswell, editor of the *Stoke Sentinel*.

How we view the past and how we live time seemed in that place, Etruria, so concentrated and yet so profuse as to defy understanding, the continuous present a puzzling place. So many pasts and times: the pasts of generations, the way pasts come together in the same time yet bring different understandings of time to this meeting, the three generations of the Coates family and what that family's links to the city betoken when plotted out over time. Especially when the links are to do with football, which possesses intimate connections with place in Britain, as here, now a century and a half old.

In Burnley the team is just as important as in Stoke, and now more successful. It has Mike Garlick, a.k.a. Michael Bailey Associates management consultants, as its owner, the proud bearer of the title of poorest club owner in the Premier League. He is said to be worth only £50 million – an infinitesimal amount for the lords of the universe who own the big clubs. He is a Burnley-bred man – though I note that the northern name of Garlick has been lost in the transition to the London-based 'Michael Bailey Associates'. He is the same animal but of a different stripe to the Coates and to Burnley's owner in the glory days of the 1960s, Bob Lord – butcher boy made good, self-styled outsider against the establishment, antisemite, friend of Edward Heath, the kind of local 'card' Arnold Bennett wrote about in his great literary accounts of the Potteries at the turn of the twentieth century.

But it is Etruria itself that provides the perspective. In 1771, Josiah Wedgwood built the factory village of Etruria on the outskirts of Stoke-on-Trent, close to the new canal system he had already had a large hand in developing. He named the set-tlement after the ancient civilization of Etruria, where, on the Italian peninsula at the time, black porcelain dating to Etrus-can times was being excavated. The remarkable beauty of these artefacts and the profit motive were his joint inspiration, and he became a seminal figure in the history of capitalism. His first major success was the mechanical production of the orig-inal porcelain in the form of what he called 'black basalt'. His products went on to have huge, worldwide economic success. But so too have the products of Denise Coates, the china cup replaced by the gambler's dream, all that is solid melting into the algorithm (Bet365's HQ is full of software engineers and systems analysts).

Josiah Wedgwood is credited with a hand in the develop-ment of the division of labour, which is the foundation of the modern factory system. He was an inventor of modern mar-keting techniques, including the money-back guarantee and the travelling salesman. But then Denise Coates is also a pioneer and innovator. Layer upon layer of history becomes apparent in this place. Josiah Wedgwood was a leading abolitionist in the anti-slavery movement. Etruria as well as exquisite dinnerware produced in great numbers the ceramic anti-slavery medallion that became the symbol of the astonishingly successful political movement that was Abolitionism. He was the grandfather of Charles Darwin. Etruria Hall was where Josiah's son Thomas, dead at just twenty-four, pioneered key developments in the invention of photography.

Etruria is home to the Etruria Industrial Museum, though amidst the roads and new developments it is difficult to find. It is the kind of heritage museum one sees throughout Britain, and these days in Ireland. Its website informs us that school parties may

> stroll along the canal towpath to learn about canals, water safety and how locks work, a step back in time to meet characters from the Flint and Bone Mill and learn about the materials needed to make bone china and going onboard a real Heritage Narrow Boat to learn about how boating families lived and worked. All workshops are linked to the National Curriculum and include Local Studies, STEM and water safety.

As in the Manchester Museum of Industry, it collects and displays objects, not joy, suffering, sadness, hardship, silence. What would a museum of historical silence look like? There have been changes in some museums, which move towards new possibilities; but not here, or at least not yet.

Such heritage museums are an important educational tool, and they excite the historical imagination. Once a visitor is excited, made alert to what the great historian Marc Bloch called the 'charge' of the past, the electricity of its difference, the provocations of its silence, many things can happen. Just as in the Etruria leisure development, the child of today may in later years look back with nostalgia at contemporary Etruria; indeed, that child looks at it now as a place even though it hardly seems like one in the continuous present, certainly compared to the time when Stoke, for good and ill, was a place like nowhere else on earth.

12

Endings

To me it seems an Echo sounds
Out of the deep distance of our grief.
Our loved ones too may be longing for us,
And send to us this yearning breath ...
A dream will break our fetters off,
And sink us forever in our Father's lap.

Novalis

Returning to London over the decades, it has felt like home, because the past of childhood and youth always lingers there. Still, I also came over time to feel dispossessed, as my kind of people, people I had known then, had been inexorably moved out to the far reaches of the city, or out of the place altogether, driven by the imperatives of the new era of the 'world city'. The city was always a monster, sucking people in and spitting them out – always a place where people from around the world came to settle, and where real Londoners were then born, for to be born there is to be a real Londoner. I was a Londoner in ways that my Irish parents were not, not so much a Londoner now as I once was, but still with a sort of birthright. These days the city is more ravenous than ever – so busy, so crowded, so polluted that it now seems to choke upon itself. This is a frightful legacy for a great city.

In 2018, I returned several times to the area around Grenfell Tower, to the Silchester housing estate, and to the tower block where I had lived half a century earlier, Whitstable House, which is part of Silchester and the nearest tall tower block to

Grenfell. The fire occurred in the previous year, but I had been too ill to visit for almost all of that year. Whitstable House is the subject of a fine multimedia feature by the *Guardian*, 'The Tower Next Door'. Whitstable has suffered over the years. The place looks shabby: bleak as it was originally, it is now bleaker still. The Westway and the overhead Underground line almost directly abut it. Like those of all these 'houses' and towers, its entrance is fortified these days.

Grenfell is on the Lancaster West estate, which is sprucer than Silchester, and in some corners much better. Some of the old shops ('Dollys, The People's Florist' among them) and some of the old pubs survived the demolition of the late 1960s for a while, when I lived there. The pubs then defined one's geography – as did the still functioning public baths, with their wash houses. Now the pubs are either gone or turned into expensive bars and restaurants. Around Whitstable they are few, and the clientele pre-selected. The biggest determinant of pre-selection is price – the price of a pint is forbidding for the people who live around here.

In the *Guardian* feature, one person stands out – Joe Walsh, who runs the nearby social club, the Maxilla, named after a street that once lay near it. Joe, like me, has Irish parents, and

Entrance to Whitstable House, October 2018.

he too went to the Cardinal Manning School, five minutes' walk away. His father, a Limerick man, tells me that in his own young days he served with the British Army in Derry, but that was before the conflict. Joe never did well at school, he tells me; his dyslexia was never picked up by the teachers. As a result, he was always in the lower 'streams' of the school. He is one of the few originals left, and he has lived on the estate for all his life in the area. Although he maintains strong Irish connections, he does not share my childhood experience of the country, and he seems to me the quintessence of the old Dale.

He was a boxer, like Mick Delaney, with whom I went to school, a fellow 'A' streamer, yet one who coached in the Dale Youth boxing club at the base of Grenfell for forty-five years, during which time I knew nothing of his local fame. Delaney was part of the Dale Irish of St Francis, who always seemed to me harder than the rest of us ('well hard, he is'), or at least they presented themselves to us as such. The family that gave the world the hard-nut footballer Dennis Wise were of the same St Francis crew. In fact, 'Wisey', Dennis's uncle, was a feared name in my young day, whose own sons are still involved with the Dale Youth Club.[1]

The Maxilla remains an important social centre in the area. Up to the mid 1990s or so, your face had to 'fit' to be a member of the Maxilla Club; that is, you had to be white. Now people of all colours share the club. It holds all sorts of musical events, and hosts funeral receptions too. The building is forbidding inside and out; there are no windows, and the thing is a giant metal box. The super-rich slum it at the club, the area still being 'trendy', to use a sixties word: it is 'the coolest place in Notting Hill', they say, even though it is not in Notting Hill. I ask Joe if he resents this, reflecting as it does probably the worst inequality in the UK, that of the 'Royal Borough'. He answers, 'You got to accept it or it will eat away at you.'

Places like the Maxilla are needed, Joe tells me, given the dire pub situation, and the meanness of council social provision;

like many around here, he loathes the London Borough of Kensington and Chelsea, and has loathed it since long before the fire itself. The club is needed because, he says, contrary to many press reports, the Grenfell area is not the shining example of local community it is sometimes made out to be in the media. It is not that people are not friendly, but thirty years ago he knew most of the eighty or so households in Whitstable, and now he knows at most a score. People are civil – they say hello coming and going – but not much else. They all have their own lives, as they come from a wide range of places outside Britain and carry many forms of community with them, which they call upon and enact in the city as their first resort. They are the same as the people of Grenfell, so many of whose lives were ended in the terrible fire.

But the schools, churches and mosques provide cohesion, nonetheless, including the Catholic St Francis. Among the congregation of St Francis are numbered several victims of the fire. There is also the Methodist Chapel, almost in the shadow of the Tower, which at its entrance displays some thirty or forty photographs of the congregation, all but one of whom is of West Indian or African origin. At the rear of the church there is a plaque to the dozen members of the congregation who died in the First World War – all English names, and probably white.

Walking around the area, I wondered what was there before the fire, on the spot where the Tower and its immediate grounds stood; I felt that, in all the publicity given to the fire and the area more generally, the actual ground itself, the immediate territory, had been forgotten: the real place, ordinary enough, but still with its own accompanying spirit of place, its *genius loci*, as the Romans called it. Across almost all world cultures there is still a belief in this *genius* – a protective, tutelary deity.

There is a photograph of the Pitcher family of Threshers Place, near Fowell Street and the Canterbury Arms. As near as I can tell, there, on what became the Silchester Road–Bomore Road–Fowell Street triangle, the Tower later stood.[2] The old

The Pitcher family, 1930s.

unregenerate Dale. The poverty there was crushing. The very poorest children in the 1950s were sown into their clothes for the winter so as to bear the cold in 'condemned' housing; it was next to impossible to keep warm. 'It was to make sure the children kept warm. The mother took a needle and thread and sewed them in so they couldn't take their clothes off, and she usually rubbed them all over with goose grease if she could get hold of it, before doing the sewing.'[3]

The spirit of this place? This old Dale is not the world of today's immigrants, for the Pitcher family in the photo above were fairly well-settled people – white, English. Nonetheless, there were Gypsy and Traveller connections in some families in the area, and the Irish had been a presence much earlier than this. The piggeries and the potteries here in Victorian times had drawn people in, many of them outcasts from central London and the building of its great rail termini.[4] If a fairly settled people by the time of this photograph, those pictured were nonetheless kin to these earlier incomers, in that the locale was always a place of coming and going, of trying to settle, but, because of the poverty of the place, finding settling difficult. By the 1930s many had decided to stay put, if only because there was nowhere else to go. The children of these people were those who were most active in the Notting Hill 'race riots' of 1958, the epicentre of which was around here. This poor place has always been surrounded by riches.

So, the largely immigrant population of today is not so unlike these former residents as might first appear, so that the spirit of place is here, on that corner of the street in the photograph, where a family shows itself in the best style it can muster, presenting its best face to the world on a street it is claiming as its own. The different generations form a line, and they are in good spirits, all together. The *genius loci* of London; a frightful place then, too.

Another London is here as well, inseparable from the plebeian one: that of empire. Grenfell Road is named after Field Marshal Francis Wallace Grenfell, 1st Baron Grenfell GCB, GCMG, PC, commander-in-chief, South Africa, who fought in the 9th Xhosa War (the Xhosa Wars lasted a century, and were the longest-running military action in the history of African colonialism), the Anglo-Zulu War (1879) and the Anglo-Egyptian War (1872). He next became commander-in-chief of the Egyptian Army, and eventually commander-in-chief, Ireland, before retiring in 1908, a year after my father's birth.

His is the world of South Kensington, not North, however. A twenty-minute walk from Grenfell Tower takes one to the junction of Kensington Church Street and Kensington High Street, firmly within the territory of the South. I have passed there many times, as a child waiting for the bus that would take my mother and me to the eye hospital I attended. Never, as child or adult, did I think to look into the church on the corner, St Mary Abbots, the parish church of Kensington, both North and South. Inside lie the tombs of the empire-builders, the children of the very people they ruled over now making up the population of the poor North in towers like Grenfell. I pass the monument of a lady who died in Poona, which was a place of summer retreat for the British. Having finally retreated there, she is memorialized here; South Kensington was a haven for the sons and daughters of the empire-makers, as well as their retired or expired parents – the children's English home. My cousins across the years, hands across the Royal Borough.

Inside the chapel there is another monument, to William Lit-
tlejohn O'Halloran of the county of Limerick, one of a line of
O'Hallorans who served the British Empire faithfully for over
a hundred years. The Irish were empire-builders too.

In January 2015 I sat talking with a group of students in
St Charles Catholic Sixth Form College, in North Kensington.[5] Founded in 1990, it is the successor to the Cardinal
Manning Secondary Modern School for Boys. Only one of the
group I talked to was Catholic, or Irish; the backgrounds of
her classmates were Somalian, Eritrean, Nigerian, Ghanaian,
Caribbean, Kosovan and Slovenian, among others. They were
chiefly Christian, though of very different traditions, and at
least 20 per cent of the school's students were Muslim. Some
80 per cent were 'non-white', and around 40 per cent African
in background. About 25 per cent were Afro-Caribbean. Most,
but by no means all, had been born here to immigrant parents.

The school is very successful – 'outstanding', a 'beacon'. I
sensed this talking with the students and the principal. A very
high proportion of students get to university and college,
including the elite 'Russell Group' universities; most will be the
first in their family to go to university. But these children are
far from those of the elite, highly selective schools of Catholic
west London, such as the London Oratory (where Tony Blair
and Nick Clegg sent their children, and where I was refused
entry in 1961) and the Cardinal Vaughan School. Again, as so
often with London, everything happens and nothing changes,
and finding endings is not so easy as one might think. Both of
these elite schools are now, as they were then, pretend public
schools, still highly selective.

What is striking about the students of St Charles is their
strong sense that London and the school have much to offer
them. In our time we did not feel this, much as we thought
well of the school. We did not know that we were schooled
to have low expectations – which was not surprising, because
being schooled not to know that this was the case was part

of the schooling. The end-product was all the better achieved because we were the A boys, who, if we learned not to have great expectations, looked around us at the rest of our fellows for whom there were no expectations at all.

These students nowadays have, as the principal says, a belief 'in what they will become'. They are not 'negative people'. London education has improved immeasurably in the last twenty years or so, and the school is rightly proud of its role in this. It now draws students from all parts of London, unlike in the 1950s and 1960s, when it was intensely local. The school bonds the students, and they are immensely proud of it. It serves as a kind of 'house' for them, in fact – a second home. Whereas in the past the school cemented bonds that were already real, bonds of Irishness and Catholicism, religious and pedagogic institutions now have deliberately to create them anew. An atmosphere of aspiration pervades the school. This has its good and bad sides – the bad in the reality of expectations encouraged by the now pervasive rhetoric that success will be the inevitable result of believing enough, aspiring enough. The school website features a roll-call of its own success stories – students who became lawyers, doctors, financial traders, community workers, one even an adviser to Tony Blair.

This now-deliberate creation of the social bond is evident even with the Church. While there Catholicism still provides a widely shared identity, the local parish priest of St Pius X church in St Charles Square tells me that he sees his role as being that of a pontifex – a bridge-builder. His business involves reconciling West African, East African, European, Filipino, Caribbean, Irish and English Catholicism, not unlike the headmaster's role. 'Community', home-making – 'place-making', in fact – have now been given over to God's professionals as well as man's. The students I met are highly self-motivated, and highly motivated also by their parents, who are mostly relatively recent immigrants – people who have come to London having frequently tried other destinations first in their own personal odysseys. When I suggest that it seems from what they say that their parents are living their lives through them, they agree enthusiastically. Their loyalty to parents who have struggled for them is touching. One girl wants to 'make it all better' for her parents, who 'depend' on her. They want to 'build them a better life'.

The parents of some of the students I talk with have made a deliberate choice to send their children here, and so come from homes dotted around the city. Catholic schools have a good reputation. The students – pupils, as I would think of them – have an outlook that is both global and London-centred, belonging to communities outside Britain to which some of them return with various degrees of regularity, as did we, the Irish, in the fifties and sixties. Most were born here. They feel, they say, British. 'English' means nothing to them at all. They associate Britishness with 'being fully integrated', with 'a sense of community'. Those who were born outside Britain, on the other hand, feel differently, and cleave to the nation of their birthplace, which they put first, before Britain.

But they are far from representative of people of their age in schools outside London. Theirs is a particularly intense (and extensive) immigrant experience, and an experience of a city that has gone through astonishing changes since 2000 or so. The London of the post-war decades had a static, and then declining population; their London is one of increase, and of an expanding if often poorly paid job market, at least for their parents. This is inner London – though they will probably, wherever they work, eventually live in outer London, given the nature of the property market. They may remain on the estates, despite this generally being seen as a badge of failure. They are unrepresentative also in being the higher achievers in the school: happy, indeed eager, to speak to me. So they may, after attending university – as many in this group will – be able to get out of the estates, or 'off', as they say in Hattersley.

Beyond the Paddington of my youth to the north and west lies the large London borough of Brent, stretching out as far as

Wembley. A good number of the students attending St Charles's are recruited there, travelling in from this outer west to the inner. Our former experience of travelling to school as pupils of the long-vanished Manning was the collective experience of walking, picking up and shedding friends as we went to and from school, mine being one of the longest walks. The walk to school was a social event then, memorable to me still. These contemporaries are much more dispersed than we were, Brent being a huge borough. This is their world, and that of their immigrant parents, just as it was the London immigrant world of my parents before marriage, the world of what is now Brent; Stonebridge, Cricklewood, Harlesden and Willesden – Pevsner's dreary inter-war suburbs. This being London, there are pockets of prosperity in Brent, but one-third of the borough's population now lives in poverty. Brent has been one of the worst centres of Covid-19 infection and death not only in London, but in the whole of Britain. The feeling locally was that 'people were abandoned'.[6] In 2017, poverty stood at 27 per cent in Greater London – above the national average. The scandal that is London is overshadowed by the boosterism of London as a 'world city'.

The students I talk with are aware of class and social inequality, though less so in the case of those who do not live in the Royal Borough. One student who lives in now-expensive Pimlico shares my psychogeographical sense of class, that of the divided borough: 'They are trying to push us out', he says. Most come in and out of the area by public transport, and do not tarry as we once did. They are perhaps less aware of how glaring class distinctions can be than we were (within as well as between classes), sealed as they are in buses and trains, and separated by their mobile phones from their immediate reality. They tell me they come from places where people feel pretty much alike, and go to a school where the same is true.

The college is now far removed from London's youth gang culture, having for years fought strongly and with success against its influence. It has been a hard fight, as that influence was once tragically strong here. It is still an issue in London, of course, though not for the students I talk to – though, again, I was aware that they were not entirely representative. In 2010, in the middle of a crowded Victoria Station, a gang of twenty or so students from St Charles brutally murdered a student from a Fulham school. The conflict was over who had rights to the turf of the station itself, as it was through Victoria that students from several institutions moved uneasily each day. This uneasiness drew on both local and school loyalties, the bleaker loyalties of belonging coming to the fore. Eventually, in the biggest case of joint enterprise in British legal history, three of the St Charles students were convicted and sentenced for murder.

There was another sort of violence that concerned the government and school authorities in 2015, when I visited – that of 'terrorism'. Ten young men from the Ladbroke Grove area had gone to fight in Syria. To me, the students revealed how their experience of racial and religious discrimination was an everyday thing, something apparent in the little, indirect observances of everyday life as well as the big ones of institutions. School was the one institution completely on their side, they felt. It was just going into a shop, walking home at night, that really got them riled. 'We try to mask it', one says, 'it will never change' – 'you have to deal with it' – 'you just get on and work hard'. For those who are black, it is much worse for the boys than the girls; for Muslims, it is worse for girls than boys if, as many did, they expressed their faith by wearing a head-covering. The school has done good work, so that aspiration and hope – for the time being, at least – enables them to manage the prejudice around them. But the Muslim students have to be careful what they say because, however helpful the school might be, the government's Prevent programme means that teachers must report on what they hear.

They are diverse. We were uniform, made uniform by school uniforms indeed, and our Irish, Catholic whiteness. However, there were uniforms and uniforms, some new and clean, some old, worn, dirty, and some kids went without, if their parents could not afford one, though the fabled and ever-generous headmaster stepped in if this was the case. The Irish tide in inner west London has ebbed, though some remain.

In September 2014, I met with Sister Angela and Sister Margarita in the presbytery at Our Lady of the Holy Souls in Bosworth Road. Across the little park from the school is St Mary's, the infant and junior school I attended from 1950 to 1956. They have now spent over fifty years in the parish, each serving at one point as head teacher at St Mary's. They are old enough to have known some of the teachers who taught me as a child, most of them nuns in those days – the Sisters of Mercy have taught in the parish since 1895. Catholicism is an extraordinary constant here and in other British cities. At one time in the very early days, there were over 500 pupils in the school. The size of schools in the area during the late nineteenth and early twentieth centuries would be almost unbelievable to us now: one local infants' school was said to be the largest in London.[7]

What was once the sisters' busy convent in Marylebone is there no longer; the sisters now live nearby. Over the decades, they have progressively shed the nun's habit. The presbytery in which we sit was once the hallowed sanctum of the priest, which the nuns were never allowed to enter. The priest hardly ever visited the school; now he is always there, wanting like a good professional to be seen on the job. The presbytery is shared with the priest and the congregation. Like other priests, he is fed up with the lingering legacy of the old Irish, the social clubs-cum-drinking dens. He is much too clever and up to date for that sort of thing – not a great deal of *craic* about him, it seemed to me; not that that sort of thing would get you very far these days. However, in London, because of its great immigrant population, the Catholic tide is still strong – a tide of Africans, West Indians, and especially Filipinos now having taken our place (the Spanish and Portuguese have mostly gone).

Both Sister Angela and Sister Margarita are from County Clare. Like my Wexford mother, they still sound as if they have never left home. Although Ireland was poor when they left, they were shocked to see the poverty in W10 when they arrived. At home one was poor, but never short of food or space. Here it was at least four families to a house, including the basement. They talk of two Irish families whose matriarchs washed and shared the only decent blouse they had between them, taking turns.

Poverty in the area today can be bad, but it is nothing like it was back then, they tell me. Other things have changed, too. They no longer make home visits – part of the mission of the Sisters of Mercy, whose special devotion is to the poor. What they once did is now done by the state – except it is not, as there is no devotion to its poor in these times. They are full of praise and delighted remembrance of the 'Catholic mothers' of the parish, women like my mother. There is not now the old friendliness, they say, and parents do not push their children as they did in the past. The Filipinos keep more to themselves, although they also bring great faith and help to the parish. Though most of the Irish have moved out west and north, many into Brent in fact, the Irish endure; even second- and third-generation Irishness still has a presence. But where once all were Irish at Sunday Mass, now it is mostly the elderly among the Irish who are to be found in the pews.

The parish priest in St Pius mentions the old Irish ladies who are still there – how they talk about the terrible shrinkage of the congregation, even though it remains strong, the new non-Irish elements now included, yet invisible to the old eyes of the ladies. Even if sometimes they see more clearly still they will say, 'Sure, father, aren't we all Irish in the sight of God?' In the area in the north of England where I have lived for so long, the tide of Catholicism has gone out far; as the local parish priests say, you need immigrants to flourish. Both local priests are of Irish descent. They think there will not be many more like them. Away from the Church so long, I am struck by their conservative outlook. They are not the same as the priest in St Pius in London – not up to date. Their congregations are old but tenacious, and the parish would be nothing without them. My mother would have fitted perfectly among them. The faith of old women across the world – sometimes I think it is the only thing that holds the world together.

My school compatriots were destined at best for the skilled working class and the clerical life of the lower middle class. I remember some of the lower-stream boys leaving to be delivery boys for shops: 'butcher boy' was one job title. Some of them, at least in the A stream, did better, climbing up the ladders of seemingly endless exams and qualifications that then existed so as to be 'selected', and to 'better' themselves. I was the only one of them who went to university – indeed, the only one for many years after from the school. Around 1960, only around 5 per cent within the appropriate age range went to university. If we left school with some qualifications, we also left with an almost complete lack of direction, most encountering jobs we were simply dispatched to by a 'career adviser' – jobs that many of us did not like and quickly saw as dead-ends. A good third of my class emigrated to Australia without their families on the assisted passage schemes then available, almost all in the first few years after leaving school. This is staggering when I think of it now: children, really, gone halfway around the world to fend for themselves. Some held on to the green more than others; as one said to me, 'It is second nature for us to be British or English, but first nature to be Irish.'

I return in reflection now once again to those who gave us children life – my parents' generation, and the generations before them, immigrants of all kinds. Thomas J. Cottle's West Indian immigrant testimonies capture this flow of time and lives, in one of which my father was once a part just as I am now. He recounts the words of Margaret Jane, who in 1978 was a seventy-eight-year-old resident in her new home of London but born in Barbados. She talks about what she calls 'the current': 'You make the current to begin with, you could sort of say, then the current takes you the rest of the way. Current was being prepared about the time I was born.'

She continues, changing from the metaphor of the current to that of the bridge:

> People's lives, you see, are like a human bridge. Instead of going across a valley or a river, this human bridge goes across time. One generation starts the bridge, the next one carries it on a little further … No one sees the end … The biggest and most important job is to be a member of that bridge … I can see the bridge, even if many people can't, people my own kind too … What's the use, what's the point of it all? The answer is right there before people's eyes.
>
> And we're the time, we're the people whose lives are being used up to help the time pass. It is my life, my children's lives, my grandchildren's lives that are being used up with time. How many generations have to pass before the job is completed? … Our task is to be the generation that starts the move. Our lives are meant to help the time pass. The children cannot see this, they aren't meant to. But as you get older you see it so clearly it begins to frighten you. You don't have to talk about it with people your own age; they know. They figured it out the same way you did.[8]

The currents and the bridges of time are also apparent in *The Irishmen*, an hour-long film about Irish construction workers made by Peter Donnellan in 1965. It pictures a time when I was a young man, when many of the Irish immigrant building workers flooding into London were the same age, men building the new 1960s London. Some stayed and made families here; some went back, unable to navigate the current that had taken them to the city.

The film was never shown by the BBC – pulled because it was

supposedly 'formless'.⁹ In fact it has an acute sense of poetic form, one aspect of which is the sight and sound of the great *sean nós* singer Joe Heaney (Seosamh Ó hÉanaí) singing *The Rocks of Bawn* as the punctuation of the film's progression to an ending. In the early sixties I had heard Heaney, a native of Carna in Connemara, sing this song in London, and other songs, mostly in Irish, voicing in his austere way the great laments of his people.¹⁰ The mostly English audience in the Singers' Club, home of the folk revival, were reverential, honouring Heaney at a time when his own country ignored him; but I felt transported to my father's world with an intensity I had not often felt before. This was a year or so before his death.

The Irishmen discloses the physical shock of urban England, and I ask again the question of my father – the question most of us want to ask when it is too late: 'What was it like?' The film conveys an answer to this question, an answer given more than thirty years after my father's time on the buildings: 'It was just daybreak when I got to Manchester. Everything was black. Even though the day was coming out, it was as if it didn't want to, as though Manchester wasn't entitled to daylight.' 'Where are the cows?' another young man asks, without irony, for this is a landscape he cannot understand.

The simple fact of difference announces itself again – something so often missed because the English language is shared. There is an acute commentary on the film by the critic Hugh Leonard, made over thirty years after the film itself was lost to public awareness. He considers 'the aggressive resentment at being treated like a lower and – more engaging – amusing species ... the Irishman as a wounded beast, part nomad, part squatter ... The Irishman in England today is no longer the wounded beast at bay, believing in Brendan Behan's exhortation: "Trust in drink."'¹¹

Many did so trust; I saw such men, the souls of generosity, come to our house to visit. Drink was their companion until they grew old. But those in the film are mostly young men and

the spree is for them now, whether it will be their life companion or not (these young immigrant men were to wise up
in time, as they became better educated). In the film there is
the repeated sight of the sign for the giant construction firm,
'Cementation', on machinery, on the backs of workers' jackets,
as if branded there: the Cementation Company. My mother's
brother Michael, older than these young men at the time but
still labouring on in old age, served for decades in the Cementation fusiliers as a labourer, and then a 'gangerman'.

In the middle of Donnellan's film there is a remarkable scene
of an older man, surrounded by his family at home, talking to
the camera: he cups a cigarette in his hand; he is wearing a suit
and a clean shirt, so it may be Sunday. There is anger in how
he talks of the prejudice he felt against him during his time in
England – and desperation, too, perhaps brought on by the
condition in which the family lives: the kitchen, or so I take it
to be, is bare. The children are quiet, abashed, perhaps scared
by it all. They do not speak, nor the wife, who is there too.
Suddenly a tiny detail cuts me to the quick and brings me back
to the kitchen in which we did most of our living in Ashmore
Road. The detail is the sink, and in particular what might be
below it in a curtained space.

Perhaps it was the same here, but this family is not like
us; they seem poorer. Our kitchen was made homely by my
mother, and I never heard such bitterness as this man expresses
from my father. Behind the curtained space in our house was
the 'slop' bucket, with at times the leavings of us children,
absolved as we were from the journey below to the outside
lavatory. Perhaps it was the same in the film. And what I feel
as I write this is shame – absurdly so, given the place we had
and the many years that have gone by since then: shame then
at having our leavings there, and of telling it now; shame now
at what was behind the curtain.

Stupid, this little detail; one of the hidden injuries of class, to
use words that have since become a cliché. A tiny injury. But

what sets you apart is these tiny things, too, and that, for all the flights of imaginative sympathy that are possible, those with comfortable and secure backgrounds will never know what it was like. I dream this insecurity still, just as once I dreamt my father above in the room. The writer Lynsey Hanley suggests that, to liberate oneself from the confines of insecure working-class origins, one needs a chip of ice in the heart. Being younger than I – she was born in 1975 – she says she has the feeling all the time that the new life she has may be taken away. You carry that insecurity with you, that sense of never quite feeling at home – for me, not being or feeling working class, but not being middle class either, at least in the sense of carrying security of the self with you as a birthright. The historian Carolyn Steedman writes of shame to great effect in her *Landscape for a Good Woman*, though she, in nearby Hammersmith, was slightly above us in the social pecking order. Even so, she did not have the shield of Irishness to protect her, like me, nor a father who was there.

I think again of my father, of my uncle, of my cousins who came over to work on 'the buildings'. *I Could Read the Sky*, a novel by Timothy O'Grady and Steve Pyke, summons up the lost world of England's immigrant generations. The narrator is an older man – an unmarried itinerant labourer looking back on his wasted life in England. Something of dislocation and loss, but also of the connections of the experience of immigration, is contained in a list of what he could not do in England:

Eat a meal lacking potatoes. Trust banks. Wear a watch ... Drive a motor car ... Wear a collar in comfort ... Acknowledge the Queen ... Perform the manners of greeting and leaving ... Take pleasure in work carried out in a factory. Drink coffee ... Follow cricket. Understand the speech of a man from west Kerry ... Speak with men wearing collars. Stay afloat in water. Understand their jokes ... Kill a Sunday. Stop remembering.[12]

I was there, part of the current, and I am a historian by trade. I offer therefore a kind of parallel witness, another P. J., in fact, than that proffered by a character in O'Grady and Pike's novel: 'We are the immortals', says P. J. He has a few jars on him.

> We have one name and we have one body. We are always in our prime and we are always fit for work. We dig the tunnels, lay the rails and build the roads and buildings. But we leave no other sign behind us. We are unknown and unrecorded. We have many names and none are our own. Whenever the stiffness and pain comes in and the work gets harder, as it does for Roscoe, we change again into our younger selves. On and on we go. We are like the bottle that never empties. We are immortal.

The portrait below is of my cousin Seán Joyce (Seán Seoighe) – one who stayed behind at home, unlike the immortals, a small farmer-cum-peasant. He would not have used the second term, did not know the word; nor would most of his countrymen have used it. Yet he is one nonetheless. I use the term broadly but not inaccurately. He is part of an ending that now seems irrevocable, a real ending this time, among all the uncertainties in using that word 'ending'. This is the end of the European peasant and small farmer – and before too long, perhaps, of the peasantry in most of the world.[13]

He looks at the camera as from a distance – stern, distrustful. This was not how one should be photographed, not posed properly; the photograph must record only certain events, and record them in the correct fashion.[14] He would have had to be talked into it. He is a local man and the photographer is an outsider. The photograph was taken by an American man who visited unannounced from time to time, a man with a central European name, perhaps of peasant origin himself, who seemed to be in search of some authentic Ireland, a peasant Ireland perhaps. Being by himself much of the time, Seán eventually made friends with the photographer. I never saw

Seán Joyce, 1940–2002.

that look on his face; despite his congenital headstrongness, he could be and mostly was the most genial of men. In Josef Koudelka's great photograph, where he is the figure on the right, a remarkable thing happens with the advent of the digital image: with the capacity to zoom in and out, it is apparent that Seán looks at Koudelka with considerable suspicion, just as in this image. This gives the subject of the photograph a new power unimagined in the original print form – a surpassingly strange development in the history of photography.

His hands are big, if only just glimpsed here, and it is the hands that tell more directly of the peasant: the hand is where toil is concentrated, and so it is enlarged, muscled and huge in ways that make it useless for other, more delicate tasks. The hands and feet are the points where the body most intimately and knowingly meets the earth, and, for what they do, the hands have their own delicacy. We do not see the feet, but they are nimble enough for their task; he has walked the fields and hills that are his livelihood since childhood. At work early, as the children were then, and then early out of school to be a farmer when still no more than a child: his father died too young just like his brother, my father.

The feet learn too, as well as the hands: in summer as a boy he wore no shoes as he walked the land taking care of sheep and cattle. Peasants have knowing bodies. Seán had to have this knowing, walking these hills. The danger persists to this day. On a winter's day in 2019 his nephew, 'after sheep', fell from a ledge on Kilbride mountain and badly broke his leg. Times change: he managed to get a mobile phone signal, and he was taken off by helicopter. He was lucky to survive, as the day was an awful one. The ocean is only five miles away over the mountains; once the Atlantic lows hit the rain and wind are immense.

Seán is in his work clothes for the day, and sits in the kitchen of his house in Dúiche Sheoighe, my father's house. The cigarettes, Sweet Aftons, are in his shirt pocket, ready for the rest of the day. The shirt is not in the best condition. His belly bulges, as he did not look after himself so well. He died in the year 2002, at the age of 61. The mountain took his life. He was out at all hours, in all weathers, until his legs gave way and he could walk no longer – a hill bachelor, as such men are called. In Seamus Heaney's great elegy, 'The Strand at Lough Beg', he wrote of men like this that they were 'herders, feelers round / Haycocks and hindquarters, talkers in byres', men who 'Spoke an old language of conspirators', who 'could not crack the whip or seize the day / Slow arbitrators of the burial ground'.

Patrick Kavanagh, in his anti-heroic masterpiece 'The Great Hunger', wrote of 'The poor peasant talking to himself in the stable door ... Nobody will ever know how much tortured poetry the pulled weeds on the ridge wrote / Before they withered in the July sun'.[15] I was not with Seán on the ridges, pulling weeds. He now arbitrates the burial ground alongside hundreds of his fellow Joyces in nearby Rosshill, just outside the village of Clonbur in County Galway. Paddy Kenny, on his right in the Koudelka photograph, died in his fifties – the same age as my father. His profile adorns the walls of several Irish bars in New York City, I am told – symbol of an Ireland gone.

With Seán's sister Sally he had five children, none of whom had to emigrate, at least permanently. Paddy Kenny's boys, like him, know every inch of the land. They know the names of every field and part of a field – know them in Irish, not English, the names of the fields in the old Seoighe place of Séan Joyce across Maskeen too which is now theirs, around my father's house.[16] And so, now, do their children, even though the land can only give them a part-living, at best. Their side of the lake prospers; the other, Kilbride, side has mostly gone back to wilderness, the ruins of the old houses long left are now buried from sight in the encroaching bog and rushes their ancestors fought for centuries. Other children of the previous generation nearer to the towns, in which the new factories have sprung up, find work there, Irish politicians adeptly playing the game of low corporate taxes and skilful manipulation of EU agricultural subsidies. To the north of Joyce Country is Westport, the town beside Croagh Patrick, and there is a factory there which, with the aid of the children of peasants, produces the entire world's supply of Botox. A world beyond comprehension to their forbears, and scarcely credible to me.

Despite the persistence of the old, much is lost, and lost forever. The old Irish that Paddy and Séan knew (the old linguistic forms that Paddy's sons call 'good Irish') is falling away, words and pronunciations both. Who needs the many words to do with turf when no one cuts it anymore? Sally, his wife, knew all the names of the people who lived hereabouts, going back generations, and the knowledge that outlives her will be of a different form from the oral tradition in which she was rooted. In Ireland the old ways have not been forgotten, and pride is taken in them. Only now, in the country as a whole, they are seen as relics that must be preserved. Religion is still strong in these rural regions, but with the passage of time has come the breaking of the once direct bonds between belief, nature and labour.

In my mother's Wexford, I learned some of the ways of a different rural world – one of tillage, of cattle, of the few milking cows, and of the cash crops of barley, wheat and beetroot; one of fishing for salmon in the tidal River Barrow at the end of the fields below the house. The men going out late at night in summer, their great white stockings and big waders pulled on, were a source of wonder to me then as a child – to go out on that wide river in the black night. And then, in my mind, their black tarred boats, 'prongs', pushed out into a night not too moonlit and with the right tide, for they might be breaking the law – though they and everyone around saw what they did as a customary right. None of them could swim; nor could the Joyces in the west who lived by water. Peasants do not swim. The farm was barely prosperous enough to support two of Kitty's brothers, out of the ten surviving children, and then only one of the eldest brother's sons (yet another Pat), and now not even that.

I am old enough to have watched the peasants in the fields of Castile and Andalucía in the Spain of the very early 1960s – Franco's Spain – and to have warmed to their hospitality as we rode together in the fourth-class wooden train carriages of the days of Spain's impoverishment, their faces full of delight at seeing us young kids from a world as far from them then as we are now from them. In the introduction to his *Into Their Labours*, John Berger wrote that peasants are survivors.[17] Already when he was writing, now three decades ago, he knew that, after millennia of time, they might not survive much longer, and that '[t]he remarkable continuity of peasant experience and the peasant view of the world acquires, as it is threatened with extinction, an unprecedented and unexpected urgency'.[18] What peasants survive is scarcity, and the peasant's experience is always one of change – change in the sky and on the earth, change in his condition of life. He is always watchful, and protects himself against this change and the insecurity it brings through beliefs, customs, practices of work, and a conception of time that, like his work, is cyclical and repetitive.

Peasants, both women and men, are thus constantly attuned to the unknown, and this makes them aware that the condition of mankind is one of ignorance. The peasant is a conservative, not a progressive; slow to move, but once moved the speed may be unstoppable, as in the countless peasant revolts in history. The unknown cannot be eliminated, and so the peasant has a stake in what outsiders call superstition and magic. Religion, in its profound conservatism, is itself almost always a central part of life. Berger conceives of time for the peasant as a road or a path – a path made of all the walking that has gone before. The cult of progress separates the past from the present whereas peasants walk in a straight line, their repeated acts of survival being the best available preparation for survival in the future.

The past is what is known, not the future. This past, this way of walking, is in fact what is called 'tradition'. Peasants return to the past because it is safe. They still carry with them vestiges of a world when people were surrounded by death and the past was home. As time is cyclical, like the seasons, life is an interlude, which greatly predisposes peasants to religion. The past and the future are always connected, as things go around in a circle. This is surely a way of life to which recourse is needed now, as the Earth and its life-systems are spurned and destruction is threatened – not least the destruction wrought by the Covid-19 pandemic: nature turned in upon itself, devouring its own children? It seems to me that, in much contemporary talk of 'nature' and its saving, it is the peasant who is the last to be remembered. Into their labours we have been placed: 'Others have laboured and ye are entered into their labours' (John 4:38).

In an essay called 'Christ of the Peasants', John Berger wrote about the work of the Czech photographer Markéta Luskačová.[19] I talked with Markéta late in 2019, in her London apartment, itself on a road in my own west London – one in which we could see the now-cladded tower of Grenfell close by. She was with Koudelka on the day he took the photograph of my kin, and herself took photographs of the pilgrims to Croagh Patrick. I marvel at a coincidence that is really only a co-occurrence.

Sebald's method was one he termed 'ruminant curiosity', which is a striving to find the connections leading from one thing, a real thing, to others – not looking for what we know already before we begin, but recognizing conjunctions as they arise, glimpsing many paths as we walk down only a few, seeing in snatches the strangeness of the world.

Markéta photographed other pilgrims, too, peasant pilgrims at the great Marian shrine of Levoča, and a peasant village, Šumiac, in the north of Slovakia.[20] Berger wrote his essay in her honour after seeing the images she made. Considering how the faith of peasants has been so little understood over the many centuries of their existence, he writes of Luskačová that she photographs as if being summoned by the dead. The people she photographs are not 'there', but 'elsewhere', with their neighbours, the dead and the living equally neighbours. I am aware, looking at these images, how religion is also a way in which peasants remember themselves, memorialize themselves. Its rituals and observances might thus be regarded as a form of history, peasant history: an archive of the things they love and hold onto, which enables them to hold onto the dead whom they love.

My mother's missal lies open before me as I write – her Mass book. It is one of the few things she was able to leave behind in this world, her document. The cover is now half-detached, the spine broken and secured on the back and side by insulating tape. Is this tape hers, ours? But the book endures, as it is still held together by its strong cotton binding, of a form in which books are no longer made. It brings her back. Catholicism is not a religion of the Word but of the object; and while this is a book, it is really more an object. It makes God real, at least for the believer, because it is a real object. As well as a book, real enough, it is a devotional tool, a tabernacle and a shrine.

One carries the Sacred Heart of Jesus around with one, in the form of a tiny metal heart enclosed within a shrine recessed in the front cover. The back cover is the same, only now a recessed crucifix set in a linen background. One feels the different planes and surfaces of the recessed cross and its surrounds, just like those of the heart. Touch and sight are engaged, reality. The book is a library, too, an archive, for in it are stored treasured prayer cards and newspaper cuttings. Her scapula was once kept inside the book – the devotional object worn front and back, joined by two bands of cloth over the shoulders. She always wore one, as did I as a child. The Sacred Heart is 'the retreat of afflicted souls', and she must remember those who have gone, and so guard against her own affliction. A man who is dead and has suffered and must be remembered: 'They have pierced my hands and my feet; they have numbered all my bones.' There is a grave obligation to remember and pray for the dead.

Berger writes that the dead now have the impression that they are being forgotten to a degree that is unprecedented in history – peasants above all. They are forgotten because, in our modern, urban societies, there is shame at the consanguinity between the dead and the living. This is not a forgetting of individual deaths and the dead, which is always present, but a shame before 'the huge, in fact countless, collective of the Dead'. 'The Dead', as he capitalizes the word, those who have summoned Luskačová to be their witness in 'a secret assignment, such as no photographer has had before'. Berger writes as W. G. Sebald once wrote in *Campo Santo* upon viewing the Corsican graveyard of the peasant dead, of how the dead are still around us, but may soon be gone.[21]

The wife of Paddy Kenny, Sally Joyce, her maiden name, died recently after a long life. Following Seán and Paddy's deaths, she was the embodiment of the old place and the old time, the most direct link to my father, and my mother too, for Kitty and her were deeply fond of each other. I was too ill to attend the funeral. The dead body in Ireland is not spurned at once. In Britain now, it seems increasingly to be the custom that the body goes to the crematorium unaccompanied – its last journey lonely and without meaning. How poor of heart this seems.

The term 'wake' is used here in England to mean the celebration after the body is hurried away, the majority of people not knowing that the true wake involves the body lying in the home of the deceased, and the people of the neighbourhood who knew the dead person calling to view the body for the last time, perhaps to pray, and to offer their condolences to the family. Family members or friends sit all night with the corpse so that it will not be alone. Even so, in Ireland itself such wakes are becoming less common. At Sally Kenny's wake, hundreds upon hundreds of people queued out and around the house to view the body, a family member always there to greet them as they passed the open coffin. The immediate family attend the final closing of the coffin, when the priest prays in Irish over the body, for the living and the dead. After the last farewell, the coffin is closed.

My mother Kitty's family are buried in the tiny churchyard at Kilmokea on the Great Island in Wexford. It is a burial place to be envied by the city-dweller, a place of beauty and peace, the River Barrow flowing in the distance below. The Irish way of death, in Ireland: the graves are visited and tended over the decades. In Clonbur and Kilmokea there are masses when families 'go on the grave' to remember. The sons of Paddy Kenny take their turn with others to dig the graves of their friends and neighbours. No one digs a friend's or relation's grave in the St Mary's of Kensal Green. The burial places there are mostly untended, the children of the dead scattered to the great reaches of outer West London and beyond. It is too far to make the journey, though kin are not forgotten; but communion with them is difficult, sometimes impossible. They linger for a while with us, but it is difficult for us to linger with them.

In the words of John Montague's 'A Severed Head', 'Decades later / that child's grandchild's / speech stumbles over lost / syllables of an old order'. The poem concerns the enforced learning of English at school in Ireland, and with it the stigmatization of Irish. It was published in 1972, a time of great trouble.[22] The hope of finding again what is lost and old is present; while there is no denial that what is lost is lost, the sense of 'over' in these lines conveys a finding of something as if by accident, stumbling over a tree root perhaps, and that something is still there to be stumbled over – just as the stumbling is over syllables that, if lost, can only now be stumbled over because the same language is being spoken.

In his 'A Lost Tradition', Montague writes:

> The whole landscape a manuscript
> We had lost the skill to read,
> A part of our past disinherited;
> But fumbled, like a blind man,
> Along the fingertips of instinct.

We have lost the skill but have the instinct, though Montague and others have the skill to follow the fingertips of instinct where they lead – poets, photographers, painters, and musicians among them; historians, too. And philosophers of history like Walter Benjamin, to whose words I have turned at several times in this book. In his 'Theses on the Philosophy of History', he writes of what he calls the secret compact between the generations of the past and the present, and of how it exists because our coming on earth was expected, we were hoped for. 'Are we not touched by the same breath of air which was among that which came before? Is there not an echo of those who have been silenced in the voices to which we lend our ears today?

Have not the women, who we court, sisters who they do not recognize anymore?'[23] Every present must recognize that a past is meant in it. The past of war, especially – that of the massacred civilian dead of Darmstadt and places like it, and the vast numbers who died in history's wars and are totally unknown.

Benjamin writes: 'It is well-known that the Jews were forbidden to look into the future', for past time was experienced as remembrance.[24] He was more interested in saving the past for the future than he was in projecting a future for the present. The Jewish mysticism to which he turned at times incorporates the figure of the holy man as the practitioner of an activity known as *tikkun*: mending the world. God's attributes were once held in vessels whose glass was contaminated by the presence of evil, and these vessels had consequently shattered, disseminating their contents to the four corners of the earth. *Tikkun* was the process of collecting the scattered fragments in the hopes of once more piecing them together.

And then there are the words of Novalis, who transposes a moral intention into one that is personal, though the two cannot be separated. One echo, of those silenced in the past, echoes another. 'To me it seems an Echo sounds / out of the deep distance of our grief / Our loved ones too may be longing for us / And send to us this yearning breath'. Benjamin writes of how elusive the past is – an echo – and how it 'flashes its final farewell in the moment of its recognizability', when, as he puts it in his version of religion, 'the narrow entrance gate, through which the Messiah could enter', is opened.[25]

Holding this moment fast seems to me to connect with a statement by Tim Robinson, the great narrator of Connemara's past and present, who died in the pandemic at the time I was finishing this book. He writes of how difficult it is to locate 'those rare places and times, the nodes at which the layers of experience touch and may be fused together'. The map was one way – Robinson was a mapmaker. The photograph is another. Koudelka and Luskačová are photographers, and both know, like Robinson, how the times of the West intersect and diverge, and do so with a degree of intensity that is sometimes overwhelming. Robinson wrote of the compilation of his map of the island of Aran, off the coast of Connemara: 'Alone again, I have gone hunting for those rare places and times, the nodes at which the layers of experience touch and may be fused together. But I find that in a map such points and the energy that accomplishes such fusions ... can, at the most, be invisible guides, benevolent ghosts, through the tangles of the explicit; they cannot themselves be shown or named.'[26]

At about the same time as Montague wrote his poem, Seamus Heaney composed 'Belderg'. The hamlet of Belderrig lies within Céide Fields, a prehistoric landscape of field systems and domestic and ritual structures said to date back as far as 4,500 BC. It is purported to be the oldest field system yet discovered. Its extent is huge, on a site sloping down to the north Mayo Atlantic coast over what has become over time a vast bogland, under which the stones lie. It lies about fifty miles north of my father's house, in the extreme north of the county. This is part of the poem:

> A landscape fossilized,
> Its stone-wall patternings
> Repeated before our eyes
> In the stone walls of Mayo.
> Before I turned to go
> He talked about persistence,
> A congruence of lives,
> How, stubbed and cleared of stones,
> His home accrued growth rings
> Of iron, flint and bronze.

Iron, flint and bronze – the ages of human culture, back to 3,000 years before Christ, the rings accrued around his home now. The site was discovered by a local man out cutting turf,

Patrick Caulfield. His archaeologist son, Seamus, went on to excavate the site. It is Patrick who talks in Heaney's poem. Five thousand years of the history of the land coming to an end, one may say. But the words speak also of recurrence, of persistence and a congruence of lives over great stretches of historical time, benevolent ghosts not deserting us.

Acknowledgements

It is to a fine historian, Breandán MacSuibhne, that I owe the greatest debt, one extending from the very beginning up to the end of the venture that became this book. His skills as a sympathetic but critical reader match his generosity of spirit. Generosity of spirit in others helped revive my morale when it flagged, as it often did, for I was doing a sort of writing I had not tried before, and long and intense periods of writing take their toll anyway whatever the task. The warmth and encouragement of my friend in Florence, Paul Ginsborg, rescued me. So did the warmth and encouragement of Alvin Jackson in Edinburgh and Seamus Deane in Dublin. The influence of Seamus is visible upon the work in several places in the book. I had the benefit of splendid editors, Ciaran Deane in its first manifestation in the form of articles in *Field Day Review*, and Leo Hollis at Verso, who knows how to make books. He curbed my tendency to digress and to give way too easily to the temptations of the literary. I thank *Field Day Review* for permission to use material from the two essays they published, in 2014 and 2015.

The book is about places, and certain places were important in the making of the book – the places where the book is set of course, and the places where it was made. Both came together in Galway, so that memory, family and academic work played one upon the other there in a manner that helped me in ways I had not expected. During the period of writing I held a Moore Fellowship at the National University of Ireland Galway, and I thank so many there for the chance to talk, for the illumination by osmosis of being among Irish academics, for when it came to Ireland the familial and personal had for too long eclipsed the scholarly. I thank in particular Niall Ó Ciosáin, Tony Varley, and Louis de Paor.

I had a Trinity College Long Room Hub Fellowship in Dublin, a grand name for a grand place, grand in the Irish sense, that is. Ciaran O'Neill was an exemplary host. In these places the book took form, as it did in the times visiting Edinburgh University. As it turned out, the Celtic fringe was a good place to view England from. I thank Edinburgh's Enda Delaney for his help with Irish history. Donald Bloxham guided me with aspects of the second section of the book, on war and destruction, subjects he is deeply versed in. The eminent anthropologist Janet Carsten was immensely generous, opening my eyes to the subject of kin, and more particularly to what riches the anthropology of the house revealed. Dawn Sherratt-Bado was very helpful on the subject of Caribbean culture.

As for the places where the book is set, the second part opens with an account of Myles Joyce and the Maamtrasna Murders, as they are called, and I thank Margaret Kelleher, Seán Ó Cuirreáin, former An Coimisinéir Teanga, and Johnny Joyce, former Dublin Gaelic football player of high renown, for their help. Johnny Joyce sadly died before this book was completed. London is a constant presence in the book: I thank Tom Vague for sharing his great knowledge of Nottings Hill and Dale, his generosity extending to organizing a talk I gave in Ladbroke Grove Library on the London Irish, to which others of my vintage and pedigree came in good numbers and illumined the day with their observations. The Central Library of the Royal Borough of Kensington and Chelsea was very helpful, other libraries too, the Local Studies departments of Burnley and Portsmouth City Libraries, and Westminster City Archives. I should also like to thank the archivists of the Imperial War Museum and the Museum of Science and Industry in Manchester.

Acknowledgements

When I was at Trinity Luke Gibbons extended a generous welcome to me at Maynooth, and when in Galway I was invited to the house of the late Tim and Mairead Robinson in Roundstone on the southern coast of Connemara, to be part there of a discussion group who kindly listened to the first, uncertain stirrings of this work. Tim and Mairead made me and my wife Rosaleen very welcome in their house. The loss to Connemara their deaths represent is great. My friend Patrick Curry in London helped enable that day and was a pillar of support as always. When it comes to pillars of support, it as well to list my long-familiar pillars here: David Vincent (who made me think again about Etruria), James Vernon and Simon Gunn. Mike Savage and Pedro Ramos-Pinto did great support work too. My dear friend Mick Moran died before he could see the completion of a work he helped shape. Our lives led in parallel directions in many respects, Mick a son of Clare and Smethwick.

On war and the bombing of the almost defenceless German cities, my biggest debt is to Joerg Arnold. In the text and notes the nature of my debt to him is set out more fully than here, as it is for others too. Dietmar Suess of the University of Augsburg took an interest in the work, and Dieter Schott of the Technische Universität Darmstadt was very helpful on Darmstadt's commemoration of that city's awful night in 1944. From Darmstadt to Derry: Eamonn Deane extended the Deane family connection of this book, in Derry telling me much about the town, and he and his wife fed me the sort of bacon-and-cabbage dinner I had not tasted for far too long a time preceding that evening.

In the last section of the book Naomi Sweeney was an incomparably generous guide to Burnley. I should like also to thank those for whom I supply only initials in the text, who are mostly friends and acquaintances in my immediate north who I had known for too long a time without finding out the details of their stories. On my periodic returns to London, in the Catholic Kremlin of St Charles Square the parish priest of St Pius, Father Wilson, invited me in warmly, and it was a delight to spend the hours with Sister Angela and Sister Margarita in the presbytery at Our Lady of the Holy Souls in Bosworth Road. Paul O'Shea, then the principal of St Charles College, was friendly and helpful when I asked to visit the College, as were the students I talked to there. The same was the case for Burnley College students. Joe Walsh of Whitstable House, hard by Grenfell Tower, was generous with his time and his experiences, as was his father. My local Roman Catholic parish priests generously met with me and talked about the state of things spiritual in our part of the North. Not the least of the pleasures of writing the book was talking with Markéta Luskačová about her remarkable photography. She shared her time and her work with me generously.

I should also like to thank Joe Moran, Lynsey Hanley, Jill Ebrey, Niall Cunningham, Richard Butler, Colin Gordon, John MacAuliffe – in whose *Manchester Review* a chapter from the book appeared in 2020 – and also my old friend Chandra Mukerji. Talking with my MP Jonathan Reynolds (Stalybridge and Hyde) and with the CEO of Tameside Council, Steven Pleasant, proved revealing. David Edgerton kindly read chapters for me and commented. I have quoted extensively from the marvellous work of Thomas J. Cottle, and my thanks are due to him.

The Joyces, Bowes, Kennnys and Malones all stood ready when needed. My memory these days being better for the distant than for the recent past, I will have forgotten others, and to them my apologies. Those I can never forget because they have been by my side for so long are my wife, Rosaleen, and my friend of seven decades Thomas Kevin Cleary. Tom and I grew up in the long-ago London I describe in the book, the London that determined our fates. Some cognitive scientists aver that memory is, physically, something not individual but shared, so that one's memory is not just simply one's own but is distributed between oneself and others. This seems true in the case of us three, so that it can be said they wrote this book as well as I. Whatever the mind, the flesh has to be kept in good order. When, writing this book, I fell seriously ill for many months, the peerless Bernard Clarke and James Hill of the Manchester Royal Infirmary, professors of medicine both, kept me alive to finish the task. Thanks. To Rose of course I owe the lot.

Broadbottom, August 2020

Notes

Introduction

1 Czeslaw Milosz, *Native Realm: A Search for Self-Definition* (London: Penguin, 2014), pp. 5–6.

2 Patrick Sheehan, 'The Road, the House, and the Grave: A Poetics of Galway Space, 1900–1970', in Gerard Moran and Raymond Gillespie, eds, *Galway: History and Society* (Dublin: Geography, 1996).

3 See Hannah Arendt, Introduction to Walter Benjamin, *Illuminations* (London: Fontana, 1973).

4 Benjamin, *Illuminations*, p. 259, from 'Theses on the Philosophy of History'.

5 Hermann Broch, *The Guiltless* (London: Quartet Encounters, 1974), p. 6.

6 Benjamin, *Illuminations*, pp. 255–6. The final line of this thesis states that 'historical materialists' are aware of this. Benjamin was however a very peculiar historical materialist, in the rabbinical not the scientific style.

7 David Lloyd, *Irish Times: Temporalities of Modernity* (Dublin: Field Day, 2008).

8 John D. Caputo, 'No Tear Shall be Lost: The History of Prayers and Tears', in David Carr, Thomas R. Flynn and Rudolf A. Makkreel, eds, *The Ethics of History* (Evanston, IL: Northwestern University Press, 2004).

1. The Journey West

1 Peter McQuillan, *Native and Natural: Aspects of the Concepts of Right and Freedom in Irish* (Cork: Cork University Press, 2004).

2 See John Wyse Jackson and Peter Costello, *John Stanislaus Joyce: The Voluminous Life and Genius of James Joyce's Father* (London: Fourth Estate, 1998).

3 Breandán Mac Suibhne, 'A Jig in the Workhouse: Space and Story, the G-word and the Issueless Tribute', *Dublin Review of Books*, April 2013.

4 Rundale was akin to the old English common field system. The wonderful term 'throughother' exists in Irish English for this relatively communal form of agriculture. These terms are explained in greater detail later in the chapter.

5 Enda Delaney, *The Curse of Reason: The Great Irish Famine* (Dublin: Gill & Macmillan, 2012).

6 Patrick Joyce, *The State of Freedom: A Social History of the British State since 1800* (Cambridge: Cambridge University Press, 2013).

7 David Lloyd, 'The Indigent Sublime', *Irish Times: Temporalities of Modernity* (Dublin: Field Day, 2008).

8 For tourist-guide versions of the Joyces, on the 'fine, stalwart fellows giving their name to this part of Connemara', see John Barrow, *A Tour Round Ireland* (London, 1835) and Charles Richard Weld, *Vacations in Ireland* (London, Longman & Roberts,1857), pp. 360–1.

9 *Black's Picturesque Tourist of Ireland* (Edinburgh: Adam & Charles Black,1872).

10 Fifth letter in the collection, 1757–62, as cited in Sean Spellissy, *The History of Galway* (Limerick: Celtic Bookshop, 1999).

11 Aalen et al., *Atlas of the Irish Rural Landscape*, p. 100.

12 E. J. Hobsbawm, *Age of Extremes: The Short Twentieth Century, 1914–1991* (London: Michael Joseph, 1994), pp. 289–95, esp. p. 289.

13 Aalen et al., *Atlas of the Irish Rural Landscape*, pp. 120, 156–7.

14 W. G. Sebald, 'Campo Santo', in *Campo Santo* (Penguin, 2006), pp. 34 and 35.

15 Ibid., p. 35.

2. The Journey East

1 Catherine Dunne, *An Unconsidered People: The Irish in London* (Dublin: New Island, 2003).

2 For a very interesting discussion, see Liam Harte, '"Somewhere beyond England and Ireland": Narratives of "Home" in Second-Generation Irish Autobiography', *Irish Studies Review* 11:3 (2003).

3 Terry Eagleton, *The Gatekeeper* (London: Allen Lane, 2001), p. 31.

4 Ibid., pp. 33, 35–6.

5 As cited in Kevin O'Connor, *The Irish in Britain* (London: Sidgwick & Jackson, 1972), pp. 168–9.

6 Timothy O'Grady and Steve Pyke's novel *I Could Read the Sky* (London: Harvill, 1997) is the most penetrating of the several accounts of the itinerant Irish labourer in Britain.

7 Co-sleeping as much as anything separates now from then. From the fifties, when in Wexford, we slept four to a bed and thought nothing of it: brothers, a cousin, an uncle all in 'the big bed'.

8 David Fitzpatrick, *Irish Emigration, 1801–1921* (Dublin: Economic and Social History Society of Ireland, 1984), p. 30.

9 There is a remarkable book on this hiddenness, a tribute to the historian's craft: Robert James Scally, *The End of Hidden Ireland: Rebellion, Famine and Emigration* (London: Oxford University Press, 1995).

10 Vast numbers of which are collected in Florian Znaniecki and William

I. Thomas's epic 2000-page work, *The Polish Peasant in Europe and America*, 5 vols (Ithaca, NY: Cornell University, 1918–20).

11 Gaston Bachelard, *The Poetics of Space* (New York: Beacon, 1994), pp. 4–8.

12 Henry Glassie, *Passing the Time in Balymenone: Folklore and History of an Ulster Community* (Dublin: O'Brien, 1982).

13 Ibid., p. 327.

14 Ibid., p. 351.

15 Ibid., p. 354.

16 This paragraph is based on John Berger, *Into Their Labours* (London: Granta, 1992), introduction; 'Others have laboured and ye are entered into their labours' John 4:38. On the family economy of the Irish peasant farm, see the classic text, Conrad M. Arensberg and Solon T. Kimball, *Family and Community in Ireland* (Cambridge, MA: Harvard University Press, 1940), which describes life in Co. Clare, in the West, immediately south of Co. Galway.

17 Glassie, *Passing the Time*, p. 360.

18 Ibid., pp. 372, 375.

19 Patricia Lysaght, *The Banshee: The Irish Supernatural Death Messenger* (Glendale, CA: Glendale, 1986).

20 *Cré na Cille*, translated by Alan Titley as *The Dirty Dust* (New Haven, CT: Yale University Press, 2015), is widely regarded as the finest novel written in Irish. It is set in a Connemara churchyard; the action, if it can be said to be action, is set underground among the unstoppably talkative dead.

21 Seamus Deane, 'The End of the World', *Field Day Review* 8 (2012), p. 225.

22 Daniel Lord Smail, *On Deep History and the Brain* (Berkeley, CA: University of California Press, 2009).

23 See the exemplary Terence Patrick Dolan, *A Dictionary of Hiberno-English: The Irish Use of English* (Dublin: Gill & Macmillan, 1998).

24 The best book on the Irish in Britain is Enda Delaney, *The Irish in Post-War Britain* (London: Oxford University Press, 2007). See also Clair Wills, *The Best Are Leaving: Emigration and Post-War Irish Culture* (Cambridge: Cambridge University Press, 2015).

25 I describe his death in Chapter 6.

26 I consider this change in a book I am at present writing, to be called *Remembering Peasants*.

27 Pierre Bourdieu, *The Bachelors' Ball* (London: Polity, 2008).

3. Time Thickens, Takes on Flesh

1 Francis J. Kirk, *Reminiscences of an Oblate of St Charles* (London: Burns Oates, 1905).

2 Francis J. Kirk, *Some Notable Conversions in the County of Wexford* (London: Burns Oates, 1901).

3 Alan McClelland, 'Changing Concepts of the Pastoral Office: Wiseman, Manning and the Oblates of St Charles', *Recusant History* 25: 2 (2000).

4 Charles Booth, *Life and Labour of the People in London. Volume 3: Religious Influences* (London: Macmillan, 1902), pp. 243–4.

5 Mikhail Bakhtin, *The Dialogic Imagination* (Austin: University of Texas Press, 1981), p. 250. See also p. 120, on the road as the 'path of life'.

6 Ibid., p. 137ff.

7 Pierre Bourdieu, *The Logic of Practice* (Redwood City, CA: Stanford University Press, 1990), p. 73.

8 *Kelly's Post Office London Directory*, for the Harrow Road, 1938, 1945, 1953, 1963, 1973.

9 For a scholarly take on the material world, especially in its nonhuman forms, as the scaffolding of memory see Patrick Joyce and Chandra Mukerji, 'The State of Things: State History and Theory Reconfigured', *Theory and Society* 46, 1–19 (2017).

10 Alan Johnson, *This Boy: A Memoir of a Childhood* (London: Bantam Press, 2013), p. 22.

11 Jerome Borkwood, *From Kensal Village to Golborne Road: Tales of the Inner City* (London: Kensington & Chelsea Community History Group, 2002).

12 Booth, *Life and Labour of the People in London, Volume 3*, Chapter 12: 'The Outer West' for more detail.

13 Kirk, *Reminiscences of an Oblate*, p. 119.

14 'How We Are: Photographing Britain', 22 May–2 September 2007, at tate.org.uk. See also Roger Mayne, *The Street Photographs of Roger Mayne* (London: Zelda Cheatle Press, 1993). Historians also now mistakenly take these photographs as canonical. See, for example, Stephen Brooke, 'Revisiting Southam Street: Class, Generation, Gender, and Race in the Photography of Roger Mayne', *Journal of British Studies* 53: 2 (April 2014).

15 'Roger Maine – Obituary', *Daily Telegraph*, 15 June 2014.

16 Susan Sontag, *On Photography* (London: Penguin, 1977).

17 Alan Johnson takes a remarkably benign view of local violence throughout *This Boy* (London: Bantam, 2013).

18 Especially 'Our Homes, Our Streets', Notting Hill Community History Series, No. 3 (1987), and 'Women Remember', in the same series. See also, on Notting Hill and Dale, the online material of HistoryTalk (the interviews of which are currently unavailable): Patricia E. Malcolmson, 'Getting a Living in the Slums of Victorian Kensington', *London History* 1: 1; Liz Bartlett, *Having a Grand Time: North Kensington Memories of Days Out and Time Off; They Were Happy Days: Memories of Growing Up in North Kensington*; An Old Inhabitant, *Kensington, Notting Hill and Paddington with Remembrances of the Locality 38 Years Ago* – all Kensington and Chelsea Community History Group.

There are many other Group publications available, which I have consulted – as I have those of the Notting Dale Urban Studies Centre and the Notting Hill Peoples' Association Housing Group.

19 Pearl Jephcott, *A Troubled Area* (London: Faber, 1964), Chapter 6.

20 Gavin Selerie, 'Southam Street', *New River Project*, 1991, copy in Royal Borough of Kensington and Chelsea Library, Local Studies Collection.

21 On the Tower, see Jerome Borkwood, *From Kensal Village to Goldborne Road: Tales of the Inner City* (London: KCCHG, 2002).

22 In 'Our Homes, Our Streets', *Notting Hill Community History Series* 3 (1987).

23 These are treated in Chapter 4.

24 Colin MacInnes, *Absolute Beginners* (London: Allison & Busby, 2011 [1959]), pp. 61, 63.

25 Keith Moore, 'Is This UK's Most Gentrified Street?', BBC News, 27 June 2012, at bbc.com.

26 Rachel Johnson, *Notting Hell: Sex, Lies and Real Estate* (London: Penguin, 2006). See also her *The Mummy Diaries* (London: Penguin, 2005).

27 Census and Press Cuttings on Ashmore Road, Westminster City Archives. From *Paddington Mercury*, 17 October 1978, 19 September 1978, 7 July, 1978; *Paddington Times* 2 July 1982.

28 It is one I tell at more length in 'Time Thickens, Takes on Flesh: The Other West', *Field Day Review*, 2015.

29 The Institute of History Research, 'Members 1820–1832', historyofparliamentonline.org, 2009.

30 T. F. T. Baker, Diane K. Bolton and Patricia E. C. Croot, 'Paddington: Queen's Park and St Peter's Park', in C. R. Elrington, ed., *A History of the County of Middlesex: Volume 9, Hampstead, Paddington* (London: Victoria County History, 1989), pp. 217–21, available at british-history. ac.uk; F. H. W. Sheppard, *Survey of London, Volume xxxvii, North Kensington* (London: University of London/London County Council, 1973), Chapter 14, available at british-history.ac.uk.

31 See the excellent Pearl Jephcott, *A Troubled Area*, Chapter 11. See also 'North Kensington Histories: Recollections of People from North Kensington, London', at northkensingtonhistories.wordpress.com.

32 On North Kensington, see Bridget Cherry and Nicholas Pevsner, *The Buildings of England. London 3: North West* (New Haven, CT: Yale University Press, 1991), p. 452.

33 Ibid., pp. 126–8.

34 Julia Drake, 'Black Caribbean Migration and Community Formation: The Remaking of Brixton and Notting Hill, 1958–1981', University College London PhD thesis (2006). See also, *Multi-Racial North Kensington*, North Kensington Community History Series No. 2 (1987).

35 A chapter title in his book, *Soft City* (London: Hamish Hamilton, 1974).

36 For an account of these writers and of literary representations of Notting Hill, see Miranda Davies and Sarah Anderson, eds, *Inside Notting Hill* (London, 2001). As well as Raban and MacInnes, see the works of Michael Moorcock and Mustapha Matura. Nell Dunn was also writing about working-class south London at this time, and the playwright Ann Jellicoe about lower-class London. Jellicoe was married to the photographer Roger Mayne.

4. Other Houses

1 Janet Carsten, 'Stories of Kinship and Shadows of Memory', Inaugural Lecture, University of Edinburgh, 2005.

2 Janet Carsten, ed., *Ghosts of Memory: Essays on Remembrance and Relatedness* (London: Oxford University Press, 2007), and *The Heat of the Hearth: The Process of Kinship in a Malay Fishing Community* (London: Oxford University Press,1997). My thanks to Janet Carsten for organizing a workshop at Edinburgh University, 'Memory, the House and the Political', in 2016.

3 Abdelmalek Sayad, *The Suffering of the Immigrant* (London: Wiley, 2004), with a preface by Pierre Bourdieu.

4 Johnny Rotten/Lydon's first autobiography, John Lydon, *Rotten: No Irish, No Blacks, No Dogs* (London: St Martin's, 1995).

5 Mark Olden, *Murder in Notting Hill* (London: Zero, 2011).

6 George Rogers. We sang this election ditty as children: 'Vote, vote, vote for Georgie Rogers, kick old Churchill down the stairs.'

7 Edward Pilkington, *Beyond the Mother Country: West Indians and the Notting Hill White Riots* (London: I.B.Tauris, 1990), which includes the 1958 poll.

8 Nancy Foner, *Jamaica Farewell: Jamaican Migrants in London* (Berkeley, CA: University of California Press, 1978); John Western, *A Passage to England: Barbados Londoners Speak of Home* (Minneapolis, MN: University of Minnesota Press, 1992); Colin Clark, *Here to Stay: The Gypsies and Travellers of Britain* (Hatfield: University of Hertfordshire Press, 2006); Mary Chamberlain, *Narratives of Exile and Return* (London: Palgrave, 1997); Sheila Patterson, *Dark Strangers: A Study of West Indians in London* (London: Tavistock, 1964).

9 Sidney Mintz, 'Houses and Yards among Caribbean Peasantries', in Philip W. Scher, ed., *Perspectives on the Caribbean: A Reader in Culture, History and Representations* (London: Wiley, 2010).

10 Ian Thomson, *The Dead Yard: Tales from Modern Jamaica* (London: Faber, 2009).

11 Michael McMillan, 'The West Indian Front Room: Reflections on a Diasporic Identity', *Small Axe* 28 (March 2008), on an exhibition about the room.

12   Daniel Miller, 'Migration, Material Culture and Tragedy: Four Movements in Caribbean Migration', *Mobilities* 3: 3 (November 2008).

13   I consider some of these differences further in 'Time Thickens', *Field Day Review* 11 (2015).

14   Thomas J. Cottle, *Black Testimony: The Voices of Britain's West Indians* (London: Wildwood House, 1978).

15   Ibid., p. 121.

16   Ibid., p. 129.

17   Cottle, 129.

18   Ibid., p. 127.

19   Ibid., pp. 135–6, 133, 134. See above, Chapter 2, p. 137.

20   Cottle, *Black Testimony*, p. 139.

21   Ibid., p. 140.

22   Ibid., p. 156; see also pp. 159, 160.

23   Patrick Joyce, *The State of Freedom: A Social History of the British State since 1800* (Cambridge University Press, 2013).

24   On the Middle Row school, see Charles Siegel, *Backward Children in the Making* (London: University of London Press, 1949), p. 46; there but for the grace of God and the Holy Roman Church ... Jerome Borkwood, *From Kensal Village to Golborne Road: Tales of the Inner City* (London: Kensington & Chelsea Community History Group, 2002), p. 107. On his own Wornington Infants School, see Alan Johnson, *This Boy* (London: Bantam, 2013), pp. 35, 57, 74–5, 252. My wife taught in this school many years later, in the 1970s, as she did in the Middle Row one, and can testify to the awfulness of local education.

25   *List of Secondary Schools in Chelsea, Fulham, Hammersmith and Kensington, Division 1* (London: London County Council, 1955).

26   Adam Smith, *The Theory of Moral Sentiments* (Edinburgh: Alexander Kincaid & J. Bell, 1759), p. 181.

27   The title of his second autobiography, *Anger Is an Energy: My Life Uncensored* (London: Simon & Schuster, 2014).

5. The Death of Myles Joyce

1   James Joyce, 'Ireland at the Bar' (1907), in Kevin Barry, ed., *James Joyce: Occasional, Critical and Political Writing* (London: Oxford University Press, 2008), pp. 145–6. For the circumstances of the death, and for almost everything about the case, see the remarkable book by Father Jarlath Waldron, the parish priest of Tourmakeady, who knew the local ground better than anyone, *Maamtrasna: The Murders and the Mystery* (Dublin: Edmund Burke, 1992).

2   'A wrongful hanging in Connemara, 1882', *Irish Times*, 20 May 2016, citing verbatim the *Irish Times*, 16 December 1882, when the newspaper's correspondent attended the execution in Galway Gaol. See also Seán Ó Cuirreáin, *Éagóir Maolra Seoighe agus dúnmaruithe*

Mhám Trasna (Connemara: Cos Life, 2016), and the excellent study of Margaret Kelleher, *The Maamtrasan Murders: Language, Life and Death in Nineteenth-Century Ireland* (Dublin: University College Dublin Press, 2018). My thanks to Seán Ó Cuirreáin and Margaret Keller for sharing information with me.

3   Waldron, *Maamtrasna*, pp. 15, 16. For the *Nation*'s account of the case, see T. Harrington, MP, *The Maamtrasna Massacre (With an Appendix containing the Report of the Trials and Correspondence between the Most Rev. Dr. M' Evilly and the Lord Lieutenant)* (Dublin: Nation Office, 1884).

4   The Ribbon Society was a nineteenth-century agrarian secret society made up of the rural Irish Catholic poor. The name is derived from a green ribbon worn as a badge by its members.

5   On peasant silence, see Alain Corbin's evocative *A History of Silence* (London: Polity, 2018), pp. 92–5.

6   Guy Beiner, *Forgetful Remembrance: Social Forgetting and Vernacular Historiography of a Rebellion in Ulster* (London: Oxford University Press, 2018).

7   There was a public commemoration in Galway city in December 2012. I have written about the case in Patrick Joyce, *The State of Freedom: A Social History of the British State since 1800* (Cambridge: Cambridge University Press, 2013), pp. 303–7. In the argument there, I consider the various houses involved in the matter: those of Galway Gaol, the English public school, and the bourgeois homes of the English governing classes.

8   Seamus Deane, 'Expunged', *Dublin Review of Books* 120 (March 2020).

9   Robert James Scally, *The End of Hidden Ireland* (London: Oxford University Press, 1995).

10 David Alton, 'The West of Ireland – The Maamtrasna Murders 3', 3 June 2011, at davidalton.net.

11 Jürgen Habermas, *The New Conservatism* (Cambridge: Polity, 1989), pp. 232–3.

12 Stuart Hall with Bill Schwarz, *Familiar Stranger: A Life between Two Islands* (London: Penguin, 2018).

13 Paul Connerton, *How Societies Remember* (Cambridge: Cambridge University Press, 1989), pp. 10–13, 72–104; and his *How Modernity Forgets* (Cambridge: Cambridge University Press, 2009).

6. Grave Births

1   US Strategic Bombing Survey figures differed considerably from the German figures. These figures are discussed in Martin Middlebrook and Chris Everill, eds, *Bomber Command War Diaries: An Operational Reference Book 1939–45* (New York: Viking, 1985).

2 Jörg Friedrich, *The Fire: The Bombing of Germany 1940–1945* (New York: Columbia University Press, 2006), p. 442.

3 Ibid., p. 455.

4 Martin Greaves, *Running with Mum/Der Weg meiner Mutter*, Seedfold Films, 2007. On the Darmstadt firebombing, see also Constantin Gropper, *Brandmale* trailer at vimeo.com/88254920.

5 The prototype Halifax L7244 was built at Cricklewood in October 1939. Alan Dowsett, *Handley Page: A History* (Stroud: Tempus, 2003).

6 'The Forgotten Volunteers of World War II', *History Ireland* 1 (Spring 1998), at historyireland.com; *Scotsman* Newsroom, 'Full Scale of Irish WWII Death Toll Revealed', *Scotsman*, 12 June 2009.

7 Lynne Sharon Schwartz, ed., *The Emergence of Memory: Conversations with W. G. Sebald* (New York: Seven Stories, 2007); W. G. Sebald, 'Air War and Literature', in his *On the Natural History of Destruction* (New York: Modern Library, 2003).

8 Sven Lindqvist, *A History of Bombing* (London: Granta, 2001), Section 391.

9 Anne Fuchs, *After the Dresden Bombing: Pathways of Memory, 1945 to the Present* (London: Palgrave, 2014).

10 Tom Allbeson, '"Where Are the Pictures?" Photography and British Public Perception of the Bombing of Germany, 1941–45', *Photo Researcher: European Society for the History of Photography* 25 (2016).

11 Various authors, *The War in Pictures*, 6 vols (London: Odhams, 1946).

12 Ibid., vol. 6, pp. 194–5.

13 Ibid., vol. 4, pp. 126–7.

14 Dietmar Süss, *Death from the Skies: How the British and Germans Survived Bombing in World War II* (London: Oxford University Press, 2014), Chapter 9.

15 Paul Connerton, *How Modernity Forgets* (Cambridge: Cambridge University Press, 1989).

16 My thanks are due to Portsmouth History Centre, Portsmouth Central Library, for their efforts to find John Joyce.

17 Friedrich, *The Fire*, p. 440.

18 Ibid., pp. 437–42.

19 On the BBC News Magazine website, 20 November 2012. See also Fred Clark, 'Bombings and Doodlebugs', *WW2 People's War*, bbc.co.uk, 23 March 2005.

20 Between September 1944 and the following March, the V2 – the world's first ballistic missile – killed 2,754 people and injured 6,523. About 1,400 fell on London. There was no escape or defence. Once launched, from Holland or Germany, the rocket took five minutes to reach its target, and left only a fifty-second window for radar detection. Of the V1s that were launched, 2,340 hit London, causing 5,475 deaths, with

16,000 injured. See the National Archives, 'British Response to V1 and V2: How did Britain respond to the threat of attack by missiles in 1943?', nationalarchives.gov.uk.

21 Friedrich, *The Fire*, pp. 447–8.

22 Ibid., p. 440.

23 Ibid., p. 448.

24 Richard Overy, *The Bombing War: Europe 1939–1945* (London: Penguin, 2013), p. 70.

25 These figures are taken from Centre for the Study of War, State and Society, 'Bombing States and Peoples in Western Europe 1940–1945', University of Exeter, n.d. Available at humanities.exeter.ac.uk. Richard Overy, one of the foremost scholars of the bombing, is the head of the centre.

26 On the extraordinary website bombsight.org, one can track almost all the bombs dropped on London.

27 William Patrick Hitler (Stuart-Houston by surname) was a nephew of Adolf Hitler, born to Adolf's brother, Alois Hitler Jr., and his first wife, the Irishwoman Bridget Dowling, in Liverpool in 1911. The family lived in a flat at 102 Upper Stanhope Street, which was destroyed in the last German air raid of the Liverpool Blitz, on 10 January 1942.

28 Richard J. Overy, ed., *Bombing, States and Peoples in Western Europe 1940–1945* (London: Continuum, 2011); Richard Overy, *The Bombers and the Bombed: Allied Air War over Europe 1939–1945* (New York: Viking, 2014); David Edgerton, *Britain's War Machine: Weapons, Resources and Experts in the Second World War* (London: Allen Lane, 2011).

29 There is disagreement on the extent to which the diversion of resources affected the German war effort, however. See Edward Luttwak, 'Opportunity Costs' – a review of Richard Overy, *The Bombing War* (London: Allen Lane, 2013). The force of this disagreement is diminished, however, by the reviewer's concentration on the example of only one city: Hamburg.

30 Donald Bloxham, revised version (personal communication) of 'Dresden as a War Crime', from Paul Addison and Jeremy Crang, eds, *Firestorm: The Bombing of Dresden* (London: Pimlico, 2006).

31 On antecedents, see Lindqvist, *History of Bombing*.

32 Friedrich, *The Fire*, pp. 310–15.

33 On Darmstadt, see Martin Middlebrook and Chris Everill, eds, *Bomber Command War Diaries*, esp. pp. 60, 183, 438.

34 Friedrich, *The Fire*. See also his *Die Brandstatten* (Berlin: Propyläen, 2003) – too long unpublished in an English version. The images are horrifying.

35 Seamus Deane, 'Expunged', *Dublin Review of Books* 126, Oct. 2020.

36 Stephen A. Garrett, *Ethics and Airpower in World War: The British*

Bombing of German Cities (New York: St Martin's, 1997), pp. 184–90 and Chapter 4.

37 The *Daily Mirror* and *The Times*, 1945–50 – online search.

38 On the bombing of Britain, and civilian opinion, see Centre for the Study of War, State and Society, 'Bombing States and Peoples'.

39 Roberto Rossellini's neorealist melodrama *Berlin Year Zero* presents the city like this.

40 Klaus *Schmitt, Die Brandnacht: Dokumente* (Darmstadt, Reba-Verlag, 1964). See also Mark R. Hatlie, 'War Memorial Complex in Darmstadt Forest Cemetery', n.d. at sites-of-memory.de.

7. The Work of the Dead

1 Ernest Renan, *Qu'est-ce qu'une nation?* (Paris: Presses-Pocket, 1992), transl. Ethan Rundell as 'What Is a Nation?' There are several versions of this free online, in French and English. See, for example, a pdf of the Rundell translation at ucparis.fr.

2 Benedict Anderson, *Imagined Communities: Reflections on the Origins and Spread of Nationalism*, rev. ed. (London: Verso, 2016).

3 As in Ireland, for which see Breandán MacSuibhne, *The End of Outrage: Post-Famine Adjustment in Rural Ireland* (London: Oxford University Press, 2017).

4 Thomas W. Laqueur, *The Work of the Dead: A Cultural History of Mortal Remains* (Princeton, NJ: Princeton University Press, 2015), pp. 393, 400–1.

5 José Saramago, *All the Names* (New York: Vintage, 2000).

6 Lacquer, *Work of the Dead*, p. 431.

7 Ibid., p. 482.

8 Ibid., p. 376.

9 Ibid., p. 379.

10 Susan Sontag, *Regarding the Pain of Others* (London: Picador, 2004).

11 W. G. Sebald, *On the Natural History of Destruction* (New York: Modern Library, 2003), pp. 7, 12–13.

12 A. C. Grayling, *Among the Dead Cities: The History and Moral Legacy of the WWII Bombing of Civilians in Germany and Japan* (New York: Walker & Co., 2006).

13 David Edgerton, *Britain's War Machine: Weapons, Resources and Experts in the Second World War* (London: Allen Lane, 2011), pp. 1–2.

14 David Edgerton, *The Rise and Fall of the British Nation: A Twentieth-Century History* (London: Allen Lane, 2018).

15 Edgerton, *Britain's War Machine* (Oxford: Oxford University Press, 2011), Kindle edition.

16 The views of German historians of the air war are valuably summarized in S. Bas Von Beda Beckmann, *The Contested Air War: German Historians and the Bombing of German Cities* (Amsterdam: University

of Amsterdam Press, 2015), and Lothar Kettenknacker, *Ein Volk von Opfern? Die Neue Debatte un den Bombenkreig, 1940–1945* (Berlin: Rowohlt, 2003).

17 Jörg Arnold, *The Allied Air War and Urban Memory: The Legacy of Strategic Bombing in Germany* (Cambridge: Cambridge University Press, 2011); Dietmar Süss, *Death from the Skies: How the British and Germans Survived Bombing in World War II* (London: Oxford University Press, 2014).

18 See the account of the extraordinary act of martyrdom by the Sisters of the Eternal Worship of God in Mainz: Süss, *Death from the Skies*, p. 487.

19 Arnold, *Allied Air War*, 'Conclusion'. See also Arnold's excellent review of Friedrich, 'A Narrative of Loss', *H-German*, November 2003, available online at h-net.org.

20 Grayling, *Among the Dead Cities*. Grayling's book is significant for promoting the idea of bombing as a war crime in the UK.

21 Frederike Helwig, *Kriegskinder* (Berlin: Hatje Cantz, 2017).

22 Ibid., translation from Diane Smyth, 'Suppressed memories of war in Frederike Helwig's *Kriegskinder*', *British Journal of Photography*, 12 December 2017, bjp-onine.com.

23 Paul Gilroy, *Postcolonial Melancholia* (New York: Columbia University Press, 2005).

24 Michael Moran, *The End of British Politics?* (London: Palgrave Macmillan, 2017).

25 Bomber Command Memorial, 'About Bomber Command', rafbf.org.

26 On opposition within parliament and government management, see Sven Lindqvist, *A History of Bombing* (London: Granta, 2001), sections 190, 200. See also section 205, on Freeman Dyson, Winchester and Trinity Cambridge, but, establishment credentials notwithstanding, the best face of England was to the fore with Freeman Dyson.

27 Charles Webster and Noble Frankland, *The History of the Strategic Air Offensive against Germany, 1939–1945*, 4 vols (Uckfield: Naval & Military Press 2006 [1961]).

28 Süss, *Death from the Skies*, p. 471.

29 Ibid., p. 469.

30 'Archive Report: Allied Forces', page for Wilbur B. Bentz, n.d., at aircrew remembered.com.

31 Rowan Moore, 'Bomber Command Memorial – Review', *Guardian*, 24 June 2012.

32 *The Lancaster: Britain's Flying Past*, BBC documentary, at bbc.co.uk.

33 Other programmes included *Battlefield Britain*, *The Battle of Britain* and *RAF at 100 with Ewan and Colin McGregor*.

34 See also *The Times* and *Sunday Times* coverage for 4, 9, and 24 September 2018.

35 'Der 11. September 1944 – Zerstörung und Wiederaufbau', 10 September 2018, at centralstation-darmstadt.de. I wish to thank Professor Dieter Schott of Darmstadt Technical University for information on Darmstadt.

36 Moran, *End of British Politics?*, pp. 62–4.

37 Ibid., p. 64.

38 Information from the Imperial War Museum Register of War Memorials.

39 'Historic Duxford', at iwm.org.uk.

40 Imperial War Museum, 'Transforming IWM London: Phase 2, Second World War and Holocaust Galleries', available at iwm.org.uk; 'How Do Audiences Relate to the Second World War and the Cold War?', Susie Fisher Group, November 2015.

41 Susan Sontag, *Regarding the Pain of Others* (London: Penguin, 2003), p. 113.

42 Ibid., p. 91.

43 Ibid., pp. 76–7.

44 Joseph Roth, *Flight without End* (London: Peter Owen, 2000), pp. 129–30.

45 Sebald, *On the Natural History of Destruction*, p. 29.

46 Gregor von Rezzori, born Gregor Arnulph Hilarius d'Arezzo, was another native of Czernowitz, and he too wrote with profundity about twentieth-century war. His literary importance is only now being recognized in the English-speaking world. See his *An Ermine in Czernopol* (New York: NYRB, 2012), *The Snows of Yesteryear* (New York: NYRB, 2008), and *Memoirs of an Anti-Semite* (New York: Viking, 1981).

47 For Arendt see Barbara Cassin, *When Are We Ever at Home?* (New York: Fordham University Press, 2014).

48 Lynne Sharon Schwartz, ed., *The Emergence of Memory: Conversations with W. G. Sebald* (New York: Seven Stories Press, 2007), see interviews by Angier, Wachtel, Silverblatt and Cuomo.

49 Samuel Beckett, *Molloy* (London: Faber and Faber, 2009), p. 10.

50 Max Picard, *The World of Silence* (London: Harvill Press, 1952), 18, Reprinted Eighth Day Press, Wichita, 2002.

51 Private correspondence with Séamus Deane, May 2018.

52 Eleanor Wachtel, 'Ghost Hunter', in Lynne Sharon Schwartz, ed., *The Emergence of Memory*, p. 47.

53 Sebald, *On the Natural History of Destruction*, pp. 38–9; Victor Gollancz, *In Darkest Germany* (London: Victor Gollancz, 1947).

54 Nichola Stargadt, *Witnesses of War: Children's Lives under the Nazis* (London: Pimlico, 2006), pp. 241–2.

55 Ibid., p. 243.

56 From Ciaran Carson, *The Irish for No* (Hexham: Bloodaxe, 1988).

57 Carson, *The Irish for No*.

58 Wachtel, 'Ghost Hunter', p. 51.

8. Other Wars

1 Keith Kyle, *Reporting the World* (London: I.B.Tauris, 2009), pp. 252–7.

2 On the O'Connor case, see the well-titled Peter Taylor, *Beating the Terrorists: Interrogation in Omagh, Gough and Castlereagh* (London: Penguin, 1980), Chapter 8.

3 The academic consideration of this 'telling' seems to have originated with F. Burton, *The Politics of Legitimacy: Struggles in a Belfast Community* (London: Routledge & Kegan Paul, 1978). See also Andrew Finlay, '"Whatever You Say Say Nothing": An Ethnographic Encounter in Northern Ireland and Its Sequel', *Sociological Research Online* 4: 3 (1999), at socresonline.org.uk.

4 Seamus Heaney, 'Whatever You Say Say Nothing', first published in *North* (1975).

5 Marianne Elliot, *The Catholics of Ulster* (London: Penguin, 2000), p. 438.

6 Graham Dawson, Jo Dover and Stephen Hopkins, eds, *The Northern Ireland Troubles in Britain: Engagements, Legacies and Memories* (Manchester University Press, 2016); Ray French, Moy McCrory and Kath Mckay, eds, *I Wouldn't Start from Here: The Second-Generation Irish in Britain* (Brighton: Wild GeesePress, 2019).

7 There is a powerful BBC2 film about the family, *A Great British Injustice: The Maguire Story*. It was broadcast in 2018, forty years after the event.

8 Figures taken from Hansard and David McKittrick and David McVea, *Making Sense of the Troubles: A History of the Northern Ireland Conflict* (New York: Viking, 2012). See discussion of figures in 'AM', 'Statistics of the Conflict and Conflict of Statistics', 23 November 2011, at thepensivequill.am. See also Elizabeth Fiona McCormack, 'Fear, Silence and Telling: Catholic Identity in Ireland', *Anthropology and Humanism* 42: 1 (June 2017).

9 On the geography of violent death, see Ian N. Gregory, Niall A. Cunningham, C. D. Lloyd, Ian G. Shuttleworth and Paul S. Ell, *Troubled Geographies: A Spatial History of Religion and Society in Ireland* (Bloomington, IN: Indiana University Press, 2013).

10 Ibid., p. 217.

11 Michael Longley, 'Songs for Dead Children: The Poetry of Northern Ireland's Troubles' – online, edited version of Longley's 2017 PEN Pinter Prize speech, available at newstatesman.com.

12 Brendan O'Leary and John McGarry, *The Politics of Antagonism: Understanding Northern Ireland* (London: Athlone, 1996), pp. 12–13.

13 See the British Army's own report on Operation Banner, *Operation Banner: An Analysis of Military Operations in Northern Ireland*, Army Code 71842 – pdf available at vilaweb.cat.

14 Breandán Mac Suibhne, 'Spirit, Spectre, Shade: A True Story of an Irish Haunting; or, Troublesome Pasts in the Political Culture of North-west

Ulster, 1786–1972', *Field Day Review* 9 (2013) – a special issue dedicated to Derry and its environs in celebration of Derry-Londonderry as City of Culture that year.

15 Iain McBride, *The Siege of Derry in the Ulster Protestant Mythology* (Dublin: Four Courts, 1997).

16 Though a small-to-medium town for much of its existence, Derry is constitutionally a city. The tangled issue of the naming of the city is well known. For details of this, see the revealingly lengthy Wikipedia entry on its 'name dispute'. On the grounds that, in 2015, the democratically elected city council voted in favour of changing the official name of the city to Derry, and that what local public consultation there is on the naming of the city is overwhelmingly in favour of 'Derry', I shall use that name in what follows.

17 Cited in Culture Northern Ireland, 'Derry's Architecture up to 1800', n.d, at culturenorthernireland.org.

18 Brian Lacy, *Siege City: The Story of Derry and Londonderry* (Newtownards: Blackstaff, 1990); William Kelly, ed., *The Sieges of Derry* (Dublin: Four Courts, 2001), esp. Brian Walker, 'Remembering the Siege of Derry: The Rise of a Popular Religious and Political Tradition, 1689–1989', which points up the collapse of liberal Presbyterianism in the city in the 1870s and the triumph of Toryism and Orangeism. One could say the Derry die was cast then – a time also when an ideologically tooled-up Catholicism came on the scene. On both this issue and the earlier failure of eighteenth-century Enlightenment in the city, see also Lacy, *Siege City*, pp. 146–9.

19 *Derry Journal*, 7 October 2016. On the Project, see International Fund for Ireland, *BBI Peace Walls Project: Peace Walls Attitudinal Survey, Summary of Results, October 2017* – pdf available at internationalfund forireland.com.

20 *Derry Journal*, 21 July 2018.

21 Rev George Walker, *A True Account of the Siege of London-Derry by the Rev Mr George Walker* (London: Robert Clavel/Ralph Simpson, 1689) – also published within *The Siege of Londonderry in 1689, as Set Forth in the Remains of: the Rev George Walker, D. D.* (London: E. Stock, 1893). Several online editions are available, and a print text is available in Rev George Walker, *A True Account of the Siege of London-Derry by the Reverend Mr George Walker* (Ann Arbor, MI: EEBO Editions – ProQuest, 2011).

22 Northern Ireland Statistics and Research Agency, 'Northern Ireland Multiple Deprivation Measure 2017', n.d., at nisra.gov.uk.

23 Mick Fealty, 'Northern Ireland's Deafening Silence', *Guardian*, 6 April 2006.

24 Susan McKay, *Bear in Mind these Dead* (London: Faber, 2008); WAVE Trauma Centre, 'WAVE Stories', available at wavetraumacentre.org.uk.

25 International Conflict Research Institute (INCORE), Queen's University, Belfast 'Dealing with the Past' project, at qub.ac.uk.

26 For a discussion of *habitus* see above, pp. 37, 61, 118–19.

27 See, among a host of books, the pioneering Chandra Mukerji, *Territorial Ambitions and the Gardens of Versailles* (Cambridge: Cambridge University Press, 1997); Ken Alder, *Engineering the Revolution: Arms and Enlightenment in France, 1763–1815* (London: Princeton University Press, 1997); and Timothy Mitchell, *The Rule of Experts: Egypt, Techno-Politics, Modernity* (Berkeley, CA: University of California Press, 2002). On Ireland, see Patrick Carroll, *Science, Culture and Modern State Formation* (Berkeley, CA: University of California Press, 2008).

28 For extensive detail, including many photographs, see James Stevens Curl, *The Londonderry Plantation 1609–1914: The History, Archaeology and Planning of the Estates of the City of Londonderry and Its Livery Companies in Ulster* (Bognor Regis: Phillimore, 1986).

29 A. T. Q. Stewart, *The Narrow Ground: Aspects of Ulster 1609–1969* (London: Faber, 1977).

30 The best known of the greatly influential Mary Douglas's works is *Purity and Danger: An Analysis of Concepts of Pollution and Taboo* (London: Routledge & Kegan Paul, 1966).

31 Anthony D. Buckley, 'Walls within Walls: Religion and Rough Behaviour in an Ulster Community', *Sociology* 18: 1 (February 1984). See also the discussion of Glassie in Elliott, *Catholics of Ulster*, p. 479.

32 Eamonn McCann, *War and an Irish Town* (London: Pluto, 1974), pp. 76–9.

33 Frank Ormsby, ed., *A Rage for Order: Poetry of the Northern Ireland Troubles* (Newtownards: Blackstaff, 1992), p. 65.

34 On intransigence, fatalism and territory in the Protestant community, see Susan McKay, *Northern Protestants: An Unsettled People* (Newtownards: Blackstaff, 2000), pp. 55–6, 62, 293–4.

35 Psalm 48:12–13.

36 Psalm 31:2.

37 Walker, *True Account of the Siege of London-Derry*, p. 105. On the importance of the siege in the Protestant historical imagination, see p. 138, note 27: 'There is scarcely a blessing which the British dominions enjoy today, and which England has diffused to other countries of the world, that was not secured by the Revolution of 1688. And that revolution was secured by the defence of Derry, now so unpretentiously begun' – the words of the Rev John Graham, Orange poet and historian.

38 Hastings Donnan and Kirk Simpson, 'Silence and Violence among Northern Ireland Border Protestants', *Ethnos Journal of Anthropology* 72: 1 (2007).

39 These religious texts are cited in McCormack, 'Fear, Silence, and Telling'.

40 Ibid.

41 I am greatly indebted to Eamonn Deane for his hospitality and for sharing his great knowledge of the city.

42 Eamonn McCann has an interesting account of the school in *War and an Irish Town*.

43 There are many accounts of St Columb's, in written and broadcast forms, including an essay by Seamus Deane and a poem by Seamus Heaney.

9. Industrial Jerusalem

1 Friedrich Engels, *The Condition of the English Working Class in 1844; From Personal Observation and Authentic Sources* (London: Panther, 1969) with an introduction by E. J. Hobsbawm.

2 W. G. Sebald, *The Emigrants* (London: Harvill, 1997), p. 153.

3 Ibid., p. 156.

4 Ibid., p. 165.

5 W. G. Sebald, *After Nature* (New York: Modern Library, 2003), Section 4, 'Dark Night Sallies Forth'.

6 Recently, most notably, see Lynsey Hanley, *Estates: An Intimate History* (London: Granta, 2007), and *Respectable: The Experience of Class* (London: Allen Lane, 2016).

7 Jonathan Charles Goddard and Louisa Hermans, 'Occupational Tumours of the Urinary Tract: The Work of Denis Poole-Wilson', 1 July 2017, at urologynews.uk.com.

8 From *Belfast Confetti*, 'Schoolboys and Idlers of Pompeii'. The opening Sebald quotation is from *After Nature* (New Modern Library, 2003), p. 98.

9 Ernest. F Lang, 'The Early History of our Firm', *Beyer-Peacock Quarterly Review* 1: 2 (1927).

10 The interviews are catalogued internally at the Manchester Museum of Science and Industry (MOSI), and the Leonard Allen, Tim Talks and James Hicklin ones are particularly revealing. See also the MOSI interviews with Mary Sprace, John Fairbrother, Thomas and Mildred Brown, and Jean Walpole. At Manchester Central Library interviews with Dorothy Lord and Fred Lord and Cyril Bloor have also been consulted (Master: GMSA box 329). The respondents were born between 1928 and 1938.

11 Dick Sullivan, *Navvymen* (Dublin: Coracle, 1983), pp. 16–17, 49–8, 131–4. There are several books produced by itinerant/mobile Irish labourers themselves, including Dónal Mac Amhlaigh *An Irish Navvy: The Diary of an Exile* (London: Routledge & Kegan Paul, 1964), on the 1950s. See also John B. Keane's *The Contractors* (Cork: Mercier, 1993), a dull slog. In a previous chapter, I cited the best book: Timothy

O'Grady and Steve Pyke's novel, *I Could Read the Sky* (London: Harvill, 1997).

12 Anonymous, *History of Woodhead Chapel*, n.d. (1910?), available at historyhome.co.uk. See also Marjorie Bloy, 'The Chapel at Woodhead', 25 January 2019, at historyhome.co.uk.

13 Marc Augé, *In the Metro* (Minneapolis, MN: University of Minnesota Press, 2002).

14 Ágnes Heller, 'Where Are We at Home?', *Thesis Eleven* 41 (1995).

15 Wolfgang Schivelbusch, *The Railway Journey: The Industrialization of Space and Time in the Nineteenth Century* (Berkeley, CA: University of California Press, 1986) – a quite wonderful book, as are all his works.

16 Georgina Blakeley and Brendan Evans, *The Regeneration of East Manchester: A Political Analysis* (Manchester: Manchester University Press, 2013).

17 Friedrich Engels, *The Condition of the Working Class* (London: Panther, 1969), pp. 78–9 – originally published in German in 1845; first translated into English in 1885.

18 Sebald, *Emigrants*, p. 192.

19 'Tramp! Tramp! Tramp! (Confederate Lyrics)', n.d., at contemplator. com.

10. After the Fall

1 Patrick Joyce, 'Work', in F. M. L. Thompson, ed., *The Cambridge Social History of Britain 1750–1950, Volume 2: 'People and Environment'* (Cambridge: Cambridge University Press, 1990), tables on pp. 133–6.

2 David Edgerton, *The Rise and Fall of the British Nation* (London: Allen Lane, 2018), pp. 310–11, 336.

3 Paul Morley, *The North (And Almost Everything in It)* (London: Bloomsbury, 2013).

4 Alan J. Kidd, *Manchester* (Edinburgh: Edinburgh University Press, 2002); Ray King, *Detonation: Rebirth of the City* (Royal Oak, MI: Clear, 2006).

5 Arndale Centres were built across the nation, and the one in London's Wandsworth, opened in 1971, was at that time the largest indoor shopping space in Europe. Manchester's was larger still.

6 Richard Hoggart, *The Uses of Literacy* (London: Penguin, 1957); Jeremy Seabrook, *The Unpriviliged* (London: Penguin, 1973) and *City Close-Up* (London: Penguin, 1970); Robert Roberts, *The Classic Slum* (Manchester: Manchester University Press, 1971) and *A Ragged Schooling: Growing Up in the Classic Slum* (Manchester: Manchester University Press, 1997).

7 'Openshaw Memories', at openshawmemories.uk.

8 Gorton has a certain national fame for its poverty. See Raymond Holden, 'Hard Truths about Life in the Forgotten Manchester Neighbourhood',

Guardian, 20 June 2016, and his book, which is of limited illumination, although he lived there and I did not: Raymond Holden, *Nobody Cares: Forgotten Parts of British Cities* (Raymond Holden, 2016), free Kindle e-book. There are several novels set in Gorton, each woefully inept.

9 Paul Farley and Michael Symmons Roberts, *Edgelands: Journeys into England's True Wilderness* (London: Vintage, 2001).

10 Peter Fokman, Julie Froud, Sukhdev Johal, John Tomaney and Karel Williams', 'Manchester Transformed: Why We Need a Reset of City Region Policy', CRESC Public Interest Report, November 2016.

11 Georgina Blakeley and Brendan Evans, *The Regeneration of East Manchester: A Political Analysis* (Manchester: Manchester University Press, 2013), Chapter 6.

12 Ibid., p. 42.

13 William Davies, *The Limits of Neoliberalism: Authority, Sovereignty and the Logic of Competition* (London: Sage, 2014). See also William Davies, 'Populism and the Limits of Neoliberalism', n.d., at blogs.lse.ac.uk.

14 See the 'Mancunian Reunion Project', Hattersley Hub local authority library branch. See also, *From Smoke to Grass: Gamesley – The Birth of a New Community* (Matlock: Derbyshire County Council, 2004); Dick Richardson, Rachel Gee and Sharron Power, *Fresh Hope, Fresh Air: Starting a New Life in Hattersley* (Ashton under Lyne: Tameside, 2008); Hattersley Interviews at Tameside Library: Ellen Regan.

15 Lynsey Hanley, *Respectable: The Experience of Class* (London: Allen Lane, 2016).

16 Joe Bageant, *Deer Hunting with Jesus: Dispatches from America's Class War* (New York: Crown Business, 2007), p. 201.

17 Mike Savage, *Social Class in the 21st Century* (London: Pelican, 2015); Will Atkinson, Steven Roberts and Mike Savage, eds, *Class Inequality in Austerity Britain: Power, Difference and Suffering* (London: Palgrave Macmillan, 2013); Beverley Skeggs, *Formations of Class and Gender: Becoming Respectable* (London: Sage, 1997), and *Class, Self, Culture* (Abingdon: Routledge, 2004).

11. Home

1 Magnus Course, 'Houses of Uist: Memory and Dwelling in the Outer Hebrides', *Journal of the Royal Anthropological Institute* 25: 1 (March 2019). My thanks to Professor Janet Carsten for organizing a workshop at Edinburgh University on the house and the state.

2 Robert Pogue Harrison, *The Dominion of the Dead* (Chicago: Chicago University Press, 2005), p. xi, see also p. 38.

3 Ágnes Heller, 'Where Are We at Home?', *Thesis Eleven* 41: 1 (1995); see also other articles in this journal on Heller; Ágnes Heller, *Everyday Life* (London: Routledge & Kegan Paul, 1974).

4 'End Child Poverty Has Published New Figures (May 2019) on the Level of Child Poverty in Each Constituency, Local Authority and Ward in Britain', n.d., at endchildpoverty.org.uk.

5 See the website of the National Literacy Trust, at literacytrust.org.uk.

6 Jeevan Vasager, 'Poverty and Envy Fuel Racism in Burnley', *Guardian*, 30 June 2001.

7 'It Is So Wrong to Hate', *Daily Mirror*, 3 April 2007.

8 David Watkinson, 'Burnley Riots 10 Years On: What Happened on that Shocking Weekend', *Lancashire Telegraph*, 23 June 2007.

9 Jon Lawrence, *Me Me Me: The Search for Community in Post-War England* (London: Oxford University Press, 2019); Emily Robinson, Camilla Schofield, Florence Sutcliffe-Braithwaite and Natalie Thomlinson, 'Telling Stories about Post-War Britain: Popular Individualism and the "Crisis" of the 1970s', *20th Century British History* 28: 2 (2017); Florence Sutcliffe-Braithwaite, *Class, Politics, and the Decline of Deference in England, 1968–2000* (London: Oxford University Press, 2018).

10 David Edgerton, *The Rise and Fall of the British Nation: A Twentieth-Century History* (London: Allen Lane, 2018), p. 26.

11 Michael Moran, *The End of British Politics?* (London: Palgrave Macmillan, 2018).

12 *Golden Years of Burnley* (Halifax: True North, 1998). See also newspaper cuttings files on 1960s Burnley, Central Public Library; *Burnley Official Guide 1974*, and annually; Burnley Civic Trust, *Burnley Express* newspaper archive, at bcthic.org. See also, for example, oldburnley.blogspot.com.

13 Andrew Porter, *Suicide Squad: The Story of a Hooligan Firm* (Preston: Milo, 2005). Milo Books specializes in books on 'international drug cartels, gang wars, football hooliganism and far-right terrorism'. It claims to be the largest nonfiction publisher in the north of England.

14 For corroboration of my view of Burnley and, later in this chapter, of Stoke, see Deborah Mattinson, *Beyond the Red Wall: Why Labour Lost, How the Conservatives Won and What Will Happen Next* (London: Biteback Publishing, 2020). The author studies Accrington, next door to Burnley, and if anything in an even more parlous condition.

15 Tony Bell, *Owt and Nowt: The Story of a Working Man's Club, The Burnley Miners'* (Tony Bell on Behalf of Burnley Miners' Publishing, 2002), pp. 156, 163.

16 Chris Waters, 'Representations of Everyday Life: L. S. Lowry and the Landscape of Memory in Postwar Britain', *Representations* 65 (Winter 1999) – an excellent study.

17 R. H. Tawney, *Equality* (London: George Allen & Unwin, 1931), Chapter 1.

18 There are numerous examples of the renewed interest in nostalgia – for example, Svetlana Boym, *The Future of Nostalgia* (New York: Basic,

2002); Owen Hatherley, *The Ministry of Nostalgia* (London: Verso, 2016).

19 Thomas Dodman, *What Nostalgia Was: War, Empire and the Time of Deadly Nostalgia* (Chicago: Chicago University Press, 2018), Chapter 6 and afterword.

20 Heller, 'Where Are We at Home?'

21 There is the marvellous example of Alison Light, *Common People: The History of an English Family* (London: Penguin, 2015).

22 This has given rise to several notable examples of intellectual provincialism in the history field – for example, Richard Evans, *In Defence of History* (London: Granta, 1997).

23 Patrick Joyce, *The Rule of Freedom: Liberalism and the Modern City* (London: Verso, 2003).

24 Arthur Aughey, *The Politics of Englishness* (Manchester: Manchester University Press, 2007), introduction.

25 Jeremy Paxman, *On the English: Portrait of a People* (London: Penguin, 1999), pp. 260–1. See also his *The English* (London: Penguin, 2007).

26 Paxman, *On the English*, p. 264.

27 Emily Robinson, *History, Heritage and Tradition in Contemporary British Politics: Past Politics and Present Histories* (Manchester: Manchester University Press, 2010). See also James Cronin, *New Labour's Pasts: The Labour Party and Its Discontents* (Harlow: Longman, 2004).

28 The sense of British nationhood in the general population, as across the two main parties, has always borne the deep imprint of political institutions – if not today parliament, then still the monarchy, the armed forces, the institutions of 'the rule of law', and the invisible institution of the Constitution.

29 Richard Jobson, *Nostalgia and the Post-War Labour Party: Prisoners of the Past* (Manchester: Manchester University Press, 2018).

30 Robert Saunders, 'Nostalgia Is Good for You: The Myth of Brexit as Imperial Nostalgia', *Prospect*, 7 January 2019; Robert Saunders, 'Myths from a Small Island: The Dangers of a Buccaneering View of British History', *New Statesman*, 9 October 2019; Robert Saunders, *Yes to Europe! The 1975 Referendum and Seventies Britain* (Cambridge: Cambridge University Press, 2018).

31 There are some interesting insights on Brexit that bear on this point in James Meek, *Dreams of Leaving and Remaining* (London: Verso, 2019).

32 On Etruria, see Sharon Gater and David Vincent, *The Factory in the Garden* (Keele: Keele Life Histories, 1998).

33 Martin Fletcher: blog, at martinanthonyfletcher.com.

34 Niles Pratley, 'Bet 365 Chief's Pay Is Less Fascinating Than Where Its Revenues Are Made', *Guardian*, 18 December 2019.

35 'Bet 365 Owner: The Bets That Built the £90m House', *Daily Express*, 5 December 2018.

12. Endings

1 Jack Watson, 'How Boxing Is Helping the Grenfell Community Fight Back', *Independent*, 1 October 2018.

2 Location based on cross-referencing between the 1916 Ordnance Survey map, early 1980s *A to Z*s and Royal Borough of Kensington and Chelsea maps. Information supplied by and discussed with Tom Vague.

3 There is a remarkable account of schoolmistress teaching in the area at this time: 'I think I must have had one or two of the last of the children that were sewn into their clothes. My mother had had some of those in the 1920s when she was a teacher in Leeds, in Hunslet.' Josephine Battersby, '"You Don't Have to Push Children on the Whole – They're Pulling You"', *Guardian*, 17 May 2002.

4 See 'The Potteries and the Bramley Road Area and the Rise of the Housing Problem in North Kensington', at british-history.ac.uk.

5 A 'sixth-form college' usually caters to students between the ages of sixteen and eighteen, although many secondary schools have their own sixth form. The last two years are usually seen as preparatory to university or some other advanced qualification. The 'sixth form' covers the last two years of secondary education – years twelve and thirteen of education overall. Until 2013, students could leave at sixteen years. In 1947, the school-leaving age was raised to fifteen, and in 1972 to sixteen – a decade after I left.

6 Aamna Mohdin, '"People Were Abandoned": Injustices of Pandemic Laid Bare in Brent', *Guardian*, 27 June 2020.

7 Jerome Borkwood, *From Kensal Village to Golborne Road: Tales of the Inner City* (London: Kensington & Chelsea Community History Group, 2002), Chapter 8 and p. 107. See also Alan Johnson, *This Boy* (London: Bantam, 2013).

8 Thomas J. Cottle, *Black Testimony* (London: Wildwood House, 1978), pp. 163–5. See also pp. 88–98.

9 By contrast, Donnellan's no less superb film on the West Indian community in Birmingham, *The Colony*, which was not judged 'formless', was shown.

10 For a recent study, see Sean Williams and Lillis Ó Laoire, *Bright Star of the West: Joe Heaney, Irish Songman* (London: Oxford University Press, 2011).

11 Peter Lennon, 'Where Are All the Cows?', *Guardian*, 20 October 2000.

12 Timothy O'Grady and Steve Pyke's novel, *I Could Read the Sky* (London: Harvill, 1997), p. 71. I make my own list from their longer one.

13 Patrick Joyce, *Remembering Peasants* (forthcoming).

14 Pierre Bourdieu and Marie-Claire Bourdieu, 'The Peasant and Photography', and Pierre Bourdieu, Richard Nice and Loïc Wacquant, 'The Peasant and His Body', *Ethnography* 5: 4 (2004).

15 See also 'The Hill Farmer', in William Trevor, *Nights at the Alexandra* (London: Penguin, 2015).

16 Hughie O'Donoghue has painted the fields of his mother's north Mayo, with great passion and complex meaning. See his *Naming the Fields: Hughie O'Donaghue: New Paintings* (Dublin: Rubicon Gallery Catalogue, 2001). My thanks to Hughie O'Donaghue for the chance to talk about his work with him.

17 See the discussion of circularity and continuity in Chapter 2, above.

18 John Berger, *Into Their Labours* (London: Granta,1992) – the first of his three works on the rural–urban transformations of peasant life.

19 John Berger, 'Christ of the Peasants' in John Berger and Geoff Dyer, eds, *Selected Essays of John Berger* (London: Bloomsbury, 2001).

20 Markéta Luskačová, *Pilgrims: Photographs by Markéta Luskačová*, catalogue of Luskačová's exhibition at the V&A (London: Victoria & Albert Musaum, 1983–84). The catalogue text is also available at marketaluskacova.com.

21 John Berger, 'Pilgrims- Markéta', from the foreword to the catalogue of Luskačová's V&A exhibition, 1983

22 John Montague, 'A Severed Head', in *The Rough Field* (Oldcastle, Co. Meath: Gallery, 1972).

23 *Illuminations* (Fontana, 1973), Walter Benjamin, 'On the Concept of History', transl. Dennis Redmond, 2005, at marxists.org.

24 'Addendum B' on Jewry in Walter Benjamin, *Illuminations* (London: Fontana, 1973).

25 Ibid.

26 Cited in Fintan O'Toole, *The Lie of the Land: Irish Identities* (Verso, 1997), p. 11. Tim Robinson, I am pleased to say, has written about the Joyces. See Tim Robinson, 'The Joyces and the O'Malleys', in his *Connemara: A Little Gaelic Kingdom* (London: Penguin, 2007). See also Tim Robinson, *Connemara: Part 1: Introduction & Gazetteer* (Roundstone, Co. Galway: Folding Landscapes, 1990).

Index

Index